Call Sign Revlon

Call Sign Revlon

The Life and Death of
Navy Fighter Pilot Kara Hultgreen

Sally Spears

Naval Institute Press
Annapolis, Maryland

Library of Congress Cataloging-in-Publication Data
Spears, Sally, 1938–
    Call sign Revlon : the life and death of Navy fighter pilot
  Kara Hultgreen / Sally Spears.
       p.   cm.
    ISBN 1-55750-809-7 (alk. paper)
    1. Hultgreen, Kara, 1965–1994. 2. Air pilots, Military—
  United States—Biography. 3. Women air pilots—United
  States—Biography. 4. United States. Navy—Aviation—
  Biography. I.Title.
  V63.H86S64 1998
  359.9'4'092—dc21
  [B]   98-19084

Printed in the United States of America on acid-free paper ♾

05 04 03 02 01 00 99 98   9 8 7 6 5 4 3 2
First printing

For Dagny and Kirsten

Keep safe

Sound sound the clarion,
Fill the fife,
Throughout the sensual world proclaim,
One crowded hour
Of glorious life
Is worth an age
Without a name.

"OLD MORTALITY," THOMAS MORDAUNT, 1791

Contents

 *Author's Note*

"Writing letters on my computer is like keeping a journal," Kara wrote her friend Pamela Kunze on 16 November 1992. "I'll need these when I write my memoirs." She said it in the light, half-joking way she had, but she was serious. Kara recorded her life in handwritten diaries and later on her laptop computer. She had twelve photo albums and a scrapbook of newspaper articles. She kept letters and cards from family and friends and official navy documents and memoranda that were important to her in a large loose-leaf binder, all in perfect order.

Kara meant to do something special with her life, and as her career progressed, she became aware that she might have a place in history. "I'm going to be famous," she would say. "It's my *density*." The rearrangement of the letters in *destiny* was deliberate. She loved the play on words and she laughed when she said it, but she made sure she wouldn't forget anything that happened to her along the way. She wrote it all down in her own unique and sometimes biting style, finding humor even in the most depressing set of circumstances.

Her records provided the outline and much of the content of this book, and I quoted from the navy documents and memoranda she kept and from her diaries and letters throughout. Some of Kara's friends thought a few of her journal entries were too personal—that she never would have voiced the things she wrote in her diaries and would not have wanted her emotions publicly exposed. But I think the honesty and intensity of her feelings drew people to her and her words shouldn't have to be "blanded" down. Her journal was a gift. Few people today keep one, and fewer still record their true emotions.

Her friends also worried that if I told about mistakes she made it might detract from her memory, that people with their own agendas would use them as examples to prove whatever point they were trying to make about women in general or Kara in particular. But I believe Kara's journals show her ability to learn from mistakes and put that knowledge to positive use. They reveal a maturing process, a tempering over the years. In the early days her reactions were very intense, very black-and-white. I didn't attempt to soften them, or justify her. She had setbacks but never lost sight of her goal. She learned a lot about people and about herself between her twenty-fifth and twenty-eighth year, and that knowledge served her well when she found herself in the challenging F-14 fighter pilot community.

Some publishers, to whom the proposal for this book was sent, reacted to the prospect of "the mother" writing about Kara with disdain. Conscious of that, I tried very hard not to paint her as a saint or a prude or always in the right, a plastic perfect heroine. But I do not deny that Kara was my heart. I loved her fierce determination and passion, her drive, her irreverent sense of humor, and her inability to suffer stupidity.

Kara spent her first tour of duty flying EA-6As in an electronic warfare support training squadron in Key West, Florida, before the Tailhook fallout polished the phrase "political correctness." She was a young woman whose bold self-confidence was both a requirement for success and an irritant to a few of her male superiors. I changed names when her stories about people were extremely negative. The attitudes she described haven't changed much since the early 1990s. A powerful culture that deems certain jobs unseemly for a woman still exists. These ingrained prejudices operate to subdue women and to foster a climate conducive to harassment.

Naval officers who read the manuscript were uncomfortable about the "girly" descriptions of wardrobe and makeup and any mention of sexual attraction. They said Kara was a dedicated professional officer. If I emphasized the normal young woman rather than the naval officer, remember that the mother, and not a naval historian, is the author. I thank Paul Wilderson of the Naval Institute Press for not insisting that I have a "professional" writer stylize the book.

The prologue and the epilogue are written in the first person because those events happened after Kara's death. I wrote about her life in the third person because it was her story, not mine, and I think it reads better. I didn't do it to try to mislead the reader that this book is an objective biography or a learned analysis of women in a male-dominated career path. I interviewed third parties not to supplement what Kara said about an incident or to provide another side to her story but to try to put Kara's journals in context. I reconstructed some conversations in the book from stories people (including Kara) told me. The dialogue may not be exact but the stories are true.

Lt. Cdr. Harry Ennis, who shared his memories of Kara during two of her years at Key West and who educated me about A-6s and P-3s and life in general at Kara's squadron in Key West, died suddenly on 5 July 1997. He was a mentor to Kara and a wonderful friend to me after her death. He read a draft of the manuscript, and I am grateful I had a chance to thank him for his help days before he died.

Kara's friend Lt. Pamela Kunze helped me greatly, not only with the book but also personally. Thanks to Monique Kleck, who shared Kara's early letters and in many other ways allowed me to lean on her. The friendship formed in high school between Kara and Monique, both remarkable young women, remained true as each traveled her own separate road.

Thanks to Kara's friends and fellow naval officers, Suzanne Parker, Amy Boyer, Linda Heid, and Brenda Scheufele, who also shared their memories of Kara and their letters from her with me, and to Janet and Mike Marnane and Wayne Lockley, who read several chapters for accuracy. And many thanks to my agent, Ellen Geiger, who had faith in me, to my friend Patricia Beveridge for editing my drafts, and to Cdr. Tom "Sobs" Sobieck who guided me through Kara's training to fly the F-14 and helped me understand what happened the day she died.

Call Sign Revlon

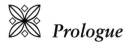 *Prologue*

"Revlon"

"Were you responsible for sending me her helmet?" I asked Commander Galpin. "It was the only tangible comfort I had during the early days after I was notified that Kara had been lost at sea and was presumed dead. It's just the right size—I can circle my arms around that helmet."

The actual helmet Kara wore when she crashed had been found, but all the survival equipment after a mishap is impounded so that it can be examined by experts to try to learn how to improve it. The squadron had a new one made and sent it to me. The call sign lettered down the back of the helmet was "Revlon."

The Blacklions also sent me Kara's flight jacket, which had been rescued thirty-seven hundred feet below the surface of the Pacific Ocean. It was retrieved from the cockpit of her plane by the remote-control mechanical arm of an unmanned deep submersible vehicle, Scorpio II. The fabric, slick and strong, was marred by nicks and scratches from the metal pincers—fingers of a robot hand.

I tried to sleep with that jacket, an attempt to hold Kara to me—but the material was too cold.

Kara's other possessions were sent to her sisters in Los Angeles so, for a while, Kara's helmet and flight jacket were the only things of Kara's that I had. Sending her mother the last things close to Kara was a kind and gentle thing for those warriors to do. Of course, warriors, especially carrier aviators, have experience to draw upon in comforting the grieving mothers and next of kin of their lost comrades. The media made much over the fact that Kara was the first female fighter pilot to die, but her squadron mates just reacted to the death of one of their own. They sent her helmet and flight jacket—her armor—just what warriors would send and what the mother of a fallen warrior would want.

The brave and talented aviators who earn the opportunity to take the F-14 Tomcat on and off an aircraft carrier form an exclusive circle. Kara Hultgreen was the first woman ever to win a place in that circle. She became "one of the boys" in the world's most restricted boys club.

The F-14 is a sinister aircraft—sleek, elegant, menacing. Learning to fly the thirty-two-ton fighter, with its supersonic speed and complicated electronics and weapons systems, is a forbidding task and requires much more than motor skills. During the rigorous year she trained, Kara concentrated completely on her work. She spent hours in the classroom, hours poring over her books, and more hours practicing instrument flying and emergency procedures in a simulated cockpit on the ground. She sought to be distinguished from her classmates only by excellence in her performance. In every other way, she desired nothing more than to blend in.

In most ways she was a fit. Like the men she trained with, she was intelligent, quick-witted, and loved to have a good time. She had a great sense of humor, a vast repertoire of jokes, and she could mimic perfectly everyone's favorite comedy routines.

The pilots kidded that they were "a manly group." They included Kara because she was bold and fearless, even though she couldn't satisfy all the physical requirements. She had a very womanly figure and a feminine face with delicate features. Her eyes were light brown with gold flecks, her hair was a honey color, and her smile was warm and ready. Taller and stronger than some of the men, she had the healthy, clean-cut look that seemed to be a recruiting requirement for fighter pilots. Her call sign in her previous squadron was "Hulk"—the incredible Hultgreen.

Soon after Kara completed flight training in the F-14 Fleet Replacement Squadron, she showed up in the Ready Room of her new squadron at Miramar Naval Air Station in San Diego, California, in her flight suit and full makeup. With false eyelashes, mascara, blusher, and lipstick, she didn't just look healthy and clean-cut, she looked gorgeous. Her new squadron mates did a double-take, and though she explained to the formerly all-male Blacklion den of Squadron 213 that the makeup was for a television interview, they teased her unmercifully and bestowed upon her a new call sign— "Revlon."

I told her I liked "Revlon" much better than "Hulk." Kara laughed and said that was typical Mom. She used to do take-offs on me in the squadron Ready Room when everyone was lounging around telling jokes. She would sit up straight in her flight suit, with her long hair neatly braided, and press her knees together primly, purse her lips, lift her eyebrows, and pronounce that her mother always told her to sit like a lady.

Kara's squadron commander, Mike Galpin, didn't like "Revlon." "It was too 'girly,'" he said. "I didn't want my female pilots to be thought of as girls. I wanted them to be thought of as fighter pilots," he told me the morning of the funeral, unintentionally reinforcing the dogma that being a female and a fighter pilot were mutually exclusive.

Commander Galpin; Tim Trant, the head casualty assistance officer; Lt. Dave Waterman, the public affairs officer; Kara's sisters, Dagny and Kirsten; and I were gathered in Admiral Bowman's office at the Pentagon preparing to watch the PLAT (aircraft carrier videotape) of Kara's F-14A airplane crashing into the Pacific Ocean. Kara's dad, Tor Hultgreen, hadn't come with us. His daughters had always teased him about being a stoic Norwegian—but he was the one who was too emotional to watch the tape.

We watched the videotape of Kara's accident twenty or thirty times. It was only a few seconds long. There was no sound. We saw the plane come into view of one of the cameras located on the carrier. Commander Galpin pointed out the crosshairs on the camera lens and showed us that Kara was coming in a little right of the centerline.

"She was overshooting a little," he explained, "not an irreversible error. After you have brought a plane around to land on a carrier several hundred times you have a feel for the turn. A perfect approach would have her about 1.2 miles from the boat at this time. Kara was probably about 1.1 miles. The landing signal officer would be telling her to correct to the left. She had plenty of time to make the correction at this point. You see the nose of the plane swing left but the plane doesn't follow the nose. Instead, something happened here. We believe the left engine went out. The right engine is still powering the plane and it causes the right wing to swing around until it almost points to the carrier."

"It looks as if the plane is skidding," I said, "just like driving on ice and losing traction."

"Exactly," agreed Commander Galpin. "Then you see the nose come up," he continued.

"That must be where Matt said he thought she was going to recover the plane." About a week after the "airplane mishap," as the navy labels it, I talked over the telephone to Lt. Matthew Klemish, Kara's radar intercept officer (RIO) when the plane crashed. Matt had described the events I was seeing now, and his account was making sense to me as I watched the tape.

Matt had called me soon after the accident. I hadn't been home and he had talked to Dagny and Kirsten. They told me what he had said about the accident and I didn't call him back. Several days later, while talking to Rear Adm. Jay B. Yakeley, I asked how Matt was doing. Admiral Yakeley was the commander of Carrier Group Three, Kara and Matt's carrier group. He said that Kara and Matt had flown together a lot and Matt was taking her death very hard. He was second-guessing himself, wishing he had ejected them earlier.

I had been so wrapped up in my own anguish that I hadn't thought of how Matt must be feeling. If Kara had lived and not Matt, Kara would have been devastated, guilty because she survived. I called him immediately. I thought he needed to know that I was glad he had made it, and that I knew he and Kara both had done the best they could.

As Commander Galpin explained, in an F-14 both the pilot and the radar intercept officer have two ejection handles and either can eject, but where the pilot is struggling to control the plane, the RIO is most likely to make the decision. No matter who pulls or pushes the handle, both are ejected in a timed sequence. First the canopy is blown off with an explosive charge. A fraction of a second later, the RIO sitting in the back is exploded out to the left of vertical. Four-tenths of a second later, the pilot is ejected to the right. Actually, the seats are ejected. The humans are just along for the ride. The canopy is blown away and the human beings strapped to their seats are carried away from the plane by small controlled rockets. It is a dangerous event. If all goes well, the seats will fall away from their passengers, the parachutes will open, and the crew will survive.

"The nose came up and I thought she had recovered it, that she was going to fly it away," Matt told me, "and then I heard a pop and everything went to hell. That's when I ejected us. I had to tell my story so many times to different people before they ever let me see the PLAT. In my mind it had taken twenty seconds or more for events to occur. When I saw the tape, I realized the whole thing happened in two or three seconds."

As Dagny, Kirsten, and I watched the tape together in the admiral's office and saw the nose lift, I exhaled with relief, only then realizing I hadn't been breathing. There was a moment when I was sure we had been having a collective nightmare, and that Kara had only just scared us all to death—again. Then we saw the left wing drop and the plane begin to roll. It happened so quickly that when Matt ejected, the plane already had rolled so much to the left that he was almost horizontal with the water. It was enough to allow his parachute to open and bounce once to break his fall before he plunged into the ocean. Hovering helicopters picked him up after about three minutes.

Kara and Matt had flown together eight times during the two weeks before the crash, doing unit training, practicing some air combat maneuvers, but mostly field carrier landings, and they enjoyed flying together. The day was beautiful, and they were laughing and joking on the way to the carrier. Just five minutes before the crash they had called in and reported that it was a perfect jet. It was a low-stress trip, considering that they were going to have to land on the carrier. Matt said he had done 150 carrier landings and always had butterflies in his stomach. "If you don't have them, something's wrong."

"Kara was very upbeat," Matt said. "She was laughing and joking and in great spirits." He told Dagny, "Kara was a blast. She was a lot of fun to be around, always quoting *The Princess Bride*.

"Everything was normal on the approach," Matt said. "The last thing Kara said to me was, '140 degrees, 450 ft., 5 knots fast, Roger,' and then the airplane got out of control. Kara was fighting to keep the plane flying. I pulled the eject handle before the LSO told me to, and I had the feeling that Kara was relieved. The canopy takes off and you rocket out of the plane at twenty-seven Gs. Most people black out. I hit the water at a 65-degree angle and I felt like I had broken my leg."

The plane was not upside down when Kara's seat was ejected but it was past ninety degrees angle of bank. Her seventy-degree left angle shot her into the water at what the *New York Times Magazine* described as "three times highway speed." She was still attached to her seat.

On the television screen, we saw the light of the explosion ejecting Matt and we saw Matt eject. Then we saw the light of the explosion ejecting Kara, but she was hidden by the plane and we couldn't see her. We watched the plane dive into the Pacific Ocean. It happened so quickly.

"She never had a chance," I said out loud. No one in the room disagreed.

The autopsy report prepared by Capt. E. R. Ghent, Medical Service Corps, United States Navy, said Kara's death was caused by blunt force injuries and drowning. "The exact contribution of each is difficult to ascertain with certainty," the report explained. "The decedent sustained multiple injuries and, though none are felt to be of an immediately fatal nature, they may not have been survivable, taken in aggregate. There are findings consistent with drowning, though this diagnosis must be made in the context of the circumstances of death (i.e., submersion with no apparent immediately fatal traumatic injuries)."

I was not comforted to know that Kara's spinal cord was intact, that there was no craniocerebral trauma, and that her great vessels, heart, and lungs were not damaged. Although the autopsy report didn't make the statement, the implication is that if Kara had separated from her seat instead of being dragged down by it, she might have survived her injuries with a few scars but without paralysis or other permanent disability. Life is tenuous, precious, and arbitrary.

The Caisson

21 November 1994—Funeral at Arlington

"Not every military person is entitled to be buried at Arlington," Tim Trant told me. "A full body burial is reserved for those who have died on active duty and a few special others." He said Kara was entitled to full military honors.

"The navy provided a beautiful memorial service for Kara in San Antonio. We don't need to have all that again," I protested. Then Tim mentioned that Kara could be carried to her grave on a caisson. "A caisson like President Kennedy had?" I thought about it. "Kara would really like that. She had a horse when she was a child. She loved horses."

And so Kara's silver coffin covered with the American flag, clear plastic tied around it to protect it from the rain, rested on a caisson pulled by six horses, three of which were mounted. An officer on a seventh horse rode alongside. The navy band, more than a hundred strong, was lined along the way, playing for the procession. Six pall-bearers with a petty officer in charge followed the caisson, and Kara's friends and family followed them. At the grave, an honor guard of seven raised their rifles to their shoulders and fired three volleys on command. Flags were presented to her father and me and then a bugler sounded taps, the final honor. The press, with television cameras, flash-bulbs, and tape recorders, huddled a hundred feet to the side.

Kara had everything except the flyover by F-14s. The cemetery is so close to Washington National Airport that it would have created an air traffic problem. The navy had honored Kara with a flyover at the memorial service held before her body had been recovered, and the San Antonio airport had come to a standstill to accommodate the F-14s.

Later, some people said they thought the ceremony was too elaborate, given that Kara was not a senior officer, and the presence of the secretary of the navy and the vice chief of naval operations at the funeral wasn't in accordance with proper navy protocol. Male pilots died regularly without such conspicuous attention from the navy top brass.

The family was introduced to Secretary of the Navy John Dalton and Adm. Stanley Arthur, vice chief of naval operations, in the Arlington Administration Building before the funeral. Then, in a light mist, we all walked together the three-quarters mile to the grave site.

It was strangely beautiful on that gray, desolate day behind the plastic-draped, flag-covered casket. The gathering under the tent that had been erected was small—family, friends, and navy personnel. There was no religious service, so the ceremony was brief. Admiral

Arthur, covered in medals, spoke a few words. "All of us who are naval aviators know that every person who takes off from the carrier does not always land. We accept that risk with enthusiasm. Kara accepted that risk with enthusiasm. She was one of us. We will miss her. Permission to fly solo."

Secretary Dalton gave me the flag covering Kara's coffin. "On behalf of the commander in chief and a grateful nation, I present you this flag. Your daughter was an outstanding naval officer and she made a significant contribution to our naval service." Then Admiral Arthur presented a second flag to Kara's father.

The superintendent of the cemetery, John Metzler Jr., materialized at my side. "You can touch the coffin now."

I looked sideways over at the press who were filming away. "I'll just wait until everyone has gone."

"No one can leave until you go," said Metzler.

I thought I was used to the cameras, but now I felt self-conscious, exposed. I just patted the coffin and walked away.

Navy cars and vans were waiting. Dagny, Kirsten, and I were riding together, and we followed Mr. Metzler away from the grave site back to the vehicles. As the driver was about to pull away, I asked him to stop and put down his window. I called to Mr. Metzler, "We want to go back to the grave after everyone has left."

Our van drove off and took a tour of the cemetery while the United States Navy and Mr. Metzler cleared out the cameras. When the only people left at the grave were the cemetery workers, our driver took us back to the grave. The casket was gleaming but everything looked bleak and vacant as new sections of cemeteries do, especially when the grass has been trod into mud around the freshly dug hole in the earth. There was only one flower arrangement. At Kara's first memorial service, there had been dozens.

We gazed forlornly at the silver coffin.

"Which way is her head?" Dagny asked Mr. Metzler before he walked back to the road and sat in his car to wait.

I walked to the end of the box where he said her head rested and sat on the wet artificial turf. I put my arm around the coffin and pressed my cheek against it. Dagny and Kirsten stood on the other side. We looked at each other. The day was moist and gray, and the caretakers were pretty far away.

None of us knew what to do. For the first time since Kara died, we were totally without activity to divert us, and we were confronted with the finality of what had happened. We were quiet, still.

Then Kirsten walked over to the coffin. I expected her to caress it gently, but instead she knocked on it, hard, several times. The noise was loud.

"O.K., Kara," she said. "The joke's over. You win. You can come out now."

Dagny and I were so shocked that we started laughing.

"It's just like you, Kara," continued Kirsten. "You couldn't just have one ceremony. You had to have us come back and do it again." And then she giggled. Kirsten has a wonderful giggle and she set Dagny and me off again.

In the midst of the most terrible tragedy we could imagine, we all were laughing so hard tears were flowing. I said we must be horrifying Mr. Metzler and the workmen who were over by the cars waiting for us to leave. Dagny speculated that there could be hidden cameras and microphones around the coffin, and it seemed so funny to us that our appalling behavior would be shown on the evening news that we laughed all the harder.

Then it just got quiet and I gave the coffin a little kiss; Kirsten gave the coffin a little kiss; and then Dagny gave the coffin a little kiss. Kirsten saw that only Dagny had left a lipstick print; there was no trace of Kirsten's kiss or mine. "Now, that's the final straw."

We all understood what she meant. Kara used to touch Dagny's full lower lip and ask her where she got those mushy lips. She and Kirsten wanted lips like that. When Kara commented on her own lips, the word "lips" was always followed by "when found."

We noticed though, that during all the kissing, the gleaming silver surface of the coffin had been smudged with handprints and so we put our hands all over it. We told the cemetery people they were not to polish us away. We wanted that coffin buried smudged.

And then we drove away and left her there.

Chapter 1 *Luck of the Draw*

"He could charm snakes and people," her grandfather Adrian said about his father, J. Monroe Spears, who at age sixteen had run away with his bride to join the circus. Adrian, their seventh child, swore his father could hypnotize a man to become stiff enough to act as a tabletop between two chairs. Kara, having a flair for the dramatic herself, was fascinated. It was much less interesting to her that he later became a lawyer and was elected solicitor of Darlington County, South Carolina. "My father could remember anything he heard just once and repeat it verbatim," her grandfather told her, and Kara identified with him because she could do the same thing. Adrian remembered nothing about his mother because he was only eighteen months old when she died at age thirty-two giving birth to her eighth child.

Kara's grandmother Elizabeth grew up in a small town at the opposite end of South Carolina. Elizabeth's father was a pharmacist, and he was called "Dr. Wylie" by Clover's nearly three thousand citizens, including his wife, Sara. Strong and capable, Sara took in boarders to help support the family during the depression years when few could pay for the drugs they needed from Wylie's Drug Store. Though the schoolteachers at her table were paying guests, Sara served the noon meal formally; two women in the kitchen cooked and responded to the beckoning of her silver bell. Sara was a tall woman for her day, and her great-granddaughter Kara would be the same height, five feet, ten inches.

Elizabeth and Adrian met when she went to Darlington to teach school; they married in San Antonio, Texas, where he had moved in order to practice law with an older brother. President Kennedy appointed Adrian a federal district judge in 1961. Kara's mother, Sally, was the oldest of Adrian and Elizabeth's five children. She went to law school at the University of Texas because she had always said she would be a lawyer like her father and grandfather (it seemed to please her father when she said it) and because she had broken up with her college boyfriend and thought she would never marry (marriage being the recommended career path for young women in the 1950s). Of approximately a thousand law school students, about ten were women.

Kara's paternal grandparents were from Norway. She was only a baby when her grandfather Hultgreen, Odd, died, but her parents talked fondly about him, telling her how generous he was and how he could make a birthday special and holidays magic occasions. Odd was six feet, four inches tall with curly blond hair and rosy cheeks, and he loved life, wine, and a good cigar. A brilliant man, he earned several advanced degrees in engineering and economics in Germany.

Returning home to Drammen, Norway, he built a paper converting operation and then a factory that made inks for the printing industry. Odd was active in the Norwegian resistance during World War II, but when the socialist government imposed heavy taxes on capital after the war, he moved his family to the United States to begin again. Dagny, his wife, was a talented artist. All her children and grandchildren wanted her paintings with their bright colors, geometric designs, and thick texture. Kara inherited her grandmother's talent and her way with color and loved to paint.

Tor, the oldest of Odd and Dagny Hultgreen's three children, was fifteen when his family immigrated to the United States. A natural athlete, he skied, played hockey, and was All-American in soccer at Middlebury College in Vermont, graduating with a degree in economics. Tor (the name is the Norwegian version of Thor, God of Thunder) looked the way you would expect a Viking descendent to look; he was voted Most Handsome his senior year at Greenwich High School. He and Sally met in summer school at the University of Colorado in Boulder and married the next summer in San Antonio. A combination of such diverse bloodlines, Kara was intrigued by what she called "the randomness of life."

Born on 5 October 1965 in Greenwich, Connecticut, Kara was their third daughter in as many years. Dagny had turned three a couple of weeks earlier; Kirsten, in the middle, was twenty-one months old. Kara was not quite two years old the summer of 1967 when Tor, who sold wood pulp to paper mills, was moved by his company to the Chicago area. He and Sally bought a home in Lincolnshire, a beautiful residential suburb of about three thousand people that had recently been carved out of one of the thickest forests in Illinois. Each of the homes in the village was on a one-half acre lot dense with magnificent oak trees, with enough bedrooms for three or four children and a two-car garage.

The people who bought these homes for the most part were new to the area—high-class transients—and like Kara's parents, many of them were in their late twenties. They met each other walking their babies or wandering over to critique the newest house under construction, and they formed close friendships.

Kara was a sweet child who wanted to please. Occasionally she didn't get it quite right. At two, she christened their new house by drawing pictures all the way down the staircase wall with her mother's best lipstick. At three, she picked every one of the tulips bordering the sidewalk of the house across the street. She proudly presented the flowers to the owners with a sunny smile and the innocent and unfulfilled expectation they would be happy.

Kara was a little daredevil, always game for whatever there was to do. She wanted to swing high, skate fast, and swim deep. The first time Tor took the girls skiing, he started to demonstrate how to snowplow to slow down. Kara watched him start skiing and didn't wait to see the purpose of the lesson. She just pointed her skis straight downhill as she had seen her father do and took off. Her father and sisters watched her furious descent and saw her finally halt at the bottom of the hill, still upright, unfazed, and ready to do it again.

She and her best friend, Amy Hoffman, were eight years old the summer they sneaked out of Amy's house after her parents were asleep. When they spent the night together they always got into mischief. Once they pilfered a cigarette and poured a little brandy from a decanter (not enough so Amy's parents would notice) and went up into the hot attic, where they had a wonderful sinful time coughing and choking. This time the village police found the two little girls riding their bikes after midnight and took them back to Amy's. Kara said their plan was to ride to their school—not more than a mile away—climb a tree to a second-floor window and see if they could open it.

They hadn't thought about what they would do once they got inside.

Life in Lincolnshire was comfortable, and the family was content. Then Tor's company transferred him to Toronto, Canada, in 1973, and everything changed. In some ways, the change was wonderful. They moved into a beautiful home in a small village called Oakville, about an hour's commute to Toronto. A private road led to one and a half acres of land where their house sat surrounded by forty-foot cedar trees, the barrier broken only by a driveway. Lake Ontario was just across the street. They started heating their swimming pool in May, and on cold Canadian mornings a mushroom cloud of moisture arose from the warm water. There was even a sauna in the pool house. The girls loved that house. Their friends thought they were rich.

In other, more important ways, the move was ruinous. Sally had been working, and in order to persuade her to move to Canada, Tor's company offered her a position in its corporate law department. She and Tor left home around 7:00 A.M. and usually didn't return to the house until after the girls had had their dinner. They had live-in help—but it kept changing. The girls didn't seem to mind. They could walk to school and ride their bikes to their friends' houses. They had a great house, meals served, clothes washed and ironed, and freedom from supervision most of the time.

Dagny, at age eleven, wrote a story for school entitled "House-keepers We Have Had." She described the young black woman with a huge bosom and a tiny waist who wore a bikini three sizes too small when she took them swimming and the woman from El Salvador who spoke only Spanish, had never seen a banana, and proceeded to eat one without peeling it. She told about the English woman whose disposition was mean and whose food was bland, and the Irish woman who dressed the children for Halloween, sent them out, and was gone for good without a word before the children returned home with their trick-or-treat candy and before their parents got home from work.

Sally's job was very demanding and she was under a lot of stress, leaving her little time or energy to spend with her children. But she felt her ability to help make money for the family was the most important thing. When she was growing up, money had been an issue—never quite enough of it for five children—and she wanted everything for her own children. Besides, they were making good grades in school (parent-teacher conferences were an ego boost). Dagny was involved with her friends, and Kirsten was absorbed in sports. But Kara, only nine years old, needed more attention than she was getting.

Kara claimed she was a self-raised child. And she was. During those first years in Oakville, she remembered her mother either with a book in her hand or upstairs taking a nap. One Sunday, Kara ran away from home and no one noticed. She told her mother years later that she left early in the morning and walked all the way into the town of Oakville intending never to return. But after wandering around for a while, she realized she had nowhere to go, so she walked back home. It was late in the afternoon when she returned, and she was sure her mother and father would be distraught. She envisioned police cars with sirens wailing in front of the house. But everything was quiet and when she walked into the family room, all her parents said was "Hi, Kara, where have you been keeping yourself?" They didn't even know she had been gone.

Dagny and Kirsten didn't want to be bothered with or by their little sister. The three girls had some major battles, and usually it was Dagny or Kirsten or both against Kara. Part of the reason they excluded her was that Kara lacked the cut-off valve, inborn in some people, that signals enough is enough. You could wrestle with Kara in good-natured horseplay, tumbling on the ground and laughing, until you lay there exhausted. But Kara would never want the game to end. She would push you to continue until your good humor vanished. She would understand that your mood had changed, but she wouldn't understand why and she would be hurt.

Eventually, that persistence and single-minded pursuit of whatever it was she was interested in became a great asset, but she had to learn to channel it first, and the lessons were painful to a child who had a great heart and a sensitive soul. In order to deal with the constant overt rejection by her older sisters and the passive rejection by parents who had no time for her, Kara began to build a protective shell. Rebuffed and ignored, the child who had been the most affectionate and eager to please became angry and aggressive. Her temper was formidable because she was fearless.

If Kara broke the glass ceiling by becoming a pioneer female fighter pilot, it was an apt metaphor. She broke two glass doors fighting for her place when she was nine years old. The first one was Dagny's glass shower door.

As Dagny told it

Kara and I got in that big fight and we were trying to kill each other practically. I tried to slam the door on her body and Kara was trying to run into my bathroom and I didn't want her in there. So finally, she came into my bathroom and I said "get out." She said, "No." She hung onto the bar of the sliding glass door to my tub and I tried to pull her off. All of a sudden, Crash! and the glass broke. I just looked at her and said, "You're going to get it." We both had to pay for it out of our allowances.

The second time glass shattered occurred not long after. Kirsten and Dagny were walking down the stairs and Kara was following them. Pestering them. Dagny told her, "Get away, we don't want to be around you." Reaching the bottom of the stairs first, the two older girls ran down the hall into the family room and slammed and locked the door. It was a door that used to open to the outside, and it was made of heavy plate glass set in a wooden door frame. Kara paused at the entrance to the hallway, about fifteen feet from where Dagny and Kirsten taunted her through the thick glass barrier.

Hurt by their rejection and at the same time furious at being treated so badly by her sisters, Kara threatened, "I'm coming in there."

"Oh, no you're not," Dagny responded, smug behind the locked door.

"I'm coming through that door if you don't let me in," Kara warned them.

They laughed at her. With fierce determination and to hell with the consequences, Kara put her arm in front of her face like a football player throwing a block and ran straight at them. Dagny and Kirsten watched with disbelief as she gathered speed. They stepped back, frightened, as they realized she wasn't going to stop. Kara sailed right through the glass, landing on her feet on the other side of the door.

Tor and Sally, upstairs in their bedroom, heard the noise and came running down. They were shocked to see huge shards of glass, some still hanging from the door frame and others lying on the white carpet. But no blood. Kirsten exclaimed, "Oh man, you're really in trouble this time, Kara."

Sally was frantic. She wasn't exactly sure what had happened—the girls were standing in the family room and all of them seemed okay—but she was terrified at what might have happened. As Kirsten described it, "Mom is having a fit, she starts spanking us—all of us. Dad just stands there and goes, 'Now who ran through the door?' I was screaming, 'Arggg. Kara. Kara did it!'

"'Kara, come over here. That's incredible.' Dad said. You couldn't accuse him of overreacting. He was picking up large pieces of glass, 'That's incredible, not a scratch on her.'"

Dagny agreed. "Well, it was pretty incredible, really. That was the second piece of glass Kara and I had to pay for."

It was a defining moment for Kara. Fueled by hurt and anger, she had taken a terrible risk, and no harm had come to her. The flawed and treacherous lesson of her reckless leap through glass was that she was invincible. She also resolved that she would not be cowed by the abusive use of power. Kara may not have realized that her parents abused their power by not being sufficiently involved with her, but she knew that her sisters had actively abused their power over her. Power that she had given them by looking up to them, aspiring to be like them, and craving their company and their approval—power magnified because they were older and because they ganged up on her.

She would never be a victim again.

Sally was either working or sleeping all the time, waking up crying in the morning, too busy to name her symptoms depression. Tor knew Sally wasn't happy and was truly sorry, but when she tried to talk to him about it, he would turn on the television or signal the waiter, anything to keep the conversation from getting too personal. He just hoped everything would work itself out.

Sally knew she had to make a change in her life. She thought it would help if the family moved into Toronto and took the two-hour commute out of the equation, but the girls didn't want to leave their school or their friends, and Tor didn't want to move either. So Sally rented a furnished apartment in Toronto and moved into it, leaving everyone else in Oakville. It seemed logical at the time. She was the sad one. Why should she uproot them? When she moved out of their house in 1976 and left her three young daughters with their father,

Kara was only eleven years old. Kirsten was thirteen and Dagny was fourteen. Looking back on it, she couldn't imagine how she had done that.

Tor and Sally still worked for the same company and remained friends, but their separation became permanent. After a year or so, she and Tor sold the house on Lakeshore Road, the house the girls loved, where they could go skinny-dipping in the sheltered pool with their girlfriends, and practice kissing in the sauna with the boys. Tor bought another house in Oakville and Sally bought one in Toronto.

The children stayed in school in Oakville with Tor, but on weekends, usually one or another of them would visit Sally in the hundred-year-old three-story Victorian house in the Yorkville section of downtown Toronto that she had renovated. It was a three-bedroom railroad, or shotgun, house with beautiful old orangey red brick, high ceilings, and hardly any yard on a narrow one-way street. The girls kept pajamas and clothes there. They liked having an executive mother with her own sophisticated town house. Sally encouraged them to bring their friends to stay overnight, and she took them to Chinese, French, and Italian restaurants. Because Sally was different from their own mothers, their friends thought she was very cosmopolitan, and her daughters took some pride in this.

In Tor's new house in Oakville, they had the same young wonderful housekeeper who had been with them since before Tor and Sally separated. A small crisis occurred when she got pregnant and the father wanted nothing to do with the baby. The housekeeper continued to live in the house with Tor and the children through her pregnancy and during her baby's first year. The girls thought it was great fun to have a baby to play with. The neighbors didn't know what the story was, and for a long time most of them thought the baby was Tor's.

Dagny, Kirsten, and Kara ran their own lives. They didn't have a mom to tell them when to get up or go to bed or do their homework. There is a lot to be said for what children do when they are clothed, fed, and then left to organize themselves. They got up, dressed, ate breakfast, and took the bus to school when it was snowing or rode their bicycles on nice days. They played sports and had girlfriends and boyfriends; they never missed school, were healthy, and made good grades.

But they were affected by having a mother who had physically deserted the home. Kara asked her mother later how she could have left them with their father. He was good to them in his way, but he didn't want to know how they were feeling or what they were thinking or get involved in their interests or activities. When he talked to them at all, it was about groceries or schedules. Mostly, he just went about his business and they went about theirs.

When Sally would call home, Kara was always glad to talk to her but Dagny and Kirsten had little to say. They would talk to her for a while, and then say they were busy: they had homework or a friend was coming over. She felt like an intruder. It was a terrible realization that she had cut herself off from her daughters' lives, and after she had lived away for about six months, Sally began to return to Oakville to stay with them at Tor's house the two or three nights a week he was traveling.

After awhile, the girls adjusted to the unusual family relationships and actually loved to satisfy the curiosity of their friends' parents who couldn't understand how their father could retain an unmarried pregnant housekeeper, or how a woman separated from her husband could spend a part of every week at his house with their children.

When Kara was twelve years old, Tor rented a horse for her. The deal was that he would pay all the boarding expenses and Kara would take care of Dundee. She was devoted to that horse and would go to the stables every afternoon after school to ride, feed, and groom him. It was seven miles from her house to the stable. Her mother was living in Toronto and her Dad didn't get home until late, so there was no one to take her back and forth. She would take the bus as far as possible, then she would get on her bike and ride the rest of the way on service roads.

It definitely was not a safe bike ride. Kirsten described the journey: "She had to get from our house into the town of Oakville on the bus and that was four miles. Then she had to go several more miles on her bike on service roads that were really busy. People would go whipping down the streets." But Kara wanted to have that horse and she would do what it took to take care of it.

She took lessons and entered horse shows—all with precious little encouragement from her parents. No one else in the family was interested in horses. The shows were held outdoors in muddy fields; it was usually cold, unpleasant, and dirty. Her mother only went to one of her shows. When Sally finally visited the stables, she was horrified to see the route Kara had to take to get there. She never should have been allowed to ride her bicycle on those busy streets.

Her freshman year in high school, Kara had a huge crush on Ralph Krumme. Ralph and his twin brother, Bernie, had moved to Oakville from Germany. They were both athletic and as Kirsten said, "the cutest guys." Kara joined the swim team and the water polo team because Ralph was on them, but it didn't work out exactly as Kara hoped. Ralph was two years older and saw her only as Kirsten's little sister.

Kara went through a wild phase when she was fourteen to fifteen years old. Kirsten told the story of how when Kara was in the ninth and tenth grades, she and her friends would go to Kara's house and drink beer in the downstairs family room. Only the housekeeper was there before Tor got home from work and Kara's house became a wonderful after-school gathering place.

She accumulated a closet full of beer bottles. One day, Tor happened to open that closet door. He asked Kirsten where those cases of empty bottles came from. Kirsten didn't volunteer information but Tor asked her to verify that they belonged to Kara, which she did. Tor gathered up all those cases (Kirsten said it took him several trips to the car) and took them back to the store for a refund. He never said a word to Kara, but when Kara discovered the cases of beer bottles were gone she was really upset—not because her father had found out about the beer but because she was depending upon the refund money (approximately forty dollars) to finance more parties in the basement. It was Tor's version of crime and punishment.

Chapter 2 ✿ *Texas*

In the summer of 1981, after Kara's sophomore year in high school, she moved with her mother to San Antonio, Texas. Sally and Tor had been separated more than five years by that time. They finally divorced in January 1983. Dagny had completed her first year at the University of Texas at Austin, about seventy miles from San Antonio. Kirsten was to finish her last year of high school in Canada with her father, then join her mother and sisters in Texas.

Kara, sixteen years old, Canadian-raised, athletic, assertive, adventuresome, and natural, was transplanted to the land of big hair, red lips, and cheerleading. They moved to the suburb where her mother had grown up, and she enrolled in the high school where her mother had graduated. Alamo Heights is a rare community in today's world. Parents, grandparents, and some great-grandparents have gone to Alamo Heights schools all the way from first grade to graduation. Starting there as a junior in high school was a real challenge. But there was one big plus for Kara: for the first time, she was in a school where no big sisters had preceded her.

Kara's friends in Oakville were always telling her how pretty Dagny was, but no one at Alamo Heights knew beautiful Dagny. Nor had they heard of Kirsten, who had been named most outstanding female athlete at Oakville Trafalgar High School. Kara was no longer the irritating little sister to big sisters who had no time for her, nor did she have to live up to her reputation as the wild one. Instead, she began to bloom as she slowly realized that the words *beautiful* and *athletic* were now being used to describe her.

The first thing Kara did at Alamo Heights was to try out for the girl's basketball team. She made it easily because she had played basketball at Oakville Trafalgar High School and hardly any Alamo Heights girls wanted to play basketball. Drill team and cheerleading were the things most girls wanted to do. Water polo was the only other team sport for girls, and Kara signed up for that too.

For the first time in her life, Kara had a full-time mother focused entirely on her. She wasn't sure she liked it. She had got along fine all those years without a mother at home. She told Sally she didn't need her to start doting over her at age sixteen, and she should get to work and buy them a house and her a car, which was what she really needed.

Whether Kara needed a full-time mother or not, Sally needed to be one. She got up every morning, fixed Kara a hot breakfast, and took her to basketball practice at 6:45. Kara rolled her eyes and complained that she could get her own breakfast and drive her own car—if she had one—and her mother didn't have to try to be June Cleaver at this late date. She liked having a working mom better.

Kara played basketball the way she did everything she decided to do—wholeheartedly—but the team's record was unremarkable. What was remarkable was that Kara and her mother were the main contributors to the demise of girl's basketball at Alamo Heights. The issue was school prayer. Before every basketball game, Kara's coach would gather the players in a circle and appoint one of them to say a prayer. Try as she might to move around that circle, Kara's time came.

"All right, Kara, it's your turn to say the prayer," said the coach.

"I'd rather not," said Kara.

"It's your turn," her coach insisted.

Again, Kara declined politely. Whether because of religious zeal or because she saw Kara's refusal as an affront to her authority, the coach became very angry and threatened to suspend Kara from the team unless and until she led the prayer. "Coach," said Kara, "I do not mean to be impertinent, but I don't believe in God and I am not going to lead a prayer. I am happy to stand here respectfully if everyone else wants to pray."

The coach gave her a grim look. Kara played that night but the next day the coach talked to the principal about Kara's outrageous pronouncement that she didn't believe in God. Although the Alamo Heights community was predominantly churchgoing, and Christian student groups abounded, the principal was aware of the First Amendment to the Constitution of the United States guaranteeing freedom of religion. He also knew Kara's grandfather was a federal judge.

Kara was forced to spend the better part of out-of-town basket-ball bus trips affirming to her incredulous friends that though she did-n't believe there was a God, she believed in right and wrong and con-sidered herself a moral person. She wanted to do good in the world even if she didn't believe she would go to hell if she didn't.

Sally was dismayed. She knew that conservative Alamo Heights people were apt to be shocked by a child's proclamation that she did-n't believe in God. Kara realized that also and hadn't wanted to make an issue of it. She was new to the school and wanted to fit in, but she was pushed and she wasn't going to pray if she didn't believe in it. The concept of separation of church and state was affirmed, but the cause never should have been joined.

The incident contributed to making 1982 the last season for the coach and, for years, the girls' basketball team. The only other major sport left open to Alamo Heights girls was tennis and, unlike basket-ball, it was socially acceptable for girls to play. Alamo Heights had the best high school tennis program in the state of Texas. Most of the young men and women had been playing since childhood at the San Antonio Country Club. Kara talked to the tennis coach, Larry Oxford, after basketball season. He knew she didn't have the tennis training or experience of the other girls, and he told her he didn't think she could become good enough to make the team by the time for tryouts. He underestimated Kara. She took tennis lessons, practiced hard, and made the team.

One of the best things about the tennis experience was the friend-ship between Kara and Monique Kleck, a bond that continued through their diverse experiences as young adults. They were both beautiful, vivacious, charming, a little wicked, and the two most com-petitive women you would ever hope to see. Monique had four older brothers and had been playing tennis since she was five. Five feet, five inches tall with waist-length thick blond hair, she looked fragile—and was about as fragile as fishing line. She was so much the better tennis player that she and Kara didn't compete with each other, which was a good thing for their friendship.

Once during a tournament, Sally saw Kara throw her racquet on the ground after making what she considered to be a bad shot. On the way home, she told Kara that if she ever again saw her throw her racquet, she would not continue to support her tennis. Kara understood what her mother meant; tournament travel, new rackets, balls, lessons, clothes all cost money. She responded by staring straight ahead, setting her jaw, and saying nothing. Sally never saw Kara throw her racquet again, but neither did she see her smile graciously when she shook her opponent's hand after she had lost a match. Kara took her games very seriously.

The tennis team traveled all over, playing various high school teams, and on one of those trips, the chaperoning mothers and fathers and Coach Oxford were gathered around the coffee shop breakfast table with their sixteen- and seventeen-year-old "stars." The young players were telling stories about their parents' various oddities; the parents were countering with their own complaints about food left out, clothes strewn about, cars returned on empty.

Kara chimed in, "My mother and I have an arrangement," she said. "I keep my room clean, and she lets me live there."

At the tennis banquet, her coach said it was amazing that Kara had made the tennis team and earned a letter in her senior year. He wished every player he coached had her "courage, discipline, energy, enthusiasm, and incredibly infectious positive attitude." He went on to say that she was an outstanding athlete and if she had played for him for four years, she would have been one of the top players in the state.

Kara blossomed at Alamo Heights. She was elected to the National Honor Society in her junior year and the next year to Service Club, an honorary society for girls. She lettered in basketball in her junior year and tennis in her senior year. She was president of the Junior Engineering Technological Society and was in the Social Studies Honorary Society. She considered the highest honor being voted "Studdette" and having her picture in the school newspaper showing her in sunglasses for having the coolest stare.

Most of the time, Kara and her friends went out in groups, but in the spring of her junior year she dated Jack Williams Jr. The romance came to an end after Jack got drunk at a party but wouldn't let Kara drive home. She walked in the drizzling rain and ruined her blue silk high heels. She was mad, and Jack was mad that she was mad, and that was that.

According to Kara, she had wanted to be an astronaut since she was a child "after a healthy dose of *Star Trek*." Her mother remembered the decision being made in her junior year in high school after she did an assignment on the space program for her history teacher, Mary Zuschlag. So the person responsible for her choice has been narrowed down to either Mary Zuschlag or William Shatner, but in either case, it's true that after she decided what she was going to be, she set about being it. "I always grew up separating my life into little goals, keeping in mind the ultimate goal to be an astronaut," Kara said in a 1989 article in *Women in Aviation* magazine. "With each goal I've always thought: 'Can I really do that?' Then I just ignore the doubt, press on, and enjoy the achievement."

Kara considered two routes to her goal of becoming an astronaut: earning a Ph.D. in a scientific field or becoming a test pilot. She liked being in charge and the idea of piloting a mission into space appealed to her. She had been fascinated with speed from the time she was a child. She rode her bike as fast as she could, pretending to be a race car driver, and once thought it would be very "cool" to be a team parachutist. She decided she would be a pilot first; the advanced degrees could come later.

"Kara told her water polo teammates she was going to fly jets," her coach, Tim Henrich, told her mother later. "Many of us asked her, 'Do they allow girls to fly jets?' Her reply was, in a very matter-of-fact manner, 'They will let me.' And they certainly did."

Kara had read *The Right Stuff*, and the message was astronauts were navy pilots. She decided the logical place for her to go to college was the Naval Academy. She received an appointment from the congressman for her district, but that year the Naval Academy took only ninety-four women. She was number ninety-seven on the list. Kara was disappointed, but she didn't agonize over it. She enrolled at the University of Texas, where Kirsten would be a sophomore and Dagny a senior. Childhood trauma behind them, the three girls had become fast friends. After Kara had been in the navy for a while, she said she was glad she hadn't gone to Annapolis because the women who spent four years there were, for the most part, pretty cynical about the navy.

Aerospace engineering seemed the logical major for a future astronaut. Logical to her. Dagny was studying broadcast journalism.

Kirsten's major was "adult health fitness management." One time Kara was reviewing formulas for her physics final in the loft of the apartment she shared with Kirsten, and she heard Kirsten, who was downstairs studying with a friend, asking, "What are the components of a good running shoe?"

"You have to go to college to learn that?" Kara called down.

Tor was funding three educations at once, grateful his daughters had chosen a state university and not expensive private schools. Kirsten was always extremely frugal, which irritated Dagny and Kara. They would be out of money, and Kirsten would still have lots in the bank. However, Kirsten was the most successful at asking their father for money, so Dagny and Kara would make Kirsten write on everyone's behalf.

Though he was very generous, every now and then their father would try to impress upon them that it was expensive having three daughters in college at once. The first time Kara asked for an advance, he questioned her about how she was spending her money. Kara was stung by the implied criticism. She wasn't careless with money and she hated having to ask for anything. The next semester she got a receipt for everything. She wouldn't get a soft drink out of a machine because she couldn't get a receipt for it. She kept a list of everything she spent, boxed up every receipt she collected and sent them all to her father the next time she needed money. He never questioned her again.

But the fact that she had had to account for her spending made her vow not to have to ask for any money from him again unless she absolutely had to. Though she was taking a full course of engineering classes, more than most people could handle, she got a job at Tracor, a large electronics corporation in Austin. As she had when she needed transportation to get to her horse, she rode her bicycle for miles on heavily traveled roads to get to and from work. She used her first few paychecks to buy a Moped, which was not as strenuous as pedaling but was even more dangerous. Since riding a two-wheeled motor vehicle was practically the only thing she had ever been forbidden to do, she didn't tell either of her parents of her acquisition.

Kirsten finally told her father what Kara was doing and he broke down and bought them a car. It was a new red Renault Alliance. It had little panache—that was the whole idea—but it was trustworthy and served the purpose. Kirsten and Kara began to like it more because Dagny thought it was gross and refused to drive it, leaving the car free for them.

Kara worked at Tracor for almost two years, until the company lost the government contract that funded the project she was working on. They said there was a place for her permanently when she graduated if she wanted it. She learned about computers in her job, and that experience served her well in the navy in her ground jobs and as a pilot.

She also got her first taste of being the object of gossip when an unfriendly secretary noticed that Kara's boss left messages on her computer beginning with the salutation "Special K" and that the two of them seemed to get along extremely well. Kara loved to joke and she liked her boss a lot, but she couldn't understand how people could think she would be romantically involved with a married "older" man in his late thirties. That incident was her introduction to the concept of perceptions: it isn't what is really going on but what people imagine might be going on that hurts you.

Kara worked hard and made good grades in college, but she also dated (no serious boyfriend) and had a lot of fun. After four years at the University of Texas, she graduated in 1987 with a 3.3 out of 4.0 grade point average in aerospace engineering. According to Kara, the course she worked the hardest in was introduction to geography and she made only a C. She made an A in calculus 1 and 2. She was tapped for Spooks, a freshman service organization, and was consistently on the Engineering Honor Roll.

She signed up to join the navy at the beginning of her senior year. She had to be intellectually and physically qualified, including having perfect eyesight, in order to be admitted to Aviation Officer Candidate School (AOCS). She passed her physical examinations during the school year, and when she graduated from college only one test remained, a rigorous physical fitness test. She began training for it as soon as she got home from school.

Monique thought it would be fun to train for the test with Kara, so every day for a month they ran and did push-ups and pull-ups. Part of the test required running one and a half miles in thirteen minutes. Kara was strong, but running was not her best event. She would run too fast the first mile, then struggle to finish the last half mile. Monique, who had been on the Trinity University tennis team for four years, had done a lot of running. She knew how to pace herself, and when Kara ran with her she did fine.

On the day of the test, Monique came along to watch. She and Kara were a contrast that morning. Kara had dressed in her serious athlete clothes, track shorts and a sweatshirt with the arms cut out. Her hair was braided tightly and her face was scrubbed. Monique was wearing makeup, a sleeveless blouse, short shorts, and the appropriate gold jewelry of a young Heights postgraduate. A young navy lieutenant met them at the Alamo Heights High School track.

Kara knew she could easily do the one hundred sit-ups and sixty-seven push-ups required for a perfect score, but she was nervous about the run; she was still having trouble pacing herself. Kara passed the strength portions of the test with ease, and Monique ran over to congratulate her. She hugged Kara, then with her green eyes wide she looked up at the young male officer, batted her eyelashes, flipped her highlighted, waist-length blond hair, and said, "Gosh, I'm thinking about joining the navy too. Do you think I could run along with Kara, just to see if I can do it?"

Kara and Monique finished the run with time to spare, the young lieutenant accepting with grace the fact that he had been sandbagged.

Chapter 3   *Aviation Officer Candidate School*

"Which color polish do you like best?" asked Monique, holding up two fingers. She was in the passenger seat of Kara's new red Alfa Romeo convertible, as they headed east from San Antonio on Interstate 10. *Glamour, Vogue,* and *Harper's Bazaar* magazines were strewn at her feet. Monique was experimenting with an upswept hairstyle and manicuring her nails, on her way to a debutante party in Houston. Kara, her hair chopped off, her nails clipped short, no makeup, no jewelry, and a trunk filled with sweatshirts, sports bras, and running shoes, was on her way to Aviation Officer Candidate School.

"Keep your fingers crossed for me. I'm a little nervous," said Kara when she dropped Monique off at the home of a friend in Houston.

"I'm not worried about you," Monique told her. "I envy you. You've always known that you wanted to be an astronaut and now you're taking the first step. I'm going to graduate school, but I still don't know what I want to do."

"Short! Loud! Crisp, Long Hair! That's how you answer," Kara's marine corps drill instructor, Staff Sgt. Brian A. Snow, shouted at her, counting push-ups.

"Yes, Sir!" Kara yelled as loud as she could. She was three-quarters of the way through the one hundred push-ups assigned by her drill instructor, obviously tired but making an effort. She knew it was a game, and the object was never to quit even though the push-ups didn't really resemble push-ups anymore.

Another officer candidate had stopped trying and was lying prone on the ground. "You finished?" growled Staff Sergeant Snow to the hapless young man, prodding him with the toe of his boot. "You better be dead!" The young man tried to do one more push-up but the drill instructor (DI) put his foot on his shoulder. "Just play dead, you fuckin' knucklehead." This was 1987 and the last thing the DIs worried about was offending the sensibilities of their charges. Kara took the salty language in stride.

Staff Sergeant Snow walked over to Kara who was still doing straggly push-ups. "You want to rest, Long Hair? Is this too much for you?"

Kara's stomach was barely getting above the ground. "No sir!" she answered breathlessly.

Snow turned his head so the class wouldn't see him smiling. "All right, you pansies. Enough; get to the showers."

Kara wrote a card to Monique on Sunday, 2 August 1987, after her first week at AOCS:

> I survived poopey week! I'm just taking a break from cleaning my rifle, and shining my flight boots. AOCS—what a party! Last week was living hell—15 guys dropped from the program. Our class now has a total of 19 persons. (I'm the only "non-male," "long hair" as my drill instructor calls me.) I feel like I have 18 brothers now—they are all great guys. My DI is tough but fair—he only expects perfection. One DI is from A&M [Texas A & M and the University of Texas have a fierce rivalry] and he gave me the ol' "where you from?" line. I paid in push-ups.

The class waited at attention dressed in shorts and shirts, each one carrying a rifle. It was Monday, 3 August, the beginning of the second week. "This thing's got to weigh about a hundred pounds after a few minutes," Kara said to her classmate Scott Douglas. "I heard that the rifle run cleared out about half of the last OCS class."

"Quiet, Assholes!" Staff Sergeant Snow shouted. "All right, at my command you'll hoist your rifles and march. Keep up with me. Left, right, left, right, double time, march!"

Several of the men dropped out along the way. Kara finished the run. As she explained to her mother, "All that kept me going that last quarter mile was that I knew that if I stopped, I'd have to drop back a class and do this again."

Kara wrote Monique a long letter six weeks later. She had lots to tell.

> Things are going great here except for the fact that our class is dwindling into almost nonexistence. We now have 10 candidates after losing 4 to the Leadership and Engines finals. Our Drill Instructor was so happy on Thursday because we won the Drill Streamer (it's

a big deal—no other classes in the Battalion have a Drill Streamer). Anyway, I think Staff Sergeant Snow is pretty upset that people keep dropping from the class. It will look ridiculous when there are only five of us at graduation. Actually, you need 12 candidates to graduate and we are picking up two tonight. If we lose any more, it might delay our graduation by two weeks.

I still can't believe how fast these past seven weeks have flown by. But, Mo, I have to admit that this isn't half as bad or hard as I thought it would be. The Drill Instructors treat me really well. After making the rifle run it was instant respect. I've done great academically and I've kept up with the guys in all the P.T. (Physical Training). The boxing coach said I was the best female boxer to come through the program and he would have put me up against a guy (but it isn't legal).

My DI was hilarious the other day because he said that if I graduated in his class that I would be the first female to graduate from his class that started the first Tuesday of Poopey Week. [He meant she would have started and finished in his class with no interruptions.] He said that this would be the single most significant achievement of my life and that any future accomplishment would be shadowed. That means, he went on to say, that I could become President of the United States and I would mention this in my inaugural speech. I almost burst out laughing—that would not have been good.

So as you can surmise, I'm having a good time. One of the hardest things to do around here is not to laugh at the DIs. They try and make you laugh and punish you if you do. "On your face now—Move!" is a familiar expression. "Side Straddle Hops, 400, . . . Get 'em!" is another good one.

Anyway, Mo. Thanks for your letters—I love getting mail. Tell me more about your classes and the hunky men at A&M. You should plan a trip to Pensacola—There are tons of QTs [cuties] around here—and they all look awesome in their whites.

I'll try to write again soon but some things I will have to tell you in person—This is going to be over before I know it.

Kara's letter to Monique two days later described the mile swim.

Tomorrow we have our mile swim in flight suits. The hardest part is that I have to stand watch tonight so I will be tired tomorrow. After the mile swim we do the tread test—we put on flight boots, gloves, helmet, and an uninflated life vest (added to the flight suit) and we have to tread water for five minutes and drown proof for five minutes. No problem. Then we do the tower jump. We strip down to flight suit and boots alone and jump from a 15-foot tower—using correct form—and then we have to swim underwater for 50 feet. Actually it's all pretty easy. We do have a couple of swim rocks in the class though and we can't afford to lose any people.

Oh well, I won't think about that today—I'll think about it tomorrow, when I can stand it.

"You watch Young and I'll watch Dunlop," Kara said to her classmate Mike Barger. "They didn't even know how to swim when they got here. At least we can keep them from drowning." The class, dressed in flight suits, was required to swim one mile in a square pattern around the pool in under one hour.

Kara swam steadily and gave encouragement to Dunlop every time she passed him, but he and Young gave up about halfway through. By the last quarter mile everyone was struggling. Kara finished first. She told Kirsten she was determined to do it well because she never wanted to do it again. Her time was fifty-three minutes.

Dressed in shorts, T-shirts, and running shoes, the class gathered for another highlight of AOCS, the obstacle course. "O.K., you guys know what to do," the DI instructed. "Long Hair, you can go around the wall."

Kara was honestly perplexed. "Permission to go over the wall, Sir."

"Long Hair, I've never had a female officer candidate make it over the twelve-foot wall. Non-males don't have the upper body strength. Now, get going," Snow ordered.

Kara held her own and when she came to the wall with the rope hanging down, she headed right for it and climbed over it without any trouble. Her classmates cheered.

"I was the first girl in two years to make it over the 12' wall on the obstacle course," she told Monique. "(We get to run around it for time, but I wanted to try it.) Anyway, I think other girls have made it over the 12' wall (it's the one with the rope from *An Officer and a Gentleman*). But our instructor just hasn't had a female that could do it. I thought it was pretty easy actually. My classmates said it was inspirational."

Monique could relate to what Kara was telling her when Kara tied it to *An Officer and a Gentleman,* the movie about AOCS. For example, Monique could visualize the scene where each officer candidate was strapped in a simulated cockpit then slammed into water and flipped upside down, and she understood when Kara described that training exercise, which she thought was great fun. The movie also helped put in context Kara's helicopter dunker story.

The helo dunker is a simulated helicopter fuselage suspended over a pool. The operator can lower it into the pool and then rotate it to various positions, from full upright to full inverted, to approximate what might happen after a helicopter crash at sea. It is a confidence builder with a practical aspect—it might actually happen some day. Students generally go through four separate evolutions in the dunker: upright, eyes open; upright, with black-out goggles to simulate night; inverted, eyes open; and, finally, inverted with the goggles.

All the officer candidates agreed it was the most terrifying exercise in the program. Six students were strapped in the dunker and instructed to let the cabin fill with water before evacuating, then to exit single file. The students were supposed to pull themselves out without kicking, so they wouldn't hurt the person behind; however, many couldn't stop themselves. Kara was at the end of the line during the last evolution, when the students were upside down and blindfolded by the goggles. The classmate ahead of her was kicking like crazy, frantic to get out.

She couldn't see to dodge the thrashing boots. And she was almost out of breath. As if the circumstances weren't challenging enough, when she reached to unbuckle her seat belt, she couldn't get it to release. The safety diver signaled her to get going. She signaled that she was stuck. He came to help, pulling and tugging at her before he realized the problem. Then he couldn't get the clasp open and became very agitated.

Kara kept telling herself to keep calm. She put her hands up and let him work with the fastening until he finally got her free. When she was safe on the dock, the first thing she said was, "I don't have to that again, right? I'm cleared, right?" She definitely didn't want to do it again. She was praised for not panicking and very thankful she didn't have to repeat the exercise.

✖

"It's Sunday and I've been cleaning out my locker in preparation for the big RLP [room, locker, and personnel inspection] on Wednesday," she wrote Monique. "Wish us luck. I really want to pass this inspection. If we pass it will mean off base liberty on the weekends for the rest of the time. If we fail I won't get off base until the 14th week."

The class stood at attention in the hall outside their rooms for the room, locker, and personnel inspection. Marine corps Gunnery Sergeant Norbeck, a drill instructor from another class, was in charge. When Kara's turn came, she preceded him into her room. The door remained open and everyone could hear what was being said.

He opened Kara's locker, searching for anything out of place. "Sir," she said tentatively, "Aviation Officer Candidate Hultgreen was going to request that the Class 32-87 gear locker be opened."

"Oh yaaaa. So you could get at all your phantom gear," Gunny Norbeck growled at her. ("Phantom gear" included civilian clothes such as jeans and T-shirts, which the young officer candidates wanted to wear out on the town if they passed inspection and earned liberty for the weekend.)

"No, Sir!" Kara exclaimed innocently.

"Hultgreen, do you think the fucking cabbage truck just rolled up out front and I fucking fell off?" responded Norbeck.

After the inspection was over, Scott Douglas came into her room. "Too bad he wouldn't open the gear locker, but it was pretty gutsy for you to ask. Now we'll have to wear our whites [white uniforms] and behave ourselves," he lamented.

"I thought sure he was going to find something wrong—even if he had to sneak in in the middle of the night and mess it up himself," Kara laughed.

"That's why the drill instructors from another class do the inspections," Scott said. "It kills them to have to pass another DI's class."

"Transformer!" Staff Sergeant Sosa barked at her later, alluding to the transformer toys that looked like a car or motorcycle but folded out into a superhero. "How come your shit's always packed so tight?"

"Sir, this candidate's drill instructor demands perfection."

✖

Mail call at AOCS was the equivalent of sitting around the campfire, a relatively relaxed time. If the weather were nice, they would gather around outside the barracks. Gunny Snow (he had been promoted on 2 October) distributed mail to his class while Gunny Norbeck stood around watching. Snow called out the names, "Douglas! Barger!" They claimed their letters.

"Hultgreen!" Kara stood up and reached out for her package.

"Hultgreen," barked Snow, "you seem to get a package every day. Open it up and show it off!"

The label on the outside of the box said Camouflage Crispies. Kara removed the top; inside the package were Rice Krispies cookies—and they were colored green. The class tried not to smile, but even the drill instructors were having a hard time maintaining a stern expression.

Gunny Norbeck got into the act. "Cookies! Green cookies! Transformer, don't your friends think we feed you here?"

"This candidate's friends are bake-aholics, Sir!" Kara explained with a straight face.

Gunny Snow had to turn his head to keep from laughing. Gunny Norbeck struggled to maintain his frown.

"What else is in that package, Transformer?" asked Norbeck, attempting to snarl.

"The *National Enquirer,* Sir!" Kara held up the tabloid with a space alien baby on the cover. That finished it. Everyone roared, including the drill instructors.

Kara had enjoyed a manicure, pedicure, and massage, and was relaxing in her luxurious hotel room on her first liberty in Pensacola. She was proud of herself. Her class as a whole was outstanding, and she was competing with the best of them. She had scored 98 on her aerospace final and 95 on the navigation final. She had won the mile swim, aced the rifle run, climbed over that twelve-foot wall, and the boxing coach had said she was the best female boxer to come through the program. Staff Sergeant Sosa had told her she was "shit hot." Yet here she was alone on the first Saturday night of liberty.

Her emotions were mixed. The pampering and the privacy were welcome, but she didn't know what the rest of her class was doing that

Saturday night. For the first time since they had started officer candidate school, she wasn't part of the group. She wasn't sure just what to make of it. For weeks she had been living and working with a small group of men. They had bonded as they shared challenges, becoming close friends in the process. And Kara had never for an instant, until then, felt that she didn't belong.

The young men probably didn't think anything about it. They were guys going out on the town to let off steam. They had passed a grueling test and deserved a "boys' night out" with all its connotations. Whatever Kara's abilities in the classroom or on the playing field, she certainly wasn't "one of the boys"—nor was she fair game as "one of the girls."

After relating to all these young men on an intellectual and athletic level for weeks, it was jarring for Kara to be confined because she was female as soon as they were back in the real world.

Kara entered the fourteen-week Naval Aviation Officer Candidate School in Pensacola, Florida, in July 1987 and graduated on 6 November 1987. She was nominated as a candidate lieutenant commander. It was a small graduating class but it was an Honor Class, one of the best. Her classmates were Michael G. Barger from Howell, Michigan; Scott M. Douglas from Solana Beach, California; Richard R. Gessner from Raleigh, North Carolina; Scott M. Hogan from Rutland, Vermont; Peter J. Hoopfer from Clarkston, Michigan; James D. Macy from NAS Pensacola, Florida; Gregory K. Macintosh from Morehead City, North Carolina; and Michael T. Zimmermann from Palatine, Illinois.

James Macy, who was prior enlisted, graduated with highest honors and because the class had only nine members, he was the only one in the top 10 percent of that class. But Kara placed in the top 10 percent of the last several classes graduating and, therefore, was a Distinguished Naval Graduate. As such, she earned a regular, not a reserve, commission as an ensign in the United States Navy.

Chapter 4 *Primary Flight Training: Corpus Christi*

The certificate reads, "On the 25th day of March, 1988, Ensign Kara S. Hultgreen did, alone and unassisted take off and return to NAS CORPUS CHRISTI, TEXAS, thereby successfully completing her first solo flight." The Texas sky over Corpus Christi, with its unmatched weather and sparse competition for airspace, was friendly to future navy fighter pilots. After her solo, Kara had 19.6 hours in the single-engine Beechcraft T-34C Mentor, a turboprop aircraft used by the Naval Air Training Command since 1976.

During the twenty weeks of primary flight training from January through May, the students were evaluated and graded from ground school through takeoffs and landings. Those grades, and the needs of the navy, determined the type of aircraft they would be allowed to fly. Future training could be on jets, props, helicopters, or E2/C2s. Every student pilot wanted to fly jets and Kara was no exception. She knew she had to have top grades to be given the opportunity.

In April, Kara was riding her new white Kawasaki 500 motorcycle along the JFK Causeway from NAS Corpus Christi to her apartment on Padre Island. She waved to a fellow ensign, Arie Friedman, as she raced by his car. Arie lived at the same complex at Leeward Isles and knew her motorcycle, otherwise he wouldn't have recognized her. Her hair was still short and covered by her helmet; goggles hid her face; and she was wearing her flight suit, so it wasn't even obvious that she was female.

Going at her usual Kara clip, she also passed other cars. Unfortunately, one happened to carry the commanding officer of her squadron, VT-27. Stuck in slow-moving traffic, Cdr. James P. Sinz was irritated when the motorcycle rider zoomed past him. Then he focused on what the rider was wearing. For naval aviators to leave the base in flight suits was against regulations; they are considered working uniforms. Jack Lefler, a lieutenant commander who happened to be Kara's first flight instructor, was driving. They decided they weren't going to let the young renegade, whoever he was, get away with a double violation. They were going after that motorcycle.

Kara saw their car in her rearview mirror and recognized the senior officers. Her heart rate and her motorcycle accelerated. She knew she was in big trouble if they caught her. Her best chance to lose them was at the bridge, where the cycle would be able to pass cars while their automobile would have to stay in its lane. Her plan worked, and when she pulled into her apartment complex and parked beside her Alfa Romeo, she breathed a huge sigh of relief.

The senior officers, even angrier after they crossed the bridge, went looking for the culprit. After all, they reasoned, Padre Island isn't that big. They turned down one street and another until they saw a motorcycle parked in front of a house.

"That's the cycle!" said Commander Sinz, "I'm pretty sure. Let's check it out." They got out of the car and felt the cycle.

"Bingo! It's hot," said Lefler. They went to the door and rang the doorbell.

Mike Barger, dressed in shorts and a shirt, answered. He was very surprised to see the squadron commander on his doorstep. Mike and two other friends from AOCS had rented a house together. It was on the water and had its own dock.

"That your cycle?" asked the commander.

"No, Sir. It belongs to Brice," replied Mike.

Brice was another navy pilot in training. He and Kara had been friends since they met as aerospace engineering majors at the University of Texas, and they had gone out a few times. He had been in navy ROTC and was the one who told Kara about Aviation Officer Candidate School. He heard his name and walked over to the door. He was barefoot and wearing jeans and a T-shirt.

"That your cycle?" Commander Sinz repeated.

"Yes, Sir," answered Brice.

Commander Sinz looked at him closely, recognizing him. "Aren't you one of the new pilot trainees?"

Brice was very uncomfortable. "Yes, Sir."

"Did you just get here?" inquired Lieutenant Commander Lefler.

"Yes, Sir," Brice answered, not sure what this was about, but not liking it very much.

"Did you come from the base?" asked Lefler.

"Well, Sir, I was there earlier today. But I just came over here from my apartment about a mile from here. Is there anything wrong?" By this time, Brice was very nervous.

The two senior officers looked at each other. They didn't know whether to believe him or not, but he wasn't wearing his flight suit and they didn't have enough evidence to accuse him.

"We saw some rebel in his flight suit speeding along the causeway and lost him in the traffic. If we could have caught the bastard, he would have been in a world of hurt." With those intimidating words, Sinz turned around, and he and Lefler got into their car and drove away.

Mike and Brice looked at each other and shook their heads; then the truth dawned on both of them at the same time. "Kara," they said in unison.

The next day Mike and Brice couldn't wait to tell Kara what had happened. "You nearly got busted yesterday, Kara," Brice said. "Commander Sinz was out for your ass—and he almost got mine instead. You need to settle down on that motorcycle."

"I know," Kara said. "It's not worth getting thrown out of the navy. I can't even tell my mother I have it. She's cool with flying but she'd freak if she knew I had a cycle. It's about the only thing my parents ever forbade me to do when I was growing up."

Commander Lefler didn't let on that he suspected Kara was the phantom motorcycle rider until her solo debrief. It's a raunchy recognition given the pilots after their first solo, and Kara's mother and sister Kirsten had come to the ceremony at NAS Corpus Christi. When Lefler made a comparison between her piloting skills and her motorcycle driving, it was the first Sally had heard about the motorcycle. By then, Kara had sold the Kawasaki and had bought a larger, more powerful Yamaha from Brice. Sally was not happy about it, but then what could she say to a twenty-three-year-old woman who was flying jet airplanes?

When Kara ran into Jack Lefler about three years later at NAS Roosevelt Roads in Puerto Rico, they laughed about the motorcycle incident. She told him that her nickname for him when he was her flight instructor was "the Anti-Christ." He was inordinately pleased, as he had worked very hard to cultivate a reputation as being the toughest, meanest flight instructor around and was glad to know his efforts had not been in vain. "She was a *great kid!!*" he later wrote.

> Flying with her was easy—she was always ready and rarin' to go. She required so little instruction—she was *good!* I could relax when we flew together. She always did everything so well. Often we would finish all the required syllabus items on a hop a little early—so—for a few moments, we would go dancing in the clouds. I'd take control of the aircraft and off we would go—yankin' and bankin' . . . zippin' along . . . over, under and around the puffies . . . joking and laughing, sharing the sheer joy of the speed and the freedom that is flight. Kara LOVED IT!! At the end of the flight, by her smile, I knew that she knew that I didn't do that for all my students—just the good ones.

Kara, Mike, and Brice were in the Ready Room, discussing their futures. Kara was making a paper airplane. "It was too cool to solo," she said. "I'm so psyched, but I'm also nervous. There are only five jet slots open to women this entire year."

"It isn't only the female jet slots that are hard to get, Kara," Mike reminded her. "All jet slots are hard to get. You have to be in the top 10 percent to get jets whether you're a guy or a girl."

"You'll love helos, Kara," Brice kidded her. "Those choppers are sooo fine." She laughed and sailed her paper airplane at him.

But everything turned out all right. All three of them got orders to report to Beeville, Texas, to begin training in the T-2C Buckeye jet.

Kara was ecstatic.

Chapter 5 *A Day at the Boat* *Jet Training at Beeville*

Kara flew the T-2C Buckeye jet in her new training squadron, VT-26, for the first time on 24 August 1988. She had 71.5 hours total pilot time. Flying a jet was so much more exciting than flying a turboprop, and she was high on anticipation of the event that made navy pilots strut—landing that jet on an aircraft carrier.

Her class practiced those carrier landings at the field before actually trying to land on the moving, bouncing, floating surface. Part of the runway was painted like a carrier deck, complete with lines resembling arresting wires, and the student pilots aimed for the third of the four would-be wires. The landing signal officer graded each attempt. In between actual practice, the students watched videos and attended lectures so they would know as much as possible about what to expect.

On the first day "at the boat" flying solo in formation behind a lead instructor, Kara's heart beat furiously as she tried to assimilate all the new distractions she hadn't experienced at the field, such as the wake of the boat and the angled deck. She loved the adrenaline rush; it stoked her natural exuberance. She had to concentrate on setting up a good approach and "flying the ball." That meant following the message of the lights on board the carrier that show the glide path to the approaching pilot.

Each aviator had to do two touch and gos, four traps (landing on the carrier deck with the tailhook catching an arresting wire), and four catapult shots off the deck. Kara carrier-qualified in the Buckeye on the USS *Lexington* on 26 January 1989. She described those first carrier landings in a cover story written by Margaret Gross in the November–December 1989 issue of *Women in Aviation,* as "absolutely the most thrilling thing I've ever done."

She was twenty-four years old.

Kara's mother was relieved when she decided to sell her motorcycle. Maybe the thrill of landing on an aircraft carrier finally satisfied her lust for danger. She told Sally she knew it was time to get rid of it because she was tempted just to wear shorts and a T-shirt instead of a jacket and helmet in the one hundred degree–plus south Texas weather. Kara knew that was asking for trouble.

She got in enough trouble driving her Alfa Romeo through small Texas towns the hundred miles or so along Highway 181 to visit her mother in San Antonio. Pretty young woman, hair flying, driving flashy "ticket magnet" (red convertible with the top down on a sunny day) through revenue-hungry rural counties was a standard formula. She got something like nine speeding tickets the year she lived in Beeville, so many that she came close to having her driver's license revoked, not to mention the costly fines.

Kara was in advanced training in the TA-4J Skyhawk jet when Brice crashed. The cause of the accident was never really known. Brice was an outstanding student and an excellent pilot, but it looked as if he just flew his plane into the ground. "It happens," she was told.

It was the first funeral she attended for one of her friends. Kara described to her mother how tragic it was and how Brice's mother was crying. "It doesn't make me scared I'll die flying a plane," she said, "but it does make me realize how terrible it would be for you and Dad and Dagny and Kirsten if I did."

She and her classmates were strangely accepting. "We don't let it scare us," Mike said, "because we never believe it could happen to us."

When Kara started training in the TA-4J Skyhawk, the highlight once again was the carrier qualification. Each aviator was required to do two touch and gos, six traps, and six catapult shots off the deck. Kara was an old hand now. She had landed the Buckeye on the *Lexington;* she was just honing her skills in the Skyhawk. She was less distracted, more comfortable with the procedures, and more confident in her abilities. They weren't going to do night landings at the carrier, but they did simulated night carrier landings at the field. The landing box on the field was outlined with lights and that's all the pilot saw. It was exciting even though they were only at the field.

In August 1989, after four and a half months and more than 130 hours in the Skyhawk in Squadron VT-25, Kara earned her naval wings. She was the eighteenth female ever to receive her wings at the naval air station in Beeville.

Her dad came from Toronto for her winging. Kirsten came from Austin and Uncle Jimmy, Grandmother Spears, and her mother came from San Antonio. Dagny was working as a model in Tokyo and couldn't be there. Kara told her parents how proud she was to get her wings. "I graduated in the upper third of my class, and that's really something. You wouldn't believe how fierce the competition is. All these guys are so good."

But she was curiously subdued for such a happy and exciting day. "Everyone with my grades but me got assigned to fleet combat squadrons. I've been assigned to fly an A-6 in a 'support' squadron that trains the fleet in electronic warfare. They tell me I'm lucky to get that. There just aren't many opportunities for women to fly jets because of the law."

The law that kept the good female aviators away from some of the navy's choicest assignments was Section 6015 of Title 10 of the United States Code. Written into the books after World War II on 12 June 1948, it said that women could not be assigned duty on vessels or in aircraft that are engaged in combat missions.

An aircraft carrier is the archetypal combat vessel, and if women couldn't serve on one, they couldn't fly carrier-based A-6s, EA-6Bs, F-14s, or F-18s. Flying carrier-based aircraft is the status assignment in the navy; that's where the exciting missions are that the best pilots get. There is an intangible something that goes into creating a career, and according to Lt. Cdr. Harry Ennis, "the time spent on the carrier is considered a sort of rite of passage. There's a kind of male bonding that goes on in that tough, dirty place. Tempers flare from time to time—people live on the edge. It changes you. All of the admirals and decision makers have been through it."

That her options were limited because she was female didn't really register with Kara until she was about to get her wings. She was specifying the type of aircraft she wanted to fly and she thought she had a good chance to be assigned to fly F/A-18 Hornets as an instructor until the law changed, but she was told those slots were filled. "You can put down F/A-18 if you want to, but you won't get it," the detailers told her. "There are a couple of women flying it as test pilots, but you're too junior for test pilot school."

Kara had received the same training and had been held to the same rigorous standards as her male counterparts in Aviation Officer Candidate School and in flight school, and she had excelled. Now she confronted for the first time in her navy career something she could do nothing about. It was a fact that she was female. She couldn't study harder or practice longer in order to overcome the obstacle that created. The gender barrier was insurmountable. It was the law.

She had been vaguely aware that there were limits on opportunities for women when she entered naval aviation, but she thought changes were imminent. The navy recruiters nourished those expectations. "By the time you finish two years of training things surely will have changed," they told her. They believed it themselves.

Since flying fleet combat aircraft is what navy jet pilots do, there just weren't many other assignments. A few shore-based squadrons were performing less demanding and certainly less prestigious missions, and if a pilot was adequate in most respects but couldn't quite cut it at the boat, he might be sent to one of them.

At the time Kara got her wings, it was to these shore-based squadrons that the women were sent. Even if a woman graduated first in her class she wouldn't be assigned to a choice tactical aircraft in a combat squadron. She might be lucky enough later in her career to be assigned to fly a fighter or attack plane, but only as a test pilot in research, development, and evaluation missions.

So instead of being assigned to fly on and off carriers in a fleet squadron with her male peers, Kara was to join Tactical Electronic Warfare Squadron Three Three (VAQ-33) at Naval Air Station Key West and help train the fleet in enemy electronic warfare tactics. She would fly the EA-6A—the same A-6 Intruder that was the carrier-based attack plane of *Flight of the Intruder* book and film fame, except that it was weaponless. It had been modified to carry electronic pods instead of guns and bombs.

In 1989 the best assignment women could have was the worst assignment a man could have.

The squadron was a shore-support unit that played games with the navy's ships—a lot of straight and level flying right down on the water—going out and attacking the fleet, jamming their radar, and simulating Russian radar and missiles with electronics. There would be no more training in heart-stopping air combat maneuvers and no more adrenaline-drenching take-offs and landings on aircraft carriers. In Kara's words, "None of the fun stuff."

Chapter 6   *More Training*

Before Kara could join her new squadron she first had to learn about electronic warfare. Second, she had to learn to fly an A-6. In between, she was to receive the training that would prepare her to survive should she ever be shot down over enemy territory. It was a great incentive to her that she was to receive survival training even though she was not eligible for combat duty—as if the navy actually believed it was only a matter of time before this training would be a job requirement for her.

Kara wrote to Monique's family on 8 November 1989.

> I'm currently in Pensacola learning everything you never wanted to know about electronic warfare. It's a typical military school which forces us to memorize (binge) on massive amounts of information and purge it all out for an exam so we can binge some more on new info. I am personally suffering from information bulimia and I don't like it. I think I can survive one more week though.
>
> Unfortunately after this I'll be off to SERE (Survival, Evasion, Resistance, Escape) training in Brunswick, Maine. I'm really not looking forward to simultaneously freezing and starving—but what a great diet technique right before the Christmas pig out!
>
> I'll be in San Antonio over the holidays and I'm sure I'll have lots of salty sea stories.

Freezing temperatures, rugged terrain, and lots of snow was the way Kara described late November in Maine. The culmination of the training was that the young officers were abandoned in teams of two in the wilderness, where they put their newly acquired skills to the test, armed with a map, an assigned destination, and a Swiss Army Knife. The scenario was that they had escaped their wounded aircraft and parachuted into enemy territory. They would have to survive off the land and evade capture if possible. If they were captured, they were expected to resist their captors and try to escape.

46

An important part of the training was for the students to experience prison camp, and since Kara knew a little about what to expect from SERE School, she was not surprised when they were ambushed and captured. What was unnerving was that their "captors" were so into their roles. They were speaking a language that sounded like what she would imagine Russian sounded like. She wondered where all these navy guys learned it. And they never got out of character.

She didn't describe exactly what happened because they were not supposed to talk about it, but she said it was very intense and some of it was not what she called fun. As for being female in such a situation (she had to strip to the waist during part of the "torture"), she said it was no more intimidating and embarrassing than some things the men had to endure. They were all subjected to mental torment, prodded, and harangued. While the "captives" weren't actually hurt, they were never entirely sure that they wouldn't be. Kara said the experience would definitely help her to cope in case she ever found herself in enemy hands and she was glad she had been through it.

She told *Women in Aviation* that she looked at SERE School as an opportunity and a way to help her "earn respect as an officer, not a female or male officer, but an officer."

As for trying to hide from the enemy and escape in the snow, she told her mother that was "a blast."

Kara rationalized her disappointment at not getting to fly a fighter by taking pride in flying the A-6. In February 1990 she started training in the Fleet Replacement Squadron at Oceana, Virginia. Even though she complained to Monique that "it flies more like a truck than a sports car," she respected the Intruder as a venerable combat aircraft, the workhorse in Vietnam. She was determined to fly it well.

"I still feel extremely lucky to be here," she told Monique, describing the first time she appeared on the runway at Oceana in her flight suit.

> You should have seen the plane captain's face when I walked around the nose of the jet. The plane captain is an enlisted guy that takes care of the jet and makes sure it's ready for flight. He clearly had never seen a female pilot and his jaw dropped to the floor. It took him about 30 seconds to give me a salute and a mumbled, "uhhh . . . umm . . . You gonna fly the A-6, Ma'am?"

I started to laugh and then I told him that I was just going to taxi around the Base for a few hours and not to worry. I wish I could have gotten it on video, Mo. I could have won a lot of money on America's funniest videos.

She added another wish to her list that began with "flying something pointy with an afterburner." She wanted to fly a single-seat plane. "I'm having a tough time getting used to this crew concept. I hate having someone else do all the talking—it makes it harder to listen. You also have to treat the B/N (Bombardier/Navigator) like he's trying to kill you. My navigator *tried* to navigate me into the side of a mountain in the simulator—at least they don't have any controls."

Her spirits were high, but soon she faced a second disappointing reality. Because she was a female and therefore not slated to fly in combat, she would receive only basic instruction in the A-6 and not go through the complete training syllabus. She would learn the aircraft systems, configuration, capabilities, and flight characteristics in ground school, and then move on to simulator and flight training, but she wouldn't go on to learn to use weapons, do air combat maneuvers, or land on an aircraft carrier. She'd had to have those abilities in order to earn her wings, but that was over. Why should the navy make a further investment in teaching her those skills if she couldn't put the training to use?

Of course, she wanted to do all those things. That was why pilots loved military flying. Even if they were working for a commercial airline, many of them stayed in reserve units so they could do the kind of flying that was thrilling and exciting and challenging.

The training was also important in its most basic form—hours in the cockpit, flight time. The lack of it meant Kara would qualify to fly the A-6E with minimum hours and experience and would never be exposed to the advanced training her male peers took for granted. Not having the training meant she would fall off the learning curve. She would enter her next squadron with a handicap: only six weeks of training—32.1 hours in the A-6E.

Tony, a trim, blond, blue-eyed Italian, drove Kara up to the gate at NAS Oceana. He was a navy lieutenant and she was a lieutenant junior grade. They were both in uniform and the guard waved them through. Tony raced through the gate, then slammed on his brakes and started to back up.

"What's the matter?" Kara asked.

"Did you see that guard? He didn't salute me."

"Calm down," Kara said. "See his insignia? He's a civilian—not navy. He's just hired to do this. It's no big deal."

"It's a big deal to me," Tony fumed. "He failed to show me the proper *decadence!*" Kara just rolled her eyes and said nothing. He meant "deference," but she was used to Tony's malapropisms.

They had met when both were stationed at NAS Beeville, and the relationship was into its second year. Tony was twelve years older than Kara. He had gone to college as an enlisted man, and then on to naval AOCS. They dated for months before Tony told her he was married, but he claimed he was in the midst of a divorce.

"I'm sorry I didn't tell you sooner," he had said. "I just thought that if I told you, it would affect our relationship."

"You're right, it has affected our relationship," replied Kara. "It just ended."

But she hadn't ended it. She was already involved with him; she was young; and this was her first serious boyfriend. His estranged wife lived in another state, and because he seldom mentioned her and Kara had never seen her, the wife didn't seem real. Besides, her parents were separated almost seven years before they finally divorced, so in her experience the actual separation was the important thing, not the formal decree. Kara didn't like it that Tony was married, but marriage was the last thing she was thinking about for herself, so she didn't pressure him.

Of course, she never thought that a relationship with a "technically" married man could end her dreams. At that time, Lt. Kelly Flinn hadn't been forced to take a general discharge from the air force for falling in love with a married man. Nor had Gen. Joseph Ralston withdrawn his name as a candidate for chairman of the joint chiefs of staff because of an affair that happened thirteen years before.

Tony was persistent in his pursuit of Kara. He was crazy about her and very jealous, especially now that Kara was no longer in Beeville and he could only visit her in Oceana. She wrote Monique, "His jealousy could doom this relationship. It doesn't help that I'm the only female in the squadron. But he gets irrational. I don't know why I brought it up. I don't want to talk about it."

Kara debated bringing him to San Antonio for Christmas 1989. "*She* [referring to her mother] hates him," she told Monique. "*She* will just rip him apart." Kara had brought Tony to San Antonio many weekends when they were both in Beeville. They would spend hours in Sally's kitchen chopping onions, tomatoes, and peppers, and sautéing sausages for Tony's authentic Italian spaghetti sauce. Sally enjoyed the meals, but she decided after a while she wasn't so fond of Tony.

After Kara left for electronic warfare school in Pensacola in the fall of 1989, Tony had called Sally several times to announce he would be coming to spend the weekend at her house and to tell her when she could pick him up at Kelly AFB. Sally would try to make excuses, telling him how busy she was, that Kelly was way on the other side of town and the expressways were under construction, confusing, and poorly marked. But Tony was incapable of appreciating a subtle hint.

Once, when she apologized that she was playing in a golf tournament the entire weekend, he responded, "Oh, that's all right, I can spend time with your brother." Then he asked Kara's grandmother to take him back to Kelly, and she got so lost after she dropped him off, it took her hours to get home. Sally couldn't stand it any longer and asked Kara to talk to Tony. Kara was embarrassed for Tony, but he never understood why he couldn't continue to spend his weekends at Sally's house.

Sally wanted Kara home for Christmas and that meant Tony had to be invited too. Insecure, he never left Kara's side the whole time, and it drove her mother crazy. She couldn't have a private fifteen minutes with Kara. He tried too hard to be liked and to fit in, and he got just the opposite reaction. After ten days or so, Sally asked Kara if Tony didn't want to take some time and visit *his* family,

Kara admitted to Monique, "He acted like an idiot while he was there." But she was upset with her mother and loyal to Tony, so she took him to Austin to stay at her sister Kirsten's apartment for the rest of their leave.

The family lost the time with Kara, and Sally was mad at herself for saying anything.

Chapter 7   *The First Assignment*

In late March 1990 Kara joined her new squadron based at Naval Air Station Key West in the Florida Keys. The island of Key West is the southernmost point of the whole continental United States, the end of a chain of twenty-seven major keys formed from coral reefs stretching south and then gently west for 127 miles down U.S. Highway 1 from Florida City on the mainland. The notion that the keys are beautiful and lined with natural beaches is a carefully cultivated myth. The truth is that driving down through the keys you see mostly mangroves and shallow water. And nearly all the sand is imported.

Artists and visitors love Key West's sunshine, gentle tropical breezes, water, and mañana attitude. But after you have beheld the restored homes of Ernest Hemingway, James Audubon, and early shipwreck salvage captains, and after you have ridden the Conch Tour Train, the only other attractions in town are T-shirt shops and bars. And all of them are expensive. But if you like the water—fishing, scuba diving, swimming, boating, water skiing—the keys are the place to be.

Tourists were catered to, but the presence of the navy formed the backbone of the economy. The naval air station had annexes in four separate locations and all but one were located on the island of Key West. The headquarters for the Joint Task Force for Counter Drug Operations was located at Truman Annex, the site of the Truman summer White House. Some of the housing, the bachelor officers quarters, and an army combat diver school were on Trumbo Point, which also was home to the only navy hydrofoils in the fleet. Close by were two other navy housing areas, Sigsbee Park and Poinciana.

The hangar and runways sat on the tidal flats of Boca Chica Key about seven miles north of Key West. The main attractions in Boca Chica were two naval air squadrons and a McDonald's. The two squadrons, Kara's electronic warfare support training squadron,

VAQ-33, and an aggressor squadron, VF-45, were completely different from each other. The aggressor squadron flew F-16s, the pride of the air force, and A-4s, the sleek fighters parked on the runways in the same line of vision as the stumpy A-6s and P-3s flown by Kara's squadron.

The Naval Air Station at Boca Chica was not remarkable from the ground, but the pilots loved to be there because the flying conditions were so good. The water below looked beautiful from the air, transparent shades of bright green and blue. Because of the good weather, the navy trained most of its East Coast fighter pilots in air combat maneuvers there. Student pilots and instructors from F-14 squadrons in Oceana, Virginia, and F-18 squadrons from Cecil Field in Jacksonville were regularly sent to NAS Key West to conduct training.

If the landscape did not make Boca Chica Key an interesting place, the dynamics of life in Kara's squadron did. All the people who endured a tour in VAQ-33 would continue to have strong feelings about the time spent there long after they had gone on to other assignments. In a way, the military life is like growing up in a small town. Everyone knows your business, where you came from, who your last commanding officer was. Certainly, how he ranked you was an ill-kept secret and just as juicy as any taboo topic of conversation. In other words, your reputation preceded you.

The navy subdivisions where many of the officers and their families lived, like most subdivisions, were insular. The mommies would stroll their children together and the rank of the daddies was obvious by the size of the house they lived in. Like civilians, some of the military folks were more impressed by the rank than by the qualities of the individual. They could be critical and outraged by nonconformity.

Kara was excited to be in Key West. It wasn't too shabby a place to have to spend the next three years. She loved tennis, golf, and water sports, and people told great stories about the fun they had there. She was gung-ho about her first assignment, her first tour, her first "real" job in the navy after almost three years and over a million dollars worth of training.

"Boo" was her call sign. Caribou. Kara Boo.

She wrote to Monique on 4 April 1990:

I just got to Key West last week—it's gorgeous here! I haven't even finished checking into the squadron and I've been flying every day. I'm going to Puerto Rico on Sunday, 8 April, for a week and we are going to Hawaii on the 22nd for 3 weeks—cool eh? I'm going to try tanking tomorrow (in-flight refueling) and I'll probably fly Trans-Atlantic to Scotland in September for a month or two. . . .

More great news—my squadron will be transitioning to F-18s in October of '91—Happy Birthday to me! [The F/A-18 Hornet was the latest generation of navy combat aircraft. Every pilot wanted to fly one.] I think I would go mental with joy at the prospect of an F-18 transition. It's a truly motivating thought. I'm going to be the best EA-6A driver they have ever seen in the meantime and I'll be first in line to fly F-18s.

I had an awesome flight today—It was my big squadron NATOPS [Naval Air Training and Operating Procedures Standard-ization] check flight and I had a blast burning gas and zooming around the valleys of this cloud deck. It's like flying a low level with the guts to come within inches of the ground. The clouds are a lot more forgiving when you run into them. I LOVE THIS JOB!

Key West was charming and Kara was young, with a boundless future. She was going to Puerto Rico on Sunday and to Hawaii right after that. Her natural exuberance bubbled. She was twenty-four years old and she was flying jets for the United States Navy—one of only twenty-seven women navy jet pilots in the world.

So what if her plane resembled a mosquito with its plump little body and a probe sticking out the front making it look as if it were searching for its next meal. The EA-6A assignment was only tempo-rary. If all went according to plan, she would be flying F-18s in little more than a year. How could life be any better?

Kara also wanted to buy a condo in Key West and had visions of a breathtaking view and a vast appreciation in the market value while she was enjoying living there. She wrote her mother and her sister Dagny on 23 April, "I'm excited about buying a condo if it happens. I'll feel like an adult—almost." The next day she left for Hawaii.

"I got here yesterday," she wrote Monique, "and we have until Monday to 'adjust to the time zone'—HA! This is great! It is absolutely breathtaking here—it puts Key West to shame. We are going Hobie catting and gliding tomorrow. This jet lag story is a great scam!"

During the three weeks she was away, she talked to some older navy pilots, heard a few of their real estate stories—about how prices went down as well as up—and cooled off about the condo. It also dawned on her that she was going to be traveling a lot. Who would look after her house when she wasn't there? Then she met Leslie Kovanic, an academy graduate and a naval flight officer who was losing her roommates. Kara moved into Leslie's rented house on Cudjoe Key, which was furnished nicely and had a deck across the back overlooking the water. She was satisfied.

She made a note on her calendar on 24 April, "Dagny gets job in L.A." Dagny was going to be the entertainment anchor for "E" Entertainment Television, a new cable network. Kara thought that was perfect because she would be going on missions to San Diego and she could easily take side trips to Los Angeles. Kara loved to visit Dagny. It was great having a TV celebrity for a sister. When they went out, people recognized her and came over to talk and get autographs. Kara was very proud of her and loved to tell people about her beautiful sister with the glamorous job.

Chapter 8 *Hair and High Spirits*

During her almost three years of training, Kara had had only one female flight instructor and only one female student aviator friend. That wasn't surprising since in January 1990, out of 12,477 navy pilots, only 225 were women. Now in Key West, for the first time in her navy career, she was in a squadron where there were a number of other women officers. As VAQ-33 was one of the few assignments available for female navy jet pilots and flight officers, there were some smart and talented women in the squadron.

The woman who became her best friend, however, wasn't an aviator but a general unrestricted line officer, a category created by the navy as a way to allow women to attain equivalent rank with men. Kara and Pamela Kunze were the same age, shared the same office in the squadron's Administration Department, and had the same quirky sense of humor. Kara called her "Spammy" or "Miss Pamela."

Pam was about five feet, eight inches tall with hazel eyes and dark blond hair. She had gone to the University of Nebraska on academic and track scholarships. She and Kara would run and rollerblade together. Kara liked to hang out at Pam's because she was a good cook. She always played country and western music, and though Kara had lived in Texas, she only learned to appreciate C&W after hearing it all the time over at Pam's.

The only thing Kara didn't like at Pam's house was her bull terrier named Knucklehead. Called Knuckle for short, the dog looked like Spuds McKenzie and had emotional problems. "Knuckle's been sent home from obedience school again with a note attached to his collar," Pam would lament. Much to Kara's annoyance, Knuckle would jump up and lick her face whenever she came over, follow her everywhere, and when she sat down he'd sit down beside her. Kara saved a thank-you letter he wrote to her. It was typed and signed "Your nephew, Knuckle."

Dear Aunt Kara,

Thank you very much for taking care of me when my mother abandoned me to visit my father in Jacksonville. I really appreciate your thoughtfulness so I bought you a sweater. It's just like your green one that got stuck on my tooth a while back. I am very sorry that I ripped your sweater. I spent many hours in my kennel and attended several counseling sessions because of that isolated incident. See I'm really not a bad dog, it's just people misunderstand my intentions. I guess I'm just too darn friendly and need to relax a bit.

Linda Heid was a naval flight officer (NFO), which is a "back-seater or side-seater" in a two-position aircraft. In the EA-6A she was called electronic countermeasures officer, or ECMO. The first time the two women flew together, Kara said the event should be recorded somewhere because it was the first "unmanned" A-6 flight in history. Linda and Kara liked to work out together and play racquetball, golf, and tennis.

Linda was a "by-the-book" aviator, but off duty she loved to experiment with her image. The style and color of her hair changed monthly depending on her mood, and the color of her eyes changed according to the tint of the contact lenses she wore. Sometimes her eyes were light green and sometimes they were sky blue. Kara and Pam kidded her that she had "timber wolf" eyes. Kara liked the idea of bright-colored eyes and bought some nonprescription blue- and green-tinted lenses, but with her brown eyes they didn't make much of a difference.

Amy Boyer, another female right-seater, arrived at the squadron in the fall of 1990. The timing was good because Kara's housemate was being transferred away from Key West, and when she left Amy moved into the house on Cudjoe Key with Kara. Quiet and reserved, Amy had stunning blue eyes, and since she blushed easily the call sign "Scarlett" attached almost immediately.

There were two other women EA-6A pilots, Sue Still and Chris Riposo. Kara referred to Sue as the only other female A-6 pilot in the world until Chris came along. Chris was married so she didn't hang around much with the single women officers. Sue had arrived at the squadron about six months before Kara. She had been in the navy longer than Kara and was a branch officer in the maintenance department, a demanding job commensurate with her seniority and experience. She was four years older than Kara. She, Kara, and Linda all had October birthdays. That October (1990) Sue and Linda would be twenty-nine; Kara would be twenty-five.

Sue was intelligent, shrewd, and a capable aviator and naval officer; like Kara, she wanted to fly F-18s and dreamed of becoming an astronaut. Her dream was to come true. In 1997 she piloted two missions of the U.S. space shuttle *Columbia*. Her first mission in space was as pilot of *Columbia*'s eighty-third flight, launched from the Kennedy Space Center on 4 April 1997. She carried Kara's miniature gold naval aviator wings with her.

Sue and Kara were very competitive with each other but still managed to pal around together. Kara's joking line was, "I might as well just go ahead and hate her. It'll save time." But there was admiration on both sides.

In her leisure time, Kara often played golf or tennis with several of the men in her squadron. She, Pam, and sometimes Sue or Linda, frequently ate out at one of the many wonderful Key West restaurants. A favorite, Mangrove Mama's, arose out of the swamp at mile marker 21 on Cudjoe Key. Cats and large iguanas roamed over the restaurant, which was nearly hidden by mangrove trees and almost impossible to find if you didn't know where it was. Once disreputable as a biker's hangout, it gradually gained respectability because of its tasty seafood. Kara and Pam always ordered the coconut shrimp appetizer when it was on the menu.

After a night on the town, Sloppy Joe's on Duval Street served what the aviators called "drunk food," greasy fries, hamburgers, and nachos. Pancho and Lefty's served large portions of Mexican food that tasted great, although you probably wouldn't want to see the kitchen. Lunches were often at the Rusty Anchor, known for its fish sandwiches. After Kara introduced Pam to sushi, they would go to Kyoto on Duval Street.

Visiting fighter squadrons continually trained at the naval air station, so there were always good-looking fighter jocks for these young women to have fun with. When they weren't in the office or flying, there was boating, snorkeling, fishing, swimming, picnicking, golf, or tennis during the day and dinner and dancing at night. Pam was engaged to an F-16 pilot in the other squadron at the base, and he had a fishing boat he would sometimes let them use. Sue had a handy portable blender, so even if they didn't catch any fish, they enjoyed strawberry daiquiris and piña coladas.

Tony came to visit Kara every time he could get leave. His divorce was now final and he wanted Kara to marry him. He gave her a diamond ring, but she wouldn't wear it and tried to give it back. For a long time he wouldn't take it. Kara wasn't ready to get married to anyone and, besides, her feelings for Tony had changed. She had new friends; her life was full of adventure; and he had become even more jealous and possessive. The more distance she tried to put between them, however, the more he smothered her. By spring 1990, she was trying to break up with him, but he wouldn't take no for an answer and kept calling and coming uninvited to visit her.

Once he surprised her by flying to Puerto Rico where she was on detachment. He made a scene at the officers club, accusing her of cheating on him, and Kara's commanding officer ordered him to leave the island.

One night he called her from Oceana, and she told him again that it was over and to leave her alone. She woke up at three o'clock in the morning to find him in her house. He had told his commanding officer he was too distraught to fly, that he had to go to Key West to try to straighten things out with his girlfriend.

"You took leave? In the middle of the night?" Kara asked. "Tony, you're crazy."

Pam told her the next morning she looked terrible.

"He threatened to kill himself if I broke up with him. I felt like saying, 'Tony, just go ahead and do it and put us both out of our misery.' He's an emotional black hole," Kara sighed, "sucking the life out of me."

"He's high maintenance, all right," said Pam. "Like when he told you the guard at the gate didn't show him the proper 'decadence.'" Pam paused, "Wonder what type of decadent behavior Tony would think proper?"

As upset as she was, Kara laughed. "Remember when he said that he could use his left and right hands interchangeably and that he was 'amphibious?'"

"Aquaman," Pam declared.

That proved a prophetic label as Tony topped off his visit by almost submerging Kara's Alfa Romeo driving through a big puddle of water instead of going around it. The car Kara loved, that she kept clean and polished and running great, never acted or even smelled right after that. After that visit and several unpleasant long distance telephone confrontations, the relationship finally ended for good in the spring of 1991.

At work, the women officers were dealt with according to their rank. They insisted on it. For example, if you have a female lieutenant and a male lieutenant commander approaching a door together, the female junior officer opens and holds the door for the male senior officer.

But sometimes off duty on a Friday or Saturday night, it was fun to just be a girl for a change. Two or three of the young women might get together dressed up in miniskirts or swingy dresses with sheer hose and high heels and go out on the town, taking full advantage of the opportunity to unbraid their hair and abandon their beige polyester uniforms and stocky brown pumps. People they worked with at the Naval Air Station on Boca Chica Key every day might not even recognize them if they saw them in the evening in Key West.

Their co-workers were used to seeing the women officers on base with no makeup, their hair pulled back primly, and tiny little navy-issue round gold-colored stud earrings, which were the only recognized uniform jewelry. The men were not allowed to wear earrings in uniform so, presumably, letting the women wear them was a good way to distinguish one gender from the other in the new unisex navy. Women in the military are not backed by long tradition, and though their numbers are increasing they are still very much a minority. They continually grapple with how to fit in with a group of mostly men— without being one.

Kara had watched her mother go to work as a lawyer in male-dominated law firms and corporations and didn't find her own circumstances that exceptional, which was both an advantage and a disadvantage. On the one hand, she never felt it was necessary to imitate a man in order to do the same job. On the other hand, she didn't realize then just how different and how much more conservative the military culture was from the civilian world of her mother and sisters.

Dagny had convinced Kara that dressing up could be a lot of fun. She would give Kara some new creation she'd bought in New York and go shopping with her to make sure she had the right accessories. Kara liked it. She was doing the most macho of navy jobs—flying jets—and sometimes she needed to feel feminine.

She wrote her friend navy helicopter pilot Suzanne Parker on 17 November 1991 that she "bought about $600 worth of new clothes— some slutty outfits to be sure—all I need is a strapless push-up bra and I'll be set!"

Kara had a talent for flamboyant overstatement. She would have had a hard time looking "slutty" no matter what she put on, but when she wanted to she could dress to stand out in the crowd. "I'm sending photos. They are still talking about the outfit of the century. It was rumored that the 'Fang' [Kara's call sign after an NBC interview] wore her underwear, a scarf, and a blazer. HA!"

Because she was so intent on and so vocal about her goal of being a fighter pilot, and because for a long time her relationship with Tony had kept her from dating anyone in Key West, there was great interest in her sex life—whether or not she had one, and if she did, were her lovers men or women? Once when she had a little too much beer and displayed some public affection to a young man at a bar, it was already all over the squadron before she reported to work the next day. Everyone was speculating as to whether or not she had gone home alone that night.

Of course, the double standard was alive and well. Male pilots referred to their wings as leg-spreaders. The men were expected to go hunting for women, but if a female officer became attracted to or appeared to be attracted to someone, it was noted. If she didn't, that was noticed also. After all, she was surrounded by great-looking men. Kara decided it wouldn't do any good to worry about it too much because it was a no-win situation. If a woman fell in love more than once, she would be labeled a slut. If no one had any stories to tell about her, they would assume she was a lesbian. She and her friends joked about it, "You're not a slut, unless the guy doesn't call you the next day."

Cdr. Don Foulk quipped that finally he had been promoted to squadron commanding officer and his biggest decision so far had been whether or not his female pilots could wear a ponytail. Yes, female pilots are concerned about hair. What do you do with your hair after it has been tucked up, matted down, and crushed under your flight helmet? "Hair by helmet," Kara called it.

The navy uniform regulations said that women pilots had to wear their hair off the face and no longer than the bottom of the collar. They could have long hair if it were braided or pinned up, but the safety regulations prohibited bobby pins on the flight line. There were good reasons for the prohibition. If a bobby pin fell out in the cockpit it could jam the ejection seat, and if it fell out on the flight line it could do foreign object damage to, or FOD, the engine.

Commander Foulk finally decided the women could wear a ponytail (rubber bands were OK) if they tucked any stray tresses underneath the collar of the flight suit. The Pentagon, however, continued to do research and ponder the problem of how women pilots should wear their hair. Finally, it arrived at the conclusion that long hair was a fire hazard. "Cut it so it doesn't fall below your helmet" was the order.

Kara was not happy about that order. She wore her hair long and aimed to keep it that way. "You don't want to keep me from exploring my feminine side, do you?" she asked. She found a hood made of fireproof material that race car drivers used under their helmets and wearing that was deemed an acceptable alternative to cutting her hair. She said the hood was hot and uncomfortable and made her look like an eraser head, but she kept her curls.

There were so many females in the cockpits at VAQ-33, relatively speaking, that hair gave personality to the entire squadron. Visiting aviators looked forward not only to flying and partying in Key West, but also to seeing what color Linda's locks would be when they arrived. During training exercises, the forces were divided into good guys and bad guys. The air above the good guys on the ships and carriers was blue. The bad guys flew in orange air. VAQ-33 always played enemy and when Linda took part in the exercises, the squadron was referred to as "orange hair."

Kara loved movies. With her great grandfather's memory for dialogue, she would quote the lines word for word, her accents, emphasis, facial expressions, and body movements perfect imitations. If she had enough room, she'd reenact the whole scene, playing all the parts.

She memorized the scene in *The Princess Bride* where the hero, Westley, in pursuit of Princess Buttercup, is stopped by Andre, the good-hearted but formidable giant who offers to fight with his bare hands, "no tricks, no weapons." As Westley, Kara assumed a bemused and quizzical air. "You mean you'll put down your rock and I'll put down my sword and we'll try and kill each other like civilized people?"

But her favorite line, the one she really loved and used all the time, in or out of context, just because she liked the sound of it, was the giant's "It's not my fault being the biggest and the strongest. I don't even *essercize.*"

Monty Python and the Holy Grail was an even better source of comedy because everyone knew it. In a perfect English accent, Kara would warm up with a discussion about the difference in the wing velocity between the African Swallow and the European Swallow. She was talking to aviators who loved that stuff.

That fueled her for a rendition of King Arthur's violent fight with the Black Knight. After King Arthur cuts off his left arm, the Black Knight says, "'Tis but a scratch."

"A scratch? Your arm's off," says King Kara.

"No, it isn't." She clips her words and her eyes dance. "I've 'ad worse. . . . It's just a flesh wound."

The *Saturday Night Live* takeoff on Jacques Cousteau was another of Kara's favorites. She took two paper napkins, one in each hand, and in a French accent, waving the napkins to mimic the underwater undulations of the male and female "napkin fish," described their courtship. The men watching would groan as Kara explained soulfully how, as he approached his beloved, the male napkin fish tore off his penis on a coral reef—and then she would tear off the corner of one of the napkins. "Not to worry," she'd reassure them, clapping her hands together in the culmination of the mating ritual, "he has six more."

Little kids loved that joke and would make Kara tell it over and over again, not only because Kara was so funny but also because they got to hear the word "penis." Being pronounced in a French accent by Kara the female jet pilot somehow made the word more acceptable to parents without diminishing its delicious naughtiness to her young audience.

Chapter 9   *Lightning*

Unlike air force pilots whose primary duty is flying, navy pilots are also assigned a ground job. As officers, they are expected to be leaders and managers of people. The ground job is supposed to be their first responsibility as a naval officer and their flying duties are supposed to be secondary, but you won't find many aviators who believe that. Kara was no exception; the challenge and the fun is in the flying. In comparison, the ground job is colorless and uninspiring. Worse, it is time consuming and demanding.

Kara's first ground job was in the administration department as public affairs officer (PAO). She shared with Pam a small, austere office with metal furniture and filing cabinets; a calendar on a clipboard was the only wall decoration. Facing each other across two desks that were jammed together, they laughed so much it was amazing they got any work done at all.

It is the intent that the first job should allow plenty of time to study, to talk to other aviators about the aircraft, and just to learn your way around the squadron. But Kara found herself spending a lot of time doing this job and several peripheral ones. She complained that the job took time away from what she considered to be her real work—flying and learning everything she could about flying. She used to feel sorry for elementary education majors at the University of Texas because they had to do so much busy work; now that was what she was doing.

She hated spending her precious study time arranging dinners for visiting dignitaries down to the menu and color of the napkins, making sure their accommodations were adequate to their rank, and providing fruit and flowers if appropriate. At times, she had to entertain them. It wasn't so bad, of course, if she could schedule a golf game and complete the foursome. She didn't play enough to break 90 very often, but she could dazzle them with her 250-yard drives.

She handled requests from Key West schools for tours and information about the navy. She had to write articles for navy newspapers about squadron life and events. Kara had a fancy 35-mm Minolta camera that her mother had given her for high school graduation, along with a course of lessons on how to use it. Her father had given her a Sigma zoom lens the following Christmas, and she took that camera equipment to all squadron events.

Taking pictures was a hassle. No one was ever satisfied with the result. "You made me look fat." "Why didn't you print the one with me and the admiral?" "Will you make me an extra copy so I can send it to my girlfriend?" And then it took time to take the pictures to be developed, go to pick them up—at least two trips were necessary since they were never ready on time—and paste them in the scrapbook or post them on the bulletin board or send them to the newspaper. This was not what she had in mind when she joined the navy.

Kara was the contact person for the press. "P.S. the news people in Miami are the worst!" she wrote on a postcard to her mother on 23 April 1990. It was her duty to talk to the media, and the media took to her because she wasn't self-conscious and she was outgoing, articulate, and inordinately enthusiastic about flying. Kara may not have liked her public affairs job much, but she was perfect for it.

Sue, having been through the "first female aviator" routine several years before, took care to distance herself from the media. That was possible since her job in maintenance was much less visible than Kara's. Kara didn't have that choice because of her assignment and because of the intentional design of her seniors.

Although public affairs was a normal job for a newly assigned junior officer, having Kara in that visible position showcased the decision to place female aviators in fleet support roles. The navy had been training women to fly its planes long before they were permitted to sit in cockpits of front line fleet aircraft, anticipating that the day would come when they would be allowed to serve in combat. The policy was to be ready, when the law changed, with a cadre of proven female pilots who had been gaining experience, knowledge, and confidence in fleet support squadrons.

Commander Foulk, and his executive officer (XO), Cdr. Bruce Nottke, loved to show off their female pilots to every admiral or other "brass" who stopped in for a visit. This was especially true of Kara. Part of her enjoyed the attention, and she reacted to it with a sense of mischief and a lot of personality. In truth, she played to it. She was always on; she couldn't help it. Sue used to say, "Oh look, it's the Kara show again," which was not meant to be flattering.

Commander Foulk was an ECMO. He flew with Kara a lot and he would point her out to visitors. They saw a striking young woman with a healthy Viking look about her that raised no doubt she could handle a navy aircraft. "That's my personal pilot," he would say, "the one over there, the one with the ponytail."

Kara reported to the administration department head, Lt. Cdr. Ben Jergens. Ben looked sharp in his always-pressed uniform, like a military man should. He was married, in his mid-thirties, about five feet, ten inches tall, weighed around 180 pounds, wore glasses, and had light brown, slightly receding hair and a mustache. He and Kara disliked each other almost immediately.

After a brief association, Kara concluded that Ben never had a positive thing to say about anybody. She would mimic him to Pam, imitating what she called his standard disclaimer. Crinkling her nose and snarling through her teeth, she would say in a nasal voice, "You know it really doesn't matter one way or another to me but . . ."

Whatever she wrote had to be approved first by Ben, then the executive officer, and then the commanding officer, and they could make whatever changes they wanted. It was called the "chop chain." The document would come back with lines all through it, and she would have to change it. It happened to all the junior officers and still does. Senior officers almost always make changes to the work of junior officers as part of the teaching process. The frustration of the junior officers is expected and intended. The junior officers' take on it is that the senior officers have nothing valuable to add, but they want to believe they are having some impact on the job at hand. Of course, when the junior officers get to be senior officers, their perspective changes.

When Ben changed something, Kara called it the "happy to glad" routine. "Oh, oh, let me get this straight. I have to rewrite this because you changed happy to glad." His response was, "This is not your *baby*. I'm not calling your baby ugly; it's just a piece of correspondence." Because it seemed to her that Ben would make changes just to be ornery, she sometimes wrote flamboyantly just to give him good cause. She knew she always had to write her articles twice anyway.

Ben had done a tour in the navy as an EA-6B pilot; then he had worked for the FBI. Later, he came back to the navy. His call sign was "Lightning."

The assignment of call signs is usually the province of junior officers, but in Ben's case, his peers had a hand in it and he didn't like it much. Occasionally, a pilot will earn a call sign as a result of some incredible act of bravery, either in the air or at the officers club. Usually, however, the call sign attaches because of a particularly lame thing the pilot did. Ben got his handle because he flew through some severe weather when he should have gone around it, and his plane suffered extensive hail damage. The junior officers didn't know the story; they just thought the call sign was a great misnomer for the sometimes pompous and always humorless Ben, parodying his "lightning" quick wit and intellect.

Commander Foulk unintentionally undermined Ben. For example, he would suggest to Kara instead of Ben an article he would like to have her write, or an idea for a squadron party, ceremony, or other event that was coming up. They had a tendency to see things the same way, and he would usually just approve what she thought should be done. Then Kara would tell Ben, "the Skipper wants it this way," thereby tying his hands. Kara didn't see why she should make the intermediate stop at Ben when she was getting her instructions from the CO. It was more efficient just to go to the top.

Ignoring the chain of command isn't the military way. To go by the book when he was giving Kara directions, the commanding officer should have called in the executive and administrative officers. But that wasn't always convenient; they might be on a mission or otherwise unavailable. No matter what the reasons were, Ben didn't like being bypassed, but he didn't want to confront the commanding or executive officers to remind them of the proper chain of command, so he blamed Kara.

Kara didn't always say "Yes, Sir," "No, Sir" to Ben; she did in front of visiting officers and at appropriate functions, just not all the time. He was insulted and took it as a personal affront. After all, he was considerably senior to her, much more experienced, and most significant, he was her immediate supervisor. He decided she had a casual attitude toward military protocol.

Ben could be congenial in a social gathering, but he didn't appreciate Kara's sense of humor, especially at work. She was capable and efficient, but sometimes she would joke about something he considered important, and he was offended.

In her PAO capacity, Kara would take candid camera shots, mount the pictures, label them with names, and post the composite in the Ready Room. The Ready Room is the place where squadron members gather when they are preparing to fly or returning from flying. It is also the place where coffee is served and myths are perpetuated. Sometimes, Kara labeled the pictures with dialogue that was spicy and usually on the mark. Some of the officers featured in the montage laughed harder than others. A few didn't think she was funny at all. The captions were clever, but not always welcome from the pen of a junior officer.

Captions under pictures of Ben were likely to have something to do with his former life as an FBI agent. He prided himself on being the squadron sleuth. If there was a mystery such as who was drinking coffee without contributing a quarter, Ben wanted to investigate it, collect evidence, and "break the case." It wasn't just Kara who found this a little ridiculous, and she wasn't the only one who added dialogue underneath the pictures. But if there was something written underneath Ben's, he probably assumed Kara was responsible.

A corner of the Ready Room was designated as the duty office, and officers of the squadron were assigned as the duty officer on a rotating basis. The duty officer sat behind a counter and, in an official logbook, kept track of who was flying or scheduled to fly, who was on leave, who was sick, telephone numbers where people could be reached—that sort of thing.

Also maintained by the duty officer was an "unofficial" logbook called the "Quote Book," which was a tome noting anything someone did or said that was either inappropriate to the circumstances or a ludicrous misuse of words. Since the officers flew missions all over the world, working together during the day and socializing at night, they knew each other very well, and no frailty or foible went unnoticed. Frivolous though it might be, the Quote Book was part of the inventory of the duty officer that had to be accounted for when turning over the duty to the next person. From the Quote Book was taken a "quote of the day," which the duty officer posted on the door of the Ready Room.

When Kara was the duty officer, Ben Jergens was likely to be featured on the daily quote board and, of course, it began with "Lightning said." He didn't like being the butt of her jokes. Like Mr. Roberts and the captain—Kara played Fonda to his Cagney. She had an eagle eye for the most embarrassing entry in the Quote Book, and the more senior the officer, the better she liked subjecting him to the friendly ridicule of the Ready Room. She loved to tease some people because they could laugh at themselves and others because they couldn't.

She wasn't the first or the last junior officer to have a special knack for that kind of thing. This kind of irreverent behavior has been going on in navy Ready Rooms forever and is generally good for morale. It keeps everybody entertained and the senior officers from taking themselves too seriously. The huge joke, of course, is that most junior officers grow up to be senior officers, find themselves emulating the same behaviors that they ridiculed for years, and become the brunt of the humor for the next generation of junior officers. They never see it coming, either.

Not that Kara was spared. She was often on the receiving end of jokes. There was always a cartoon posted on the Ready Room bulletin board, with the character's name whited out and the name of an officer penned in over the white-out. *The Far Side* was usually good source material because some of the officers thought the squadron *was* the far side. One *Far Side* showed a jungle, labeled VAQ-33 naturally, with thatched roof huts and natives wearing breech cloths standing around pointing at a man who was covered by what looked like thousands of little dots or paint splatters. The man was labeled Kara. The caption read, "Crossing the village, Mowaka is overpowered by army ants. The bystanders were all quoted as saying they were horrified, but 'didn't want to get involved.'"

Kara refused to believe Ben could do her any harm. She should have had more sense. He had input into her performance report, called a "fitrep," short for fitness report. She hadn't yet learned the lesson,

"OK, I may not think too much of this guy, but he has power and I am going to have to get along with him." She had been subject to few restrictions growing up, had no previous exposure to military ways, and was at the very beginning of her naval career. It takes time to mature and become a good officer.

It got back to Kara that Ben talked about her to anyone who would listen, accusing her of having a cavalier attitude toward military formalities and of just being downright arrogant. One problem was that Kara exuded such self-confidence, it wasn't apparent just how young and inexperienced she was. Ben never told Kara he expected her to say "Sir" every time she addressed him; he just assumed she was antagonizing him deliberately when she may not even have realized she was doing it. She was coachable—if she respected the coach.

Although his difficulties with Kara were related to her performance as public affairs officer, he presumed she was just as cocky flying an airplane. He was a pilot, so he never flew in the same plane with her, but he did occasionally fly in the same section, a section being a grouping of airplanes, as few as two or as many as four.

After every flight, aircrew get together to "debrief," or discuss what happened. The flight or section leader will note any deviation from the preflight plan, mistakes made, and what improvements are necessary to correct any problem, striving always to make the next flight perfect. Debriefs are supposed to provide positive feedback and learning sessions for the aircrews. If there is to be pointed criticism toward anyone involving anything serious, it should be made privately in the Safety Office and not in the Ready Room.

But when Kara flew in Ben's section and he was doing the debriefing, she noted that he didn't observe that nicety, nor did he complain about her in the privacy of the commanding officer's office because he knew Commander Foulk wouldn't have been sympathetic to him. He would debrief her in the Ready Room with the entire aircrew present, criticizing her every judgment call, his "counsel" to her more in the form of accusation. Kara's friends told her Ben would talk about her in the Ready Room after she left and anyone could overhear, senior officers, junior officers, and sometimes enlisted men when they were filling in for the duty officer.

Chapter 10 ❋ *The O-4 Brute Squad*

The squadron had a large number of lieutenant commanders with nowhere else to go and nothing else to do except complete their twenty-year obligation so they could retire. A few thought Key West would be a great place to end their navy careers and actively sought the assignment; others, failing to be promoted to commander within the time frame allowed, found that Key West was the place their careers ended.

Kara called Lt. Cdr. Ben Jergens and his Ready Room clique the "O-4 Brute Squad"— "O-4" because lieutenant commanders were designated O-4 on the pay scale, and "Brute Squad" from her favorite movie, *The Princess Bride*. Sent by the prince to clear out the forest, Andre the Giant announced, "I'm on the Brute Squad." Miracle Max said, "You *are* the Brute Squad."

Lt. Cdr. Phil "Weasel" Mansfield, an A-6 pilot, was one who loved to hang around and hear Ben's latest Kara story. "Weasel" was in charge of running the physical readiness test, PRT for short, and had been surprised when Pamela Kunze had a better time on the run than most of the men. He had boasted, "I'd never let a woman beat me," but when his time was checked against Pam's, sure enough, Pam's time was faster.

It was no comfort to "Weasel" that he was about fifteen years older than Pam, or that she had recently been a college All-American track and cross-country star. Having a woman beat him was the important issue. Before the next PRT, he trained every day for weeks to make sure his time would be better than Pam's.

Lt. Cdr. Chuck Gardner was always there when Kara's name came up. He was an A-6 right-seater and his call sign was "Swampfox." Kara called him "Swampthang" a combination of the B-movie *Swampthing* and faithful mimicking of the pronunciation in the song "Wild Thing."

Lt. Cdr. Dave "Putt" Dominici, another right-seater in the A-6, crewed with Kara quite a bit. Kara liked him and he liked her. Nevertheless, if he were part of a debrief or gossip session where Kara was being criticized, he wouldn't risk coming to her defense.

Lt. Cdr. P. W. "Boris" Burris-Meyer, an NFO in A-3s, listened to what Ben had to say. He was the squadron safety officer, and it was his job to be alert to aircrew troubles. He had to pay attention to criticism leveled against a junior pilot by one more senior and experienced. If there were problems, his duty was to investigate. Normally, he would talk to the aircrew involved, and if a particular incident or trend was thought to be a safety concern, he was obligated to inform the commanding officer and recommend action. Ben's complaints about Kara didn't fall into that category, but they didn't do her any good in "Boris's" eyes.

Kara identified with a cartoon posted on the Ready Room bulletin board that showed a preying mantis serving snacks to two friends sitting on the couch. Someone had labeled the insects "VAQ-33 Lieutenant Commanders." One preying mantis was holding up his hand, saying, "Oh, good heavens, no, Gladys—not for me . . . I ate my young just an hour ago."

The pilots in the squadron were flying airplanes that were the last of their kind still in operation. For example, VAQ-33 was one of only three squadrons left in the navy that were still operating A-3 aircraft. Because of this, most of the pilots and aircrew of those planes had completed their careers and retired. The ones still on active duty were getting to be pretty senior, contributing to the overabundance of lieutenant commanders.

The EA-6A (an A-6 modified for its electronic warfare mission) had outlasted the pilots trained to fly it, and the navy had to scramble to find replacements. The assignment of women aviators to navy support squadrons had alleviated the problem but hadn't solved it. The squadron became the unwilling recipient of A-6 pilots and navigators who had been "screened out" of fleet A-6 squadrons. There were aviators with no career possibility in the fleet because of their inadequate flying skills sitting in the right seat of the EA-6A with new pilots like Kara who had no fleet experience and had not even completed a full category-1 fleet replacement syllabus for the aircraft. The same was also true of the P-3 officer aircrew. They were not the ideal mentors to train inexperienced pilots.

Not every senior pilot or navigator in the squadron was a fleet reject. Some had invaluable training and experience in electronic warfare, fleet tactics, and coordination, and some had cross-training in more than one type of aircraft. Their experience was prized and made it possible for the fleet to get the best possible training.

The junior officers had no trouble reaching a consensus on who was chaff and who was wheat. They were quick to identify a "fleet reject" as a "no load" without knowing the facts and could be cruel in their instant judgments. They didn't have the background experience to understand that some of the men had lost their fleet seats through no real fault of their own. Minor physical disability, fatigue, personality conflict with seniors, family problems, any one of a number of things could be the source of the problem.

But sometimes, the initial assessments by the junior officers were correct. Time would have to pass before the young men and women would gain the experience and maturity to realize that those senior officers were still human beings, shipmates, and comrades in arms, serving their country and worthy of respect.

Kara did not ingratiate herself with the officers who were insecure about their abilities or the paths their careers had taken. Not only did she talk about wanting to fly a fighter, she also said she deserved to fly one. "If I were a man, I would be flying a better plane, preferably the F/A-18," she told them, the implication being that real men flew fighters. She said she was in the top 1 percent of her peer group, and men who were as good as she was got their choice. "Who would choose to fly the EA-6A? No one, that's who." She may have been right, but she was insensitive to the fact that she had just insulted many of the senior experienced officers who had been paying their dues in the navy when she was still a baby.

She talked about fairness, about equal opportunity for women, especially women in the armed forces, and how qualified people, men or women, should be allowed to advance. Her attitude was simply that she had earned an opportunity to fly a front line fleet aircraft through her performance in training, and she wanted an opportunity to prove she could do it with the best of them. She could not understand how anyone could be blind to this logic.

The O-4 Brute Squad quickly tired of hearing about the injustice of the combat exclusion laws that kept Kara Hultgreen from being the fighter pilot she was meant to be. No antifemale sentiments were voiced, but there was an unspoken understanding among some of the men that the women in the navy were given special breaks. Kara was junior, and she was getting way too much attention from the higher-ups, they thought. And it was only because she was good-looking and female that the CO and the XO were patting her on the head and putting her in the forefront every time the admirals, commodores, and captains came to town.

Chapter 11 *The Firebirds*

Kara looked forward to going on detachment (DET), a military mission away from home base. She had already been to Puerto Rico and Hawaii. She was supposed to take part in a September detachment to Scotland, but it was canceled. "Blame it on Hussein," Kara wrote on her calendar. Iraq had invaded Kuwait and spoiled her trip. But San Diego, Virginia Beach, and Jacksonville were still on the calendar for 1990.

Thrilled to leave her ground duties in Key West, she'd pack a few clothes and fly her aircraft to another base to live and fly for several days or weeks. It was great fun visiting new places, and she made friends all over. All the aviators loved going on DET because they lived to fly, and on detachment they got to do a lot of it. There was a certain excitement about the trips for everyone involved, even though for some it caused a major disruption of their lives. A detachment was the culmination of months of planning. It meant packing and unpacking tons of equipment and families being separated.

Kara's squadron was called the Firebirds. Its mission was to train U.S. and NATO fleet units—single ships and battle groups, surface and air units—in the art of electronic warfare. Firebird planes were equipped to provide all manner of electronic jamming of communications and weapons systems. The aircraft simulated enemy tactics, enemy aircraft, weapons control, and firing systems, and sometimes even the hostile weapon itself. This training was essential for the crews of the navy vessels sailing the oceans, projecting the power of the United States, vigilantly protecting the stability of the planet.

The squadron's location at Key West was convenient to the places where East Coast fleet training was normally conducted: the Puerto Rico Operating Area, Jacksonville, Florida, and the Virginia Capes Operating Areas. Two other fleet support training squadrons, VAQ-34 in Pt. Magu (later Lemoore), California, and VAQ-35 in Whidbey

Island, Washington, provided this training to the Pacific fleet. Depending on mission requirements, sometimes both squadrons participated in fleet support training exercises regardless of where they were held. Detachments were constantly "on the road," not a particularly apt figure of speech since they were training seagoing vessels.

Before each scheduled six-month or longer cruise, a carrier battle group goes through a series of exercises, each one more intensive than the last, culminating in a FLEETEX. During that three-week exercise, occurring approximately one month before the cruise, the Firebirds and the other electronic warfare support squadrons would provide electronic warfare training. The object was to expose the crews to the enemy threats they might expect to encounter during the upcoming cruise.

Unlike most navy squadrons, VAQ-33 was a "composite" squadron. Instead of flying one type of aircraft, the Firebirds were assigned a number of different aircraft types. At one time, the squadron owned twenty A-6As, five A-3s, two P-3s, and seven old TA-7Cs. In a typical navy squadron flying one type of aircraft, all the planes have the same systems installed, the same basic weight, cockpit configuration, and weapons capabilities. A squadron pilot can be assigned to any aircraft at any time and be familiar with it instantly. But Kara's squadron had to deal with flying and maintaining a hodgepodge of fleet cast-off airplanes that were the final ones of their kinds. It was as though the squadron had gathered the lemons from every used car lot in the country—and there weren't nearly enough people to service them.

The TA-7Cs had been sent to the boneyard because of wing cracks and structural fatigue before Kara got to the squadron, but the A-3 was still around. Officially named Sky Warrior, everyone called it the Whale because it was so large, the largest jet aircraft ever to operate off an aircraft carrier. It was the fastest nonafterburner aircraft in the navy. Originally designed in the 1950s as a bomber, the Whale had become the mainstay of the electronic warfare training mission. But it was supposed to have been decommissioned in 1981, and everyone knew it was only a matter of time until the plane was abandoned. Once that happened, the pilots and aircrew would have to retire or scramble to train in another type aircraft to continue their navy careers.

When the A-3 was finally decommissioned, the squadron was left with only two types of aircraft, A-6As and P-3s. The P-3s were turboprops, not jets. A turboprop is a propeller-driven aircraft, but it has a turbine engine driving the propellers, so it has features of a jet and a propeller-driven aircraft. The P-3 was at that time limited in its capability and was used mostly to transport parts and personnel to deployment sites.

The plane Kara flew, the A-6A Intruder, was the sixth design of an all-weather attack bomber designed and built by the Grumman Corporation for the navy in the 1950s, and though it was now 1990, the Intruder was still equipped with the 1950s state-of-the-art electronics package and power plant. It had earned its place in naval aviation history as the workhorse of the fleet, but it wasn't coincidental that it wasn't the featured airplane on *Top Gun*. Nicknamed by fleet aviators "the Ugly," it was bulky and had a bulbous nose as opposed to the patrician nose of a fighter. And it had that hooked-beak probe sticking out in front. It was a precision bomber, designed to fly straight and low level. Compared to a fighter, it was a plodder and not glamorous: "Like the difference between a Mack Truck and a Maserati," Kara said.

During A-6 training at Oceana, Kara learned to fly in the latest model, the E model. In Key West she flew the earliest model, the A model. Model designations of planes change according to improvements in design and technology that increase safety, reliability, and mission effectiveness. As soon as the aircraft is under heavy daily usage in the fleet, pilots and maintenance personnel find all the little kinks and problems, and modifications are suggested and incorporated.

Every few years, when enough modifications accrue, revised and always more-costly contracts are signed with the manufacturer, and the factory begins production of the next generation of the aircraft. As soon as there was a new model, the original A-6 was referred to as the A-6A. By the time it got to the E model, it was a much different airplane.

In the late seventies, additional electronic warfare training became essential for the fleet. The navy didn't have the money for a special aircraft, but it did have twenty old and practically obsolete A-6As scattered around in marine and reserve squadrons. It decided to gather them up and send them to Key West to be modified to become

EA-6As, basically an A-6A with electronics and some A-6E bells and whistles added. However, when Kara arrived in Key West in 1990, seven of the twenty A-6As had been junked and only four had been modified to the EA-6A configuration. The modified planes were referred to as "recaps." The nine unmodified A-6As were called "nonrecaps."

The pilots in VAQ-33 had to fly both the recap and the nonrecap planes, and it was confusing to switch back and forth between them. To further complicate matters, each nonrecap plane had its own idiosyncrasies because it had been modified according to the needs of the last squadron that owned it. For example, the cockpit control box might be located in a different place in each plane, or the intercommunications systems might differ one from another, or varying weight and distribution of that weight would alter the center of gravity. Though each plane had systems essential to safety, any system that wasn't essential might not be installed in every plane, and when a plane was equipped with extra amenities, sometimes they worked and sometimes they didn't.

The recap planes were all the same until one or two special pods carrying electronic equipment were hung on the wing stations, drastically altering weight and drag, creating entirely different flight characteristics, and making it almost like flying a different model aircraft. The nonrecaps carried old jamming equipment salvaged from the Vietnam era. Internally installed in the aircraft, the equipment was unreliable, hard to maintain, and harder to operate properly, and no trained maintenance technicians, parts support, or tooling had accompanied the planes to the squadron.

Added to the Firebird mix was a variety of electronic equipment that was always being updated. Simulating Soviet and Third World threats, including various missiles, was hot stuff in the fleet training arena, but these enemy threats and capabilities were constantly changing. Third World countries had begun to acquire Chinese and Soviet advanced technology. Iraqis, Syrians, and Iranians were buying Chinese Silkworm missiles from the Chinese and the North Koreans. They would import the technology and put a different spin on it, and the simulator pods were continually being reprogrammed to mimic evolving enemy hardware.

All of these differences were distractions, making every flight a familiarization flight and keeping the pilots from establishing solid habit and instrument scan patterns. Kara and her peers had learned to fly the A-6 in a model that, though it couldn't be compared to a Lexus, was at least the equivalent of an Oldsmobile, and then they reported to the squadron to fly in a 1959 Studebaker. And some of the Studebakers were better than others.

The first tour is where the new, or "nugget," navy pilots are supposed to continue their education. When Kara first arrived at the squadron and counted those thirteen A-6 airplanes on the flight line and in the hangar, and only nine A-6 pilots in the squadron, she assumed there would be plenty of flight time. Fresh from training, she knew if you were to keep your skills and grow as an aviator you had to fly continually. If she could fly all the time, even though flying the crusty old A-6 was kind of like driving a truck, she would be happy.

Instead, she was disappointed. The squadron didn't have the budget to maintain all the tired old chunks of aluminum it owned. In 1990 and early 1991 only eighty-four technicians were assigned to maintain the thirteen A-6As. By comparison, a fleet squadron of twelve A-6E aircraft would have had more than twice as many. Probably 60 percent of the young men and women assigned to maintain the A-6As hadn't had the benefit of any formal training. They worked twelve to sixteen hours a day, seven days a week most of the time, to try to keep sufficient planes up for missions but without much success.

So few up-and-ready planes were available at any one time that the pilots in Kara's squadron had difficulty flying enough hours to maintain their flight status, let alone to fly training missions. Pilots have to have an absolute minimum number of one hundred flight hours per year to keep their NATOPS qualification as a pilot. Even more important, they have to have that many hours to be eligible for flight pay, which they consider a God-given right.

Squadrons are expected to provide essential continuous training for new and inexperienced pilots, but for the junior pilots who were unlucky enough to serve their first tour in VAQ-33, there was no formal apprenticeship. Again, the problem was money. Every hour of flight training required thirty to sixty maintenance hours and cost as much as nine hundred taxpayer dollars of fuel.

During her first year or so in the squadron, Kara flew very few hours. Unless she was on a mission, there wasn't much of a flight schedule. Her log book showed that in September 1990 she flew just 2.1 hours. That was the month the detachment to Scotland was canceled because of Saddam's invasion of Kuwait. In October she flew 7.3 hours. In November, when she went on two missions to the Puerto Rico Operating Area, she amassed 22.6 hours, but in December she logged only 6.3 hours.

In January 1991, when they were training the *Nimitz* out of San Diego and the *Forrestal* out of Jacksonville, she accrued 22.1 hours, but in February, only 8.9 hours, and in March, 9.8 hours. April's count, when she was on detachment in California, was 18.1 hours. A mission to Whidbey Island, Washington, in May allowed her 14.3 hours, but in June she flew only 1.6 hours.

In contrast, a fleet fighter pilot based on a carrier could expect to fly approximately 30 hours a month, even in peacetime. Fleets train from their home base on shore for twelve to eighteen months, and then deploy for six months. During shore training, the flying is not as intensive; pilots might fly 25 hours a month at the beginning of the training cycle and then more and more as they get ready to go back to the ship. Desert Storm carrier pilots probably flew from 40 to 60 hours a month.

The final problem that plagued VAQ-33 was its dual chain of command. That wasn't the way most of the navy operated. The squadron had to get money for missions and systems changes through one chain of command, and money for training, manpower, and aircraft maintenance and modifications through another. The squadron found the first chain easier to deal with, and got in the habit of backdooring all changes through it in order to get things done faster.

When they had to go through proper channels to get money for training, they had to "fess up" to their sins before they could get approval. Those officers who had been bypassed before resented it and assumed that if the squadron was coming to them now, what it wanted was probably illegal, immoral, or was going to cost money they didn't have. This scenario placed the squadron well outside the system that was designed to support it, and it was known far and wide as an independent or rogue outfit.

Chapter 12   *Reality Check*

On 16 January 1991, at 3:00 A.M. Iraq time, the Persian Gulf air war started. Saddam Hussein refused to leave Kuwait. Kara was taking part in a Pacific Fleet training mission at Miramar Naval Air Station in San Diego when she got the news. The air war lasted only a little over a month and when it was over, Mike Barger, Kara's buddy from AOCS through flight school, wrote her that he had "dropped over 100,000 pounds of bombs (mostly Mk-83s), dropped 4 Mk-84s, a Walleye, shot a HARM, and witnessed a number of SAM firings, none of which seemed to be guided. Pretty good for a first tour guy."

Mike had flown forty combat missions. He said his carrier, the *Roosevelt,* "hand-delivered almost five *Million* pounds of 'influence' on the Iraqi forces. (We affectionately referred to each weapon as a 'candy-gram.') It is no wonder that the ground forces had to simply sweep up the left-overs as they took Kuwait in two and a half days and proceeded to take a third of Iraq in only two more."

He signed the letter "Your Friendly Neighborhood Strike Fighter Pilot."

Kara was jealous when she got that letter. Mike had been outstanding at AOCS and flight training. He was flying F/A-18s off a carrier and had been to war. Not only was he having a fabulous time shooting real ordnance at real targets and zooming on and off the *Teddy Roosevelt* in the latest-model navy fighter warplane, but his career was soaring. Combat was an "A number one" check mark for the résumé of a future admiral.

Kara too had been outstanding at AOCS and flight training, but she was stuck in a fleet support squadron with boring, ho-hum flying in a slow, squatty, attack bomber that was old and gelded by its pod-toting mission. It wasn't fair. Her mother agreed it wasn't fair, but she was glad Kara wasn't flying in the Persian Gulf. She wrote to Mike after the war was over but while he was still on cruise:

82

Kara wants me to write my congressman and tell him that I have a daughter who is a navy pilot and that I think she should be flying combat missions. Although I do think she should be obligated to do exactly what you are obligated to do, I haven't written the letter. I couldn't write a letter asking that anyone be sent to war. I worry about you and all of Kara's friends who are in danger. It will be very glamorous when you next come to my house to dinner and amuse me with all of your war stories and I want that time to come soon.

In San Antonio, Texas, the opinions on the war were strong. Sally wrote Kara on 21 January 1991:

My women golfing buddies, Louise, Pimmie, Scootie, were all decrying the anti-war demonstrations and saying that such demonstrations shouldn't be allowed now that we were at war. I reminded them that we were fighting for the right to say what we wanted, even if it wasn't patriotic and even if it offended the servicemen and women who were defending us. They didn't agree. Louise said that we really didn't have free speech anyway and that even if we did, this kind of speech shouldn't be permitted.

I just hit my ball and the subject dropped, but I can't help thinking that Louise didn't think that *The Last Temptation of Christ* should be allowed in movie theaters. I guess the Ayatollah Khomeini had the right idea in putting out a contract on Salman Rushdie and I'm sure Saddam wouldn't permit anti-war demonstrations in Iraq.

Funny that people don't see any similarities in their thinking and the thinking of all bigots, bullies, and dictators when they say what ought and ought not be permitted. Abortion, religion, sex, obscenity, race, politics, civil rights for accused criminals, war, the flag. I wonder where we would be if expression of opinion was controlled by the proponents of God, Mother, and Country and don't let anyone tell you different.

Anyway, I know you are a good sailor and I am proud of you. Just remember that you are protecting everybody and everybody's rights, even the rights of no-good yellow-coward anti-war hippies.

Chapter 13 ❀ *Vertigo*

On Friday, 25 January 1991, Kara wrote in her journal, "I nearly kilt 'Psycho' on missed app nzc (vertigo)." Translated, that means she was coming in for a landing at Cecil Field Naval Air Station in Jacksonville, Florida, when she became disoriented and almost crashed.

Kara and Lt. Downey Ward, her navigator, call sign "Psycho," were on the next-to-last leg of their journey home from San Diego where they had been for almost two weeks working with the carrier *Nimitz*. Downey was a fairly senior lieutenant who had been an instructor in the A-3 and had also qualified in A-6s, though he hadn't been flying in them very long. Another plane was flying in their section, and both planes stopped for fuel at Kelly Air Force Base in San Antonio on Thursday the twenty-fourth. Kelly's mild winter weather and its location halfway across the country on the southern route from San Diego to Cecil made it a logical refueling stop. It was also an air force maintenance depot, and its general expertise was helpful when navy aircraft had problems.

Her mother loved it when Kara flew cross-country. She would go to Kelly and watch Kara land. Sometimes Kara could stay overnight at her mother's house and often she would bring other aircrews with her. Everyone wanted to eat San Antonio Mexican food. One time, six pilots and flight officers stayed at Sally's house, a couple of the men curling up in blankets on her living room floor. Two others stayed with Kara's bachelor uncle, Jimmy, at his apartment, which Dagny had aptly named "Filthville." No one seemed to mind, though.

The weather was bad in Jacksonville, so the two crews decided not to continue on that day. Kara made notes on her calendar that reflected her thought process. "Flyoff RON S.A.," she wrote. "Flyoff" is a navy term for launching all functioning air wing aircraft to their home bases when a carrier returns from a deployment or operations at sea. Kara stretched the meaning a little, as she hadn't actually been deployed on a carrier—but she was returning to her home base after working with one.

RON means "remain overnight en route." S.A. meant San Antonio.

"Fuel on reds," she continued, possibly reminding herself that if the weather was too bad to land at Cecil Field she needed sufficient fuel to proceed to an alternate destination. "Gear & bad WX" probably meant she anticipated a low ceiling and wet runway at Cecil and might have to take the arresting gear if the braking action were bad. To further complicate matters, the whole trip from San Diego she had had trouble with the backup flight instruments in the cockpit.

The decision to stay at Kelly was a good one. The bonus was the last note, "Fajitas at Mom's."

Early Friday morning when Kara went to Kelly, it was foggy in San Antonio; the weather at Cecil Field in Florida was not much better than it had been the day before; and Kelly maintenance hadn't been able to fix their backup flight instruments. The two crews considered holding up for another day, but Kara and Downey decided to fly to Jacksonville. They were supposed to participate in battle group operations on Saturday. They weren't on their way just to train vessels for some eventual, possible conflict. They were transporting the state-of-the-art electronic pods to be used in training the carrier *Forrestal,* which was about to leave on an emergency deployment to the Persian Gulf. The electronic warfare training was essential and the *Forrestal* was depending on them to get the equipment there.

The decision was not an easy one. They would have to leave San Antonio late because of the fog, which meant they would arrive in Jacksonville at night, in iffy weather—and their backup flight instruments were not working properly.

Kara had been flying recap EA-6As for the past two weeks in San Diego, but she had drawn one of the old unmodified nonrecap A-6As for the flight to Jacksonville. She disliked this particular airplane because it had an unusually weird instrument configuration even for a nonrecap. She couldn't locate the buttons and switches by using experience or logic; she just had to feel around for them. To accommodate the nonstandard cockpit, she had to modify her normal instrument scan pattern, which increased the workload dramatically.

Lt. Cdr. P. W. "Boris" Burris-Meyer, the safety officer, recorded in his Memorandum for the Record, "Upon arrival at Cecil after sunset, wx [weather ceiling] was 800', overcast with thunderstorms in the immediate vicinity. That meant they would be flying in the clouds until they were only eight hundred feet above the ground. As they were descending to land, Kara could see neither the horizon nor the ground, nothing but clouds and lightning.

The safety officer's report continued: "Workload in the cockpit was disproportionately increased due to perceived erratic backup flight instruments." Kara had to depend on the ground control approach (GCA) controller and his radar screen to tell her where she was, to talk her down. "Boris" noted: "The GCA controller was erratic and significantly below the norm in observing trends and responding with timely calls." When Kara asked for landing instructions, they were delayed and unclear, and the lousy weather created static, making the radio crackle so that even when he said something she could hardly understand him.

The airplane was carrying an ALQ-170 electronic pod underneath one wing at station two, two ALQ-167 pods underneath the other at station five, and drop-tanks at stations three and four. The ALQ-170 was the heaviest pod the navy owned, weighing close to eighteen hundred pounds and worth more than a million dollars a copy. There were very few of those assets in the navy and they were irreplaceable, so they really were worth much more than just the cost to build them. Each ALQ-167 pod weighed about three hundred pounds, and each was valued at around a million dollars.

The aircraft handled differently because of the pods and drop-tanks, and its optimum angle-of-attack airspeed on final approach was higher because of the increased weight. Kara felt like the plane was slipping.

Landing an unfamiliar airplane with unreliable backup flight instruments, carrying three heavy pods and drop-tanks, the weight unevenly distributed under the wings, and flying in the dark through lightning, rain, and clouds is extremely challenging. If, on top of that, no answers or directions come from the GCA controller, about the only other bad thing left to happen would be to get vertigo—and Kara did. She felt that her surroundings were whirling about, spinning, and it made her nauseated.

Pilots are trained to handle vertigo. They are indoctrinated to have complete faith in the instruments and in the instructions from the GCA controller. But Kara didn't trust the flight instruments in this plane, and the controller didn't seem to be speaking English. She scanned outside the plane for any landmark or field lights, and Downey tried to help her, but they couldn't see anything and she couldn't get her bearings. She swallowed hard and tried to concentrate on her scan.

Imagine flying along in pitch black, lightning off in the distance, no horizon, rain spattering on your windshield, the dim red glow from the instrument panel the only light in the cockpit. Your instincts no longer tell you whether your head is pointing toward the sky or the earth, and you know you won't be able to see the ground until the plane practically reaches the runway. Your training says to trust the instruments, but you have good reason not to. You're certain only that you're somewhere between heaven and earth flying in God only knows which direction.

About the midpoint of the approach and still in the goo, she decided the best decision was to break it off, come around, settle her stomach down, and try it again. Downey agreed. "Clean it up and let's get out of here," he said.

She pushed the throttles forward to military power to stop her rate of descent, adjusted the nose attitude, and raised the landing gear, flaps, and slats. Airspeed was approximately 150 KIAS (knots indicated airspeed). (One knot is one nautical mile per hour, which is equal to 1.15 statute miles per hour.) Raising the landing gear reduced drag. Unfortunately she raised the flaps and slats about 20 knots below the minimum placard speed and the aircraft began to settle.

The left wing dropped. Kara applied the aft stick and full right aileron. It didn't correct. The left wing was not responding, and the nose wasn't rising.

"Get the left wing up! Get the left wing up!" shouted Downey.

She lowered the flap/slats handle. The wings leveled; the nose rose above the horizon; and the plane accelerated through 180 KIAS. The aircraft continued to respond and she flew it away. The safety officer's memorandum stated that they were four hundred to six hundred feet above the ground. With characteristic appreciation of the drama of a suspenseful situation, Kara noted in her diary that she "recovered with about 50' to spare."

Kara and Downey went into a holding pattern to catch their breath. A new GCA controller took over and she landed the plane.

Chapter 14 ✼ *Fiasco*

Battle group training operations with the *Forrestal* and its contingent of escort destroyers, frigates, and amphibious assault ships began the next day off the coast of Jacksonville, Florida. On Sunday, 27 January 1991, Kara and Lieutenant Commander Boone, call sign "Pepper," were crewed in an EA-6A Intruder, part of a section of four airplanes that were taking part in a mission to simulate striking the vessels at sea.

The four planes were to join up on takeoff from Cecil Field and fly to the operating area as a flight. In addition to the Intruder were two F/A-18 Hornets and an ERA-3B Whale, which was scheduled to lead the flight with Lieutenant Wilkens as the pilot, Lieutenant Crissman, the navigator, and Lt. Cdr. "Boris" Burris-Meyer, the electronic countermeasures officer. "Boris" was the mission commander and Kara asked him if she could lead the flight formation so she could secure her section/division lead training qualification.

Once pilots have mastered the basics, they are assigned to first practice and then qualify for various mission duties, such as flight leader and mission leader. Each qualification reflects a gradual increase in responsibility and workload and is an addition to the pilot's résumé. Usually, however, before they assume the responsibility for leading the flight formation on an actual mission, aviators have had a lot of flight time in the cockpit and experience with the mission aspect. For Kara, with just under 150 hours in the EA-6A, it would be on-the-job training. But she wanted to do it and there was no tactical reason why the EA-6A Intruder couldn't lead, so "Boris" agreed.

He noted in his Memorandum for the Record that Kara's brief for the flight "was *most* professional and thorough with the noticeably late arrival of LCDR Boone as the only detractor. Significant pains were taken to ensure that join-up, speeds and procedures were completely understood and all players were completely comfortable with the unfolding plan. I remark here that LTJG Hultgreen was follow-ing a precedent set earlier that day in training for the lead and that she was exceptionally well prepared and thoroughly professional with her brief."

During start-up and taxi, Kara's plane developed problems on the flight line, and "Pepper," her navigator, was having difficulty with the radio. The Whale and the two Hornets had to wait for the Intruder in the "hold short," which is an area just off the active runway where the airplanes taxi and remain until everyone has joined up. The planes could take off when they were ready and join up in the air, but the air-craft burns a lot less fuel waiting around on the ground.

After some delay, the planes finally got their tower clearance and taxied out to the runway one at a time. Kara's Intruder took off first, followed by the Whale and the Hornets.

Rendezvous was never completed. Kara's Intruder was slower than briefed at join-up, and the Whale was forced to underrun to the right. "Pepper" continued to have problems with the radio; transmissions to and from the Intruder were garbled, and he missed several calls from both the tower at the field and the radar controller. The Hornets briefly joined the Intruder on the port (left) side, but because of the confusion on the radio, decided to drop back behind the Whale. How-ever, when Kara asked "Pepper" if all the planes were aboard, he said yes. She accelerated and the Whale couldn't catch up.

The Whale continued trailing, its navigator trying to provide both communications and navigation assistance to "Pepper," who had to ask the vector (directions) to the *Forrestal*. It was well past sundown. Intermittent rain, thunderstorms, and layers of clouds further ob-scured visibility. Kara couldn't see the other aircraft. It was like lead-ing ghosts.

The transmission difficulties continued until "Pepper" couldn't get through to anyone on the radio. He told her he wasn't sure anymore that the other planes were with them. With no other way of knowing what was happening, Kara descended to reach visual flight conditions. She hadn't found any by one thousand feet. It was not standard oper-ating procedure to fly below one thousand feet, but the clouds appeared to be thinning and she took her plane a little lower, staying just long enough to look around to see where the water met the sky.

She saw that the Whale was behind her and the Hornets were not with her. The Hornets had taken two thousand feet step-up separation. They never rejoined. Then the Whale broke off, climbing to find fairer weather. Kara had a decision to make. She had lost the other planes in her section, her radio was not working, the weather was terrible, and she wondered whether her navigator had any idea where they were going or how to get there. Safety of flight always comes first, and she considered aborting her flight and returning to Cecil.

But she couldn't bring herself to do that. There was a war on. Exposure to this training had consequences for the *Forrestal* and the other fleet vessels that were deploying imminently for the Persian Gulf, and her EA-6A was carrying the most important electronic warfare training pods. If she didn't go, the heart of the mission was gone. Training the *Forrestal* to anticipate an enemy attack was a "real" mission, the most meaningful assignment she had had in the navy. She completed the mission. The *Forrestal* received the all-important electronic warfare training before it went to war, and even though there was no recognizable formation of planes, everyone got back to the base safely.

Kara was criticized for her performance during the *Forrestal* battle group operation because of her headwork, not her flying. Of course, it is easy to second-guess decisions after they have been made. The facts were that there was a flight plan and there were standard procedures that were supposed to be followed. When things didn't go as planned, Kara continued on when, considering her navigational and radio difficulties, it might have been more prudent to turn around and go home.

Probably, early on in the flight she should have passed the lead to the Whale, but it was not in her nature to give up. In her debrief, Kara said she was aware of the continuing errors but because of the communications difficulties, she received little information from her navigator. She elected to press on at each juncture because she felt she could carry the whole load.

Lieutenant Commander Burris-Meyer's Memorandum for the Record said that in Lieutenant Commander Boone's debrief, "It was apparent that he had lost situational awareness early in the flight and was, in fact, unaware of errors made, calls missed and SOP violations."

Chapter 15 *The Ready Room Commandos*

Pilots are supposed to share flight experiences. They tell about their mistakes so others can learn from them and know what to do or not to do in similar circumstances, and that is what Kara did. "Bad idea," she said in her diary entry. "I decided we should do an A-6 NATOPS training session about it. I ended up in front of the entire Ready Room. I'm still under the squadron's electron microscope."

Downey tried to convince her she would be better off not to talk about their close call at Cecil Field. But Kara was idealistic and thought it was the right thing to do, so he went with her to talk to the assistant safety officer (ASO) after they reported back to work in Key West. The ASO happened to be Lieutenant Crissman, the navigator of the Whale during the *Forrestal* operation on Sunday. He reported what they told him to his boss, the safety officer, who happened to be the *Forrestal* operation mission commander and the electronic countermeasures officer of that same Whale, Lieutenant Commander Burris-Meyer.

Burris-Meyer might not have attached much significance to Kara's difficulties when she was trying to get her section/division lead, but he became concerned when he found out she had had a close call two days before. The combination of the two incidents so close together made him decide he needed to bring them to the attention of the squadron commanding officer.

Don Foulk, Kara's mentor, had been transferred to the Pentagon the previous month, and Cdr. Bruce Nottke, who had been his executive officer, was the new commanding officer. He knew Kara and was well disposed toward her, but the new executive officer was an O-4 Brute Squad honorary member, Cdr. William Raymond "Billy Ray" Puckett, who had been hearing Kara stories for months from Ben Jergens.

The incidents were put on the agenda at the next All Officer's Meeting (AOM). Lieutenant Crissman was to conduct the review, and Kara and Downey were both scheduled to talk. AOMs aren't just a meeting of pilots and flight officers, but of all the officers in the squadron. The purpose is to talk about general squadron policy and things like deployment schedules, social gatherings, and mess dues. When the meeting gets around to business that only concerns aviators, the other officers don't have to stay. But this time, when it was Kara's turn to speak, few of the nonaviator officers got up to leave.

By the time the meeting took place, Kara had become aware it would be well attended. Her close-call landing at Cecil and her division lead fiasco were the hot topics of conversation. Fueled by Lt. Cdrs. Ben Jergens and Phil Mansfield, "I told you so" was ringing in the corridors.

The tension some of the senior officers felt regarding their future career options was now heightened by a war mentality. The Gulf War had revived the warrior, even in Kara's squadron, and macho pride was strong. Her bad luck in almost killing herself was nothing compared to the bad luck of having done it in wartime. The attitude was, This is serious! This is war!

She knew the Ready Room Commandos were relishing her screwup and would hold it against her, and because she was defensive, she made her biggest mistake. She made excuses for her actions. After explaining how the incidents had happened, she talked about the problems caused by lack of familiarity with the cockpit, since every A-6 she got into was different, and the fact that she hadn't had much flight time. She told about the incompetent controller and how the backup flight instruments hadn't functioned and about the bad weather and the faulty communications system. She didn't say anything that wasn't true.

What she didn't do was begin by saying, "This is what I did wrong. I raised the flaps/slats too soon. I should have known better. I certainly know better now." She was willing to stand up and tell a room full of fellow officers that she wasn't perfect, but she couldn't bring herself to take full responsibility for her bad headwork. If she had, maybe she wouldn't have given her critics such an opening. Though all her excuses were valid, they also applied to every other nugget pilot in the squadron. With a little guidance or the benefit of more experience, she would have handled it differently. As it was, she provided ammunition for those people in the squadron she had antagonized, and they used it.

Though it was supposed to be a learning session to help an inexperienced pilot who made a mistake, Kara was prepared for it to be an unpleasant ordeal. She expected some "typical aviator" rough treatment, but she never expected to be viciously attacked by senior aviators for doing something they probably had done themselves when they were junior. And attack her they did, making her go over and over each decision. Some of the men meant well, just trying to hold her feet to the fire, to push her into taking more responsibility for what happened. Others questioned her ability and judgment.

Kara began:

On January 25th, I nearly killed Psycho on a missed approach to Cecil. We're very relieved to be here to talk about it. I share this sorry tale with you in the hope that it might help if you ever find yourself in a similar situation.

I had been flying the remodeled A-6s for the two weeks we were in San Diego, but I was flying one of the old planes home, and I wasn't familiar with the cockpit layout. To add to that, we had had trouble with the backup flight instruments on the way to San Antonio from San Diego. We almost delayed another day in San Antonio. But we were transporting the ALQ pods to Cecil and the pods were needed for fleet training. So, we came on anyway.

Basically, I became disoriented in the goo and got vertigo. We decided to abort the landing and come around again. I must have raised the flaps/slats before I had sufficient air speed because the plane departed.

Downey interjected, "The ground controller was incompetent, but there was so much static over the radio, we couldn't hear him anyway."

Kara continued: "The ALQ-170 pod is heavy. It created more drag than I was prepared for. I'd never transported that pod before."

Ben Jergens interrupted in a cold voice, "When did you realize you had vertigo?"

"When I was about halfway down," Kara replied.

"When did you decide to break it off and go around again?" Phil Mansfield asked her.

"Just about that time. Downey said . . ."

Burris-Meyer cut her off, "Did you check your instruments?"

"Yes," she answered, "but the backup instruments weren't working right. I didn't trust them to . . ."

The tone of the questioning was adversarial. They hardly gave her time to answer one question before they fired another one.

Commander Puckett wanted to know if she remembered NATOPS instructions about when to raise her gear and flaps/slats.

"Why did you raise them too soon?" asked Lieutenant Commander Mansfield, not giving her time to finish her answer to Commander Puckett.

"Why didn't you lower the flaps/slats sooner?" Burris-Meyer broke in.

"I lowered them as soon as I realized the plane wasn't responding," she answered.

"You knew the situation was extreme. Why didn't you eject?" questioned Mansfield.

"It never occurred to me. I was so busy trying to recover the aircraft. I was sure that I would fly it away," Kara responded. They grilled her for two hours, the questions repetitive and relentless, and Kara felt, sarcastic and belittling.

Neither the commanding officer, Commander Nottke, nor the executive officer, Commander Puckett, stepped in to say, "OK, enough. We're accusing, not learning." They knew the difficult circumstances for new pilots in the squadron, and they were aware of the undercurrent of resentment that had built up for months about Kara, but they were convinced she was overconfident and thought this might bring her down a peg.

Kara's detractors were few in number, but they were senior and in powerful positions.

Chapter 16 *Professional Slaughter*

Kara was very upset by her ordeals in the air and in the Ready Room, but she had to laugh when Pam threatened to submit the following article to the base newspaper:

> Up Close and Personal with LTJG Kara "I don't need no stinkin' uniform regs [regulations]" Hultgreen
>
> It isn't often that one has the pleasure of meeting someone on the brink of suicide, someone who hates not only their job, their life, and their uniform pants, but also their lips (when found), and still finds the strength and perseverance to go on, never buckling under to the inner and outer pressure to quit, always able to give one more tour, take one more picture, or write one more article. Known by her mother as merely Dagny's sister, Kara is always seen as a beacon of positive thinking and oft times sought out by her squadron mater, er uh squadron mates, as a source of strength and moral support.
>
> A pillar of high moral standards, Kara is affectionately known by a tight circle of friends as the manatee woman because she has hair and is a mammal, but chooses not to mate. She has on several occasions been found dressed to the nines on a Friday night, surrounded by broken hearts and an occasional admirer (who may have the pleasure of sharing her company, but never her bed) only to return home alone at the end of the evening.

Lieutenant Commander Burris-Meyer described the Ready Room review of the incident in his Memorandum for the Record.

> The assistant safety officer, acting on our direction, conducted a review for the Ready Room with LTJG Hultgreen and LT Ward recounting the actual chain of events. The atmosphere was *most* defensive and LTJG Hultgreen was later heard to remark on numerous occasions as to how LCDR Burris-Meyer had unfairly advised

her to bring this to the wardroom's attention, leading her to professional slaughter.

Disparity in dates of the incident and its initial reporting to safety was not explained. It is my impression the aircrew were too much on the defensive and wished not to disclose their errors. LTJG Hultgreen was involved in another incident on 27 Jan and this may have delayed any decision on her account.

Kara and Downey hadn't intentionally delayed reporting their close call at Cecil Field on Friday evening, 25 January; there just wasn't the opportunity while they were in Jacksonville. Battle group training operations with the *Forrestal* began on Saturday and everyone was occupied. On Sunday, Kara was flying. The detachment flew home on Monday, 28 January, and Kara didn't go back to work at the squadron until Thursday, 31 January.

The aviators had been away from Key West since 11 January. If aircrews are away from home base for more than two weeks, they get a couple of days off when they get back, to run errands, do laundry, and regroup, so Kara had Tuesday the twenty-ninth and Wednesday the thirtieth off.

Burris-Meyer's report stated, "At no time did either aircrew mention ejection or jettison." The decision not to jettison shouldn't have been a criticism since it was a judgment call as to whether to dump the expensive electronic pods. He continued, "My belief is that the navigator—an A-3 navigator instructor—had not yet made the ejection option part of his conscious thought process. Further discussion with the pilot rendered, 'I didn't jettison the stores [pods] because I was a woman and I knew I'd catch *so* much shit.'"

Kara wrote Mike Barger's mother about her close call; she didn't tell Mike. Mike wrote Kara from the *Roosevelt:*

Glad to hear that you are doing well in your squadron, not that I ever doubted your ability. Interesting little story you had for my mother—funny that you didn't include it in my letter. Actually, it's those types of "near misses" that make each of us respect our vulnerability and look at our jobs from a "mortal" standpoint. This makes it easier for Hornet guys to hold conversations with those unfortunate members of the lesser communities. Ha Ha. Seriously we FAGs are really spoiled, as you know from the simulator.

FAG stands for "fighter attack guys." On the macho scale, their position is so secure that they made up the nickname themselves.

After the verbal assault on Kara by the Ready Room Commandos, life in her squadron deteriorated for her. She finally had made a mistake in the air that the O-4 Brute Squad could use to teach her a lesson. Instead of helping her, they labeled her dangerous, and their remedy was to "watch" her closely. They criticized everything she did and were openly antagonistic any time she talked of the possibility of women flying combat aircraft.

Other senior officers were reluctant to take up for her because they didn't know what to make of her. They faulted her for the mistakes of inexperience and for being brash and naive. Refusing to let anyone sell her short, she invariably got in the last word, especially when talking about the place of women in the military. Not fitting anybody's stereotype and pushing the structure, she made everyone uncomfortable.

She was only twenty-five years old, junior, and no threat to them, but her confidence and natural ability inspired the kind of jealousy usually reserved for those competing directly with them for the same job. She beat the guys at everything: tennis, golf, swimming, and she always scored 300 on the physical readiness test. That perfect score required that she swim five hundred yards in under eight minutes, just like the men, and do the same number of pushups as the men, sixty-seven. She could have done less than the men and still been classified "outstanding," but she wouldn't settle for that.

On 9 May 1991, almost four months after the controversial AOM, Lieutenant Commander Burris-Meyer wrote the following memorandum to Commander Nottke via Commander Puckett:

SUBJ: LTJG HULTGREEN, PERFORMANCE AND PERCEPTION OF

Sirs,

I feel most strongly that issues and innuendoes concerning Kara's performance and abilities are now most *unfairly* represented. Liken to beating a dog when he is down, the wardroom attitude toward this officer is unprofessionally and unfairly out of control.

Unquestionably, there is documented justification for concern and attention based on *past* performance. As discussed, however, we must recognize that given the obvious aggressive (Thank God) attitude coupled with frighteningly limited experience and current flight time restrictions, *we* must accept the cause for her training failures. Basic instructor guides continuously warn us to pay special attention to the overconfident. In this specific case *we* have allowed a trend to develop—in fact we have fanned the flame with our inaction. We owe her a better shake.

I most strongly urge she be given the opportunity to return to the RAG [Replacement Air Group] post-haste for warm-up and refresher training and flights. A[n] SOP for other fleet outfits, this is a non-punitive—*good* investment. I further request that the Executive Officer provide the wardroom with one of his *very* effective recalibration briefs concerning SOP/BRIEFS/DEBRIEFS. I would be delighted to provide subject text.

Concerning wardroom attitude toward Kara—I am *most* concerned as I see this as a burden further demoralizing an obviously stressed *officer*. Again, I think we owe her better. Though the intent was honorable, I deeply feel the ready room debrief of her 25 Jan 91 incident en route Cecil Field was quite skewed in its delivery and management. The result has *not* been beneficial.

In discussion with LCDRs Small and Dustin I've found little support for action on *our* part. I ask here for *your* action.

VR, "Boris"

Nothing ever happened as a result of that memo. When Lieutenant Commander Burris-Meyer left the squadron, he gave Kara copies of all of his memos along with an undated handwritten cover letter that said:

Kara,

The enclosed are items I've culled from *my* files—I believe you should have a copy.

I was obliged to provide the two memos (re 25/27 Jan.) to go into your training jacket. I've no idea if they were ever entered.

The last item is a memo I sent the CO/XO as my tenure in Safety was ending. I still feel very strongly that you were denied proper training and adequate flight time. *Your* longevity is more a credit to your own talent than *our* efforts. For this I'm very sorry.

Please understand. I feel it's important to know that there were those who *did* support and defend you. People who cared. Positional authority and the need to support the chain-of-command precluded more "visible" support. Not my choice, but it was my job.

There is always "more," but I'd need a beer and a retirement check first. Until *that* time, fly your best, study hard, but *don't* miss the fun.

Anon,
"Boris"

Chapter 17 ❋ *Ten Days on the* Lincoln

Kara recovered from her "trial" at the All Officers Meeting. She decided Ben Jergens and the rest of the O-4 Brute Squad weren't worth worrying about. They would either be leaving the navy or going on to other assignments soon. The squadron was scheduled to begin flying F/A-18s in the fall, and when the combat exclusion laws were repealed, she would be off to a fighter squadron.

In the meantime, she had good friends, she was traveling to great places, meeting other pilots, and learning a lot. The frustrations of flying old ugly slow planes, her "idiot" boss and his Neanderthal buddies, and the busy-work public affairs job were only that, frustrations. Things were going to get better.

Of course, it irritated her when her articles were chopped, or when she was criticized, unfairly she thought, for courting attention from visiting brass and basking too much in the media limelight. But she was determined to do her best in this assignment so she would be ready to take her place in the fleet when the law changed, flying something sleek and lethal.

She wasn't the only one having an eventful winter. On 11 February 1991, the EA-6A piloted by Ben Jergens with Linda Heid as the navigator suffered a complete hydraulic failure and they had to eject over the water at fifteen thousand feet about ten miles south of St. Augustine, Florida. They lost the plane, two three-hundred-gallon drop tanks, and two electronic pods, a scarce ALQ-170 and an ALQ-167. Ben was in the water for approximately forty-five minutes and Linda for an hour before they were rescued and taken to NAS Jacksonville.

The skipper, Commander Nottke, the XO, Commander Puckett, and Kara, with camera in hand, calling herself "the ever-present PAO," were waiting for them when they returned to Key West. Kara wanted to know all the intricate details of the entire experience: Was

Ben scared when he saw that the wind was blowing him away from the coastline or when he had difficulty climbing into his raft? He wasn't anxious to dwell on the part about difficulty climbing into the raft, but Kara pressed him about it in the most solicitous way. And, of course, she referred to him as Ben "Lightning" Jergens.

She asked Linda how she felt when she found that her radio didn't work and that she had lost her glasses and couldn't see the coastline. She wrote about how the rescue diver grabbed hold of Linda's harness and asked, "Are you OK?" When Linda replied, "I'm fine," and he realized she was a "she," his hands went in the air and he said, "Pardon me, Ma'am!!!!"

Linda laughed and said, "Kara wrote the story for the base newspaper as only she could write it—funny, satirical, and quite the drama. No one could embellish a story like Kara."

On the day after Valentine's Day, Kara and Amy Boyer went on a cross-country trip to San Antonio. Marina Pisano of the *San Antonio Express-News* met Kara and Amy when they landed at Kelly Air Force Base; Gloria Ferniz took pictures of them in the cockpit and standing by the EA-6A in their flight suits.

Kara asked for and received permission from Commander Nottke to give the interview. The Kelly media representative sat in on the interview conducted on the base in a VIP lounge. A civilian, he could not have been more disinterested in the subject of Kara and Amy's quest for equality. As far as he was concerned, his afternoon had been completely wasted.

They stayed in San Antonio far longer than planned because the jet had hydraulic problems and wasn't fixed until Tuesday. The jets were always sick. Kara noted in her journal that on 11 March 1991 in Key West, she tried two different jets but she never got off the deck. On 14 March her jet was down with a fuel leak. On 11 April she was returning to Key West from San Diego detachment; she and Amy stopped at Randolph Air Force Base in San Antonio for fuel and repairs.

They stayed overnight with Kara's mother, and although they were able to take off the next day, they had trouble with fueling and the air conditioner en route to Key West and had to make an emergency landing in New Orleans. To Sally, the constant mechanical problems only meant that Kara often spent time in San Antonio on her way back and forth to the West Coast, and she got to be with her. It didn't register with her that each time Kara flew one of those old and fragile jets she was risking her life.

"I'm writing you from the lovely Mary Todd suite on the USS *Abraham Lincoln*—that's right, the Navy's newest and greatest nuclear powered *Nimitz* class aircraft carrier," Kara wrote her high school friend Mimi Hinton on 5 May 1991.

> I'm sure it has not slipped past your notice that Mary Todd was Lincoln's wife's name. The *Lincoln* is the only carrier with a 4-man bunkroom and nearby head (or bathroom) dedicated to female visitors. No, I'm not permanently assigned to the ship. I'm here as an on board observer for 10 days while my cohorts & squadron mates are attacking from Miramar (San Diego).
>
> This has been an awesome experience. I am amazed at the amount of coordination and teamwork it takes to run a flight deck, and that's just a drop in the bucket when you are dealing with an entire battle group. I've been able to witness operations from the command and control centers. I've flown in an A-6 tanker (great catapult shot) and an SH-60F—a brand new helo (flying video game). I'm really having a great time—and I'm learning a ton.
>
> I had better go and get on with my standard 18-hour day on this ship. People work around the clock here. It is very motivating to watch.
>
> Please write your senators & congressmen. We need to abolish the combat exclusion laws! I'm ready to fly F/A-18s off of these ships.

Kara was inspired by the experience. She said it wasn't scary being under attack by fake missiles, but it was intimidating to have to open the doors of the fleet squadron Ready Rooms below the decks of the carrier and announce, "Hi, I'm Lt. Kara Hultgreen." The receptions varied. Some of the men just stared at her and then ignored her, but a lot of them were interested in her reaction to carrier life and made her feel very welcome.

When Kara got back to Key West, she had lunch with Suzanne "Zanner" Parker, who was being "stashed" at the squadron after Aviation Officer Candidate School while she waited to begin flight school. "All Kara could talk about was how cool the *Lincoln* was, watching the carrier OPS, and how cool it was to fly jets," Suzanne said. "She couldn't wait to fly off the carrier—she longed for the day. . . . She was like a kid in a self-created fantasy playground, no time for negativity, just the reality of how much fun flying was."

Chapter 18 ❁ *The Combat Exclusion Laws*

On 8 May 1991 Representative Pat Schroeder announced to the House Armed Services Committee that she would offer an amendment to the 1992 Defense Authorization Act. The bill she introduced was "To amend title 10, United States Code, to repeal the limitations in that title on the assignment of female members of the Air Force to duty assignments in aircraft that engage in combat missions."

After input from Les Aspin and Beverly Byron, both Democratic members of the House at that time, Schroeder's amendment was recast to include the repeal of the navy's prohibition against women flying combat aircraft. The combat exclusion laws that restricted the use of women in the air force, navy, and marine corps—air force law (10 USC 8549) and the aircraft portion of the navy's law (10 USC 6015)—would be repealed.

In 1948 the Women's Armed Services Integration Act had been passed, which permanently integrated women into the U.S. armed services. Carl Vinson, a congressman from Georgia, had been chairman of a House Armed Services subcommittee that had conducted hearings on the proposed legislation. If the congressman had had his way, women wouldn't have been allowed even to serve in what he considered to be his personal navy. He hadn't accomplished that, but he had been successful in keeping women off the ships.

Women pilots were allowed to fly navy planes, but only those that were based on land and not on carriers, and there was great resistance to changing this injunction. It was unarguable that for women to live on carriers, enormous changes would have to be made. First, existing ships would have to be refitted with quarters to accommodate women—an expensive and time-consuming undertaking. However, that was a practical problem and could be solved. The interesting debate was cultural. In 1948 women were also excluded from boardrooms, operating rooms, and courtrooms, and from serving on police forces and in fire departments, or from maneuvering heavy equipment. The words "proper" and "moral" were often heard.

The arguments seemed particularly valid when applied to warships. Would the usual fireworks men and women generate escalate to nuclear proportions if they were thrown together in crowded spaces for six to eight months at a time? Would pregnancy cause a woman to be returned to shore, and if so, would that be her punishment or her excuse to get off the ship? Weren't women too fragile and emotional for such demanding duty?

As the years passed, women successfully demonstrated their abilities in formerly all-male occupations. Men did not always welcome their participation, but law did not prohibit it. In fact, the only thing women were prohibited from doing by law was going into combat. As the decade of the 1990s began, probably the thought that the last bastion of the all-male domain might fall was the biggest barrier to women getting onto combat ships. The men who had served on carriers seemed to fear that women on carriers and combat ships would somehow taint the atmosphere.

Kara and other women naval aviators were writing letters supporting repeal of the combat exclusion laws to the members of the House and Senate Armed Services Committees. They asked all their friends and families to contact committee members, circulating addresses, telephone numbers, and fax numbers. Lieutenants Tammie Jo Shults and Pam Lyons flew F/A-18s in VAQ-34, one of the West Coast electronic warfare support training squadrons. Tammie Jo had been Kara's roommate in Key West when Kara was carrier-qualifying in the T-2C Buckeye in January 1989. Pam, a year ahead of Kara at the University of Texas, had been a sorority sister of Dagny's. Like Kara, she had been an aerospace engineering major.

Tammie Jo's letter reminded the legislators of the tremendous contributions and sacrifices that U.S. military women made during Operation Desert Storm, as in World War II, saying it should erase any lingering doubts concerning the ability of these individuals to perform under fire or as a team with male counterparts.

The Gulf conflict illustrated, once again, that innocents in or out of uniform are not spared the war's horrors. Enemy soldiers, conventional or chemical weapons, and Scud missiles do not practice chivalry. More significantly, it clearly demonstrated the public's sad but proud acceptance of women returning from war in body bags, as POWs, and as heroines like Maj. Rhonda Cornum, USA. In the context of modern warfare, repeal of these laws would simply allow women the right to fight back.

Removal of the combat exclusion laws is not a revolutionary step but an evolutionary one. We have had 20 years of successful integration in the operating forces. Operation Desert Storm has proved that now is the time. For the future, repeal is not an issue of women's rights but of national security. We can no longer afford the luxury of discriminating against half the population in recruiting the kind of talent that is essential to victory. Most importantly, as stated in the *Air Force* and *Navy Times* May 6, 1991, editorials, it is the right thing to do.

Kara had her mother writing the senators from Texas, Lloyd Bentsen and Phil Gramm; her congressman, Lamar Smith; and two congressmen in bordering districts, Albert G. Bustamante and Henry B. Gonzales.

"I'm the little stick monkey flying the plane," Kara told Marina Pisano in the two-page article that ran in the *San Antonio Express-News* on 10 March 1991. The title was "On the Wings of Women"; the subtitle said, "Navy pilots are flying high but not in combat." Kara said she wanted to be deployed in the Gulf war zone. "I'm not saying, I want to travel to strange new lands, meet interesting people and kill them. Nor do I especially want to be in harm's way myself. But people enter the military to defend what they believe in—to fight for freedom."

When Marina asked her how she felt about the policy against women flying combat missions, Kara replied, "It just never occurred to me that being female was a birth defect."[1]

Her mother enclosed the *Express-News* article in the letters she wrote to all the members of the Senate Armed Services Committee after the House voted to repeal the combat exclusion laws. The letters were all similar to the one she sent the secretary of defense, Richard B. Cheney, on 9 May 1991:

[My daughter] flies EA-6As. She wanted to fly F-18s, but that was not one of her options when she earned her wings. It was one of the options of men with comparable grades who earned their wings at the same time.

If I had a son, I wouldn't choose to have him go to war. But if he chose the Navy as his career, I would support his choice and his obligation to defend his country. I do have a daughter who has chosen the Navy as her career and who has promised to defend her country. I support her choice and her obligation, and I believe she should benefit from the opportunities that accompany the obligation.

On 28 May 1991, at a Department of Defense briefing, several weeks after the House approved the amendment [H.R. 2100], the secretary of defense said he supported the House action. Cheney stated, "We welcome the legislation, because it gives the Department of Defense the authority to decide where the limits should be drawn, rather than having Congress set the limits on where women can serve."

The question was asked, "What is the Department of Defense [DoD] current policy on women in combat?" The written response was "DoD policy extends from the combat exclusion laws which are found in Title 10 of the U.S. Code section 6015 (Navy), and section 8549 (Air Force). These laws preclude the assignment of women to combat vessels or aircraft. Title 10 section 3013 gives the Secretary of the Army the authority to assign, detail and prescribe the duties of members of the Army. Under this the Army's combat exclusion policy functions in consonance with the policies of the other services, which are derived from law."

The tone of the Department of Defense answer clearly was "If it is left up to us, this is the way it will stay." Dick Cheney knew exactly where he intended to set the limits.

Kara and her mother then wrote all the senators on the Senate Armed Services Committee: Republicans John McCain of Arizona, Robert Smith of New Hampshire, and John Warner of Virginia, and Democrats John Glenn of Ohio, James Exon of Nebraska, Edward Kennedy of Massachusetts, Robert Byrd of West Virginia, and Al Gore of Tennessee. They also wrote Sam Nunn, Democrat from Georgia (a distant relative of Carl Vinson), and Strom Thurmond, ultraconservative Republican from South Carolina, though Kara and Sally considered them lost causes from the beginning. Sally got her friends to write letters also.

The female aviators were on the cusp of change, but they had to wait for the public to pressure Congress to make a political statement. It didn't matter that Kara thought she should be flying F-18 Hornets or F-14 Tomcats; it mattered what they thought in Iowa or Nebraska or Texas or Maine. And though the media was spotlighting the issue and many people were sympathetic to the women's point of view; much of the public was either ambivalent or horrified by the prospect of women in combat.

But even if the combat exclusion laws were repealed, Kara and her peers feared they were going to have to wait for a new administration in the White House before any changes would be implemented.

Chapter 19 ❋ *The NBC Interview*

Naomi Spinrad came to NAS Key West on 31 May 1991 to produce a television story for NBC. The topic of lifting restrictions on combat roles for female pilots was hot. Kara's job as public affairs officer was to help NBC in every way to put the story together and she was nervous and didn't sleep well the night before.

NBC wanted its photographer to take pictures from the cockpit of a plane flown by one of the female pilots and Kara intended to be that pilot. But the executive officer, "Billy Ray" Puckett, decided Sue would be the pilot instead, which upset Kara. After all, she had been the one actively working to promote repeal of the combat exclusion laws.

That decision, as bitter as it was for Kara, meant she spent more time with the producer, and after Naomi got to know Kara, she couldn't resist putting her on camera. Tom Brokaw began the 3 June *NBC Nightly News* report "Women in Combat" with the words, "Next month the Senate Armed Services Committee is expected to approve legislation giving American women a combat role."

Fred Francis, the Pentagon correspondent, narrated the story and started off with female army boot camp recruits doing calisthenics: "They did not join the army to be warriors, but since Desert Storm, these boot camp recruits and 200,000 other women in uniform may soon change the face of war.

"Like twenty-year-old Jacqueline Casey," said Francis, the camera focusing on a beautiful girl—even in camouflage gear, no makeup, and her hair pulled straight back—with clear skin, perfectly shaped eyebrows, white straight teeth, and a serious expression, "today's female soldiers want careers and equal chance at promotion, but that has been impossible since women are kept out of combat jobs." Ms. Casey said, "I think that women have proved themselves ready to share the burden and the glory."

Francis continued, "In the eyes of Congress and the nation, Desert Storm did more than vanquish the Iraqi Army; it wiped out cultural taboos that American women should not be wounded, captured, or killed facing an enemy. Major Rhonda Cornum's ordeal alone debunked the myth that women have no place on the battlefield."

Rhonda Cornum had survived a helicopter crash that killed five of her comrades. She had been taken prisoner by the Iraqis, and with the detachment and dignity of a soldier bearing insult the best way she could, told how she had been fondled by one of her guards. She knew the story would titillate some, but it was important that it be told. In her book, *She Went to War,* she said she hadn't been raped because of her screams "and the fortunate impossibility of getting me out of my flight suit with two broken arms."[1]

Rape almost happened. She had faced what all opponents to women in war considered to be the "fate worse than death," the most terrible thing that could befall a female, yet Major Cornum related the incident in a matter-of-fact way. The important thing to her was that she had survived.

When the NBC camera lights shone on VAQ-33, Lt. Sue Still was the star. There she was on the runway examining her jet in her flight suit, blond hair freshly washed, shining, and gathered in a soft braid in back. In the next sequence, she had her helmet on and was climbing into the cockpit, unsmiling and intense; then there was video of the plane taking off. In the right seat beside her in the aircraft, the bright blue Key West sky in the background, the photographer taped Sue verifying that being a pilot "doesn't take a tremendous amount of physical strength; it takes a lot of endurance and some amount of physical strength."

Fred Francis said about Sue, "At twenty-nine it will be too late for her to start flying the combat version of this A-6 from aircraft carriers." Then the focus shifted to two young women standing on the tarmac in uniform skirts and wings on their shirts. "The change in the law would put lieutenants Linda Heid [although Linda was also twenty-nine] and Kara Hultgreen on that most exclusive of male clubs, the aircraft carrier." Linda in her khakis looked relaxed and pretty and said, "I can do anything a man can do in a jet or any other airplane in the navy."

The camera shifted to Kara in her white uniform gazing into the sun, squinting slightly and smiling. Her hair was pulled back in a French braid and her mouth was a little tight, the only sign that she was nervous. "My fangs can grow as long as anybody else's when the time comes." Then she scrunched her eyebrows and got that very determined look she had when talking about combat exclusion laws and continued, "And, I mean, I don't like to lose."

A handsome young male navy F-14 pilot on the carrier *Forrestal,* Lt. Chris Green, wrapped up the piece with, "You can't deny a woman who has killer instinct the opportunity to try to express it."

Kara's comment earned her a new call sign, "Fang." After "Pancho" and "Boo," and before "Fang," her call sign had been "Hulk" or "Hulkster." It was a toss-up which call sign was worse, her mother thought. She had been horrified to hear her daughter referred to as "Hulk"; Kara thought it was pretty cool.

Chapter 20 ❊ *Jealousy*

The navy hierarchy was allowing much more latitude than usual on media coverage of the women's issue. The O-4 Brute Squad was annoyed that the interviews with the women were being conducted in squadron spaces and in uniform. It hadn't been that way during the Vietnam era—not by a long shot. Then, the navy had insisted that the military interview be off base and out of uniform, so there could be no confusion, no appearance that the navy condoned the opinions expressed. But times were changing, and the navy had to take civil rights into consideration. As long as what the women said was presented as their personal opinions and not the navy's, the interviews were allowed to take place on base and in uniform.

The national TV coverage provided the squadron with some recognition and Commander Nottke liked that, but some of the senior officers were extremely irritated that the women's issue made national television, and that Kara, a junior grade lieutenant fresh out of training and unproven as yet, was getting media attention. Those senior aviators had been serving their country a long time; they had done more and flown more. Kara was getting noticed on national television just because she was young, pretty, and female. They had a point, but it was hard for them to put it into words without sounding petty.

At least, Linda and Sue both had some real time in the navy. Kara was a junior officer, and she was supposed to keep a low profile. Within the experience of the senior officers, it simply wasn't proper for a junior officer, or any military officer for that matter, to be involved as an active proponent for one side of a political issue. They couldn't order the women to shut up about it because of the civil rights "nonsense." Distaste for expanding women's roles in the military was combined with extreme discomfort about all the new emphasis on sexual harassment issues. The whole situation was complex.

Kara was the woman most actively involved in working to influence the repeal of the combat exclusion laws, and she was a lot better at articulating her position on women's issues than the men were at defending theirs. That caused much of the resentment the men had in general over these issues to be directed at her. Kara knew she wasn't doing herself any good with the O-4 Brute Squad by talking to the press. Her mother warned her that the people who put themselves in the line of fire might make change happen, but they usually suffered so much damage from the battle that they rarely survived to benefit from it.

Kara felt she had no option but to actively fight, because if she had any chance of benefiting from change, it had to happen soon. It hadn't been her intention to carry a torch for womankind, but at the same time, in order to get where she wanted to be, she had to fight the larger battle.

The press began to focus attention on her, and she responded to it. She couldn't help it—it was her nature. The media took to her because not only did she look the part but she gave a great interview. She was photogenic and she always had a pithy quote. She was spirited and genuinely warm, and it came through on camera.

After the House voted to repeal the combat exclusion laws, the women's campaign to influence the Senate began in earnest. After the NBC interview, Kara wrote an article about it for the *Southernmost Flyer,* an official navy publication that was a newspaper about eight pages more or less, intended solely for base military and civilian personnel and printed at taxpayer expense. Most of the articles in the paper were submitted by public affairs officers from the various squadrons and commands and were about who was visiting whom, who had been promoted, that kind of thing. The paper would not be standing in line for any awards.

Excerpts from the first two paragraphs of the article Kara submitted read "A few of the Firebirds finest female fliers were questioned by a team from *NBC Nightly News.* . . . The law would open up carrier assignments to female aviators like those of VAQ-33. . . . With the barriers broken, the services will be able to base assignments on performance as opposed to gender."

With a blue marker, Ben "Lightning" Jergens drew six or seven short vertical lines through each of the next four paragraphs. Sentences such as "Living on and flying off of an aircraft carrier is something most aviators are proud to complain about" and "The women will be proud to share in the misery and the satisfaction" were among those deleted.

Chopped also was her statement that the Senate would be voting on the proposed legislation in July and "to have your views represented, the Senators can be contacted at the following address." The names and addresses of the senators on the Senate Armed Services Committee were crossed out. He said that information wasn't *Southernmost Flyer* material. Kara didn't hesitate to tell Ben if she thought he had made a dumb correction or an inappropriate change. It wasn't as if he were saying this isn't *New York Times* material.

"Not *Southernmost Flyer* material? Encouraging the democratic process is not *Southernmost Flyer* material? Why not let the paper decide that?" Kara said, incensed.

But Ben wasn't swayed. It was his position that a military newspaper printed at taxpayer expense was not supposed to encourage active duty military personnel to take a political stance because it might be construed that the military was campaigning to do away with laws that had been conceived in Congress by civilian leaders. A navy newspaper can encourage personnel to take part in the political process by urging them to vote, but that's as far as it can go. For example, even though the subject would be of acute interest to the military reader, you won't find articles in navy publications telling service members what Congress is trying to do to reduce their retirement benefits.

Either Ben didn't bother to explain his position to Kara or she just didn't buy it, because she was very angry about it. To her, it was just another one of "Lightning's" attempts to ruin her life.

Kara, who had written the senators on the Senate Armed Services Committee, was elated when Sen. John McCain answered:

> The performance of American women in Operation Desert Storm in Southwest Asia and Operation Just Cause in Panama has prompted me to reexamine the restrictions that prevent women from serving as combat pilots and in other combat roles in the military.
>
> After conferring with the Chairman of the Armed Services Subcommittee on Manpower and Personnel, we have agreed to begin this reexamination by holding a hearing on the issue of women in combat on June 18, 1991.

The hearing had been postponed, however, and there was talk it would be postponed indefinitely. In a letter dated 17 July 1991 to Suzanne Parker, Kara lamented, "I heard that the Senate is not going to vote on the women in combat issue for another year. Too controversial or something. What bullshit."

Kara was excited when she learned later that week that the hearing was on again and on 24 July, she took leave to go to Washington, D.C. The next day, Thursday, there was a press conference at 9:30 A.M. "Very interesting," she wrote in her journal. "Educating Senate. Called XO." Barb Bell, Dave Howe, Lori Melling, Lucy Young, and Rosemary Mariner were part of the delegation. Kara stayed at Commander Mariner's house.

The military women, including Kara, dressed in their uniforms, dropped by senators' offices. It wasn't against the law for them to wear their uniforms when they visited the lawmakers, but it certainly wasn't in accordance with military policy. A civilian went with them to talk about the issue. The aviators just talked about what they did.

Kara had met Barb Bell in Key West when Barb had flown down in the back seat of an F-14 to talk with the women of VAQ-33 about career opportunities. Barb had just finished Test Pilot School and wanted to encourage other women to do the same. Sue needed no encouragement; she was actively seeking the assignment. It was also on Kara's agenda for the future. Barb had been the second woman NFO to complete the school. She and Kara had hit it off from the start. Barb said Kara was "the kind of officer that sets the standard for others to follow." They "talked and talked about flying and the navy and how we were going to change the world—or at least the navy."

On 31 July, Kara was in Puerto Rico on DET. She played golf at Las Palmas in Del Mar. "Gorgeous!!" she wrote in her diary and then she noted, "Senate votes Yes!!" To top it off, she had a night flight. That day got two stars on her calendar.

The Senate Armed Services Committee version of the Fiscal Year 1992–93 Defense Authorization Bill directed the establishment of a presidential commission to study the role of women in combat assignments. It also included an amendment to repeal the statutes barring women from flying combat aircraft sponsored by Massachusetts senator Edward M. Kennedy and Sen. William Roth of Delaware.

One amendment that all the women aviators supported didn't make it through the joint House and Senate conference. Introduced by Sen. John Glenn, it would have expanded the role of the commission to permit the temporary suspension of all combat restrictions for the duration of the commission's study, which would have allowed actual tests to be conducted at every level of land, air, and sea combat.

Senator Roth wrote Kara on 2 August 1991.

Dear Kara:

I wanted to let you know how much I appreciated your efforts with regard to removing the combat exclusion laws. You should take pride in having affected a decision that will touch the careers of promising aviators and, indeed, our national defense. Congratulations on a great effort that was an important part of our success.

Thanks for your assistance.

He signed it "Bill."

Chapter 21 *Overstress*

Kara and Linda Heid flew together to Whidbey Island, Washington, for the Prowler Symposium on 19 May 1991. There had been a lot of talk about Kara and Linda transitioning from EA-6As to EA-6B Prowlers. The Grumman EA-6B Prowler, which was derived from the A-6, was the navy's first aircraft specifically built for tactical electronic warfare. Prowlers were huge, expensive airplanes filled with state-of-the-art electronic equipment—a very responsible flying assignment. Linda was considering it. Kara was fighting it. The Prowler had four seats, and in Kara's eyes it was just a bigger, uglier version of the plane she already flew. She desperately wanted to fly a single-seat aircraft.

About an hour from Whidbey, their canopy suddenly popped open at twenty-six thousand feet. After a few anxious moments, they got it closed. It made their hearts beat faster but they were able to continue on to Whidbey.

Sometime after Kara and Linda returned to Key West, more than one hundred fuel leaks were discovered in the wings of the plane they'd flown to the symposium. The leaks had been caused by a major overstress, and the repair job was long and complicated. A plane flown beyond its engineering parameters or in such a way that the pull of gravity becomes too great can be severely damaged. For example, pilots attempting to "look good in the break" have overstressed aircraft by pulling too hard as they hit the numbers and turn downwind to land.

Linda told Commander Nottke she thought Kara had overstressed the airplane coming into the break at Whidbey. Two pilots had flown the plane since Kara, and the normal procedure would have been for Commander Nottke to talk to all three pilots to see who would own up to the overstress. But Nottke only talked to the other two pilots and Linda—not to Kara.

A 7 ½ G click on the G meter, an accelerometer mounted in each wheel well, was noted by ground maintenance personnel at the same time that the leaks became apparent. When the plane experiences a change in gravitational or G force, the accelerometer clicks forward a notch. For each G change, the number increases by one. Plane captains are required to record those readings after each flight on an A sheet, which goes into the aircraft discrepancy book and is reviewed by maintenance managers and the next aircrew. The effects of gravitational forces on an airplane are cumulative, and when the A sheets show a G change of 7 or more, the aircrew is contacted to determine whether that amount of in-flight stress occurred at one time. If so, a major inspection is required.

Kara wrote in her diary that the plane, GD 117, "was subsequently overstressed by Lieutenant Commander Looney. Looney denied it. C. Riposo denied it. But did the buffoons ask me? Heck no. They asked Linda, 'Do you think Kara overstressed the jet into Whidbey?' and Linda—my good friend—wasn't speaking to me for about three weeks—I wasn't paying enough attention to her—she said, 'I really think she did overstress it, but I didn't look at the "G" meter. I thought I could hear the rivets popping while we were in the break.'"

Either the pilot or the NFO is supposed to check the G meter after a flight and note the readings, but neither Kara nor Linda had done so. However, the maintenance data clearly showed that the plane had been flown twice since Kara last flew it, and that it started leaking fuel immediately following the second flight. After a major overstress, damage usually doesn't take long to show. If Kara had overstressed the plane, fuel leaks probably wouldn't have waited to appear until after two more flights.

When she heard how Linda had responded, Kara's comment was "Oh fucking great answer." Her language had deteriorated in the last few months.

Kara wrote Suzanne about it on 7 July 1991:

What a nightmare. . . . "They" naturally assumed that I was responsible for the overstress and that I covered it up—so they talked to the other two pilots and instead of me they asked Linda. This was when Linda wasn't speaking to me.

Of course, no one has the balls to confront me but they talk to everyone else about me. This squadron . . . what can I say. If I survive this tour professionally, it will be a miracle. . . .

So I spoke to the XO ["Billy Ray" Puckett], the Ops O [operations officer] and the MO [Wayne Lockley, who had just become the maintenance officer] and I'm going to be less aggressive, less cocky & a 3 "G" pilot for awhile. . . . The XO played dumb—like he had no idea this was going on or that any blame was directed at me. The MO said he didn't know if anyone *should* talk to me. He explained that the perception of me was that I didn't know my own limitations and I blatantly disregarded the aircraft's limitations. I was trying to fly the EA-6A like it was an F/A-18.

I told him I was painfully aware that the A-6 was *not* an F/A-18 every time I strapped in. But I guess I need to change the perception, regardless.

They are even taking the fun out of flying by making me fly with O-4s.

Wayne Lockley knew Kara hadn't been responsible for the overstress. The maintenance department knew exactly who was piloting the plane when it had been overstressed. Regulations require that A sheets be saved for ten flights. On the eleventh flight the sheet for flight one is thrown away. Wayne had saved all the A sheets for Kara's flights and the succeeding flights and had shown them to Commander Nottke. There were no abnormal readings for Kara's flight, but Nottke seemed to ignore Wayne's documentation proving Kara wasn't guilty. He believed Linda. She was an experienced aviator, and she said she thought she could hear the rivets popping. The accusation had become fact and Kara was never exonerated.

Because Linda said Kara might have overstressed the plane and because Kara had been involved in two incidents in January, and without anyone ever saying anything to her officially, she was put under "double super secret probation." Of course, unofficially, people couldn't wait to tell her.

The overstress was the first of several incidents for which Kara would be unjustly blamed. In only a few months, Kara's ascending star had collided with the invisible but real obstacle of destructive public opinion. The undermining of her reputation had been insidious.

Kara didn't know what to think or do. Her mother wrote her:

My energetic, enthusiastic, intelligent, honest and focused daughter—beautiful, natural, quick-witted, outspoken, athletic, insightful, sensitive, kind—all wonderful qualities—all designed to inspire envy and fear in the less favored. Expect highs and lows in the public perception of you. Let each experience teach you how to influence public perception.

Don't ever change. In the end, you'll be fine.

Kara's near-accident in January had given Ben Jergens and his buddies the opportunity to voice their negative opinions about her in front of the whole squadron. When neither her commanding officer nor the executive officer made any objection, she had faced alone a vocal and hostile attack from those powerful few senior officers. Other officers may have assumed they were hearing a valid professional concern. Fact and fiction began to fuzz over.

She had no mentor in the squadron. Commander Foulk had been that for her, but he had left for a new assignment at the end of December 1990. She felt completely alone and unprotected, as if the senior officers were all taking some sort of satisfaction that she was finally getting paid back for daring to be different and trying to change the system.

It wasn't that Kara was a woman. It was the kind of woman she was.

Chris Riposo and Sue Still didn't arouse the same reactions in the men that Kara did. Chris was married, for one thing. She was nice, smart, a good pilot, and a dedicated officer. Her personality was such that she didn't place herself in the midst of controversy, and she didn't want the same things Kara and Sue did. She didn't want to fly fighters off a carrier, so she wasn't a threat. Chris wasn't driven.

Sue was driven. She wanted to fly the F/A-18 and be an astronaut just as Kara did, but Sue had a few more years in the navy and, somewhere along the way, she had decided not to get upset about whether or not her situation was fair. Maybe it was because she was four years older, more mature, and politically astute, or just more canny, but she worked within the structure and didn't waste her energy trying to change it.

Kara, on the other hand, besides organizing letter-writing campaigns to congressmen and senators, was networking with other female jet pilots in the navy who were trying to make things change. Her mentor was Cdr. Rosemary Mariner, one of the original six women to train as navy pilots. She was, in 1991, the first female serving as a commanding officer of an electronic warfare support training squadron, VAQ-34. Commander Mariner was trying to make things better for Kara and those who came after. Kara was doing it for Kara. She knew she was working within a short time frame and change had to come quickly or it would be too late for her. The window of opportunity would close soon.

Chapter 22 ❀ *Maintenance*

"I'm turning over the stinking PAO job tomorrow," Kara wrote Suzanne Parker gleefully on 1 July 1991. Suzanne was in flight school, and Kara wrote her lots of letters and postcards of encouragement.

Kara's new job was in the maintenance department, downstairs where the planes were kept when they weren't flying or when they were ailing. It was the aircraft outpatient clinic and hospital. Kara's title was branch officer, which sounded important, but her desk was one of three in a cubbyhole space, about eight feet by twelve feet, in the hangar. The other desks belonged to the division leading chief and the division officer, which would be Kara's next step up.

This assignment was a logical progression with significantly increased scope and responsibility. She was responsible for the training, morale, welfare, and discipline of sixty to seventy enlisted maintenance technicians.

She was to work for Wayne Lockley, the maintenance officer, and Harry Ennis, the assistant maintenance officer, both of whom were lieutenant commanders. Wayne had just taken over maintenance and there was a lot of work to be done. He teamed up with Harry, who had been on the job for a few months, to begin attacking the maintenance nightmare. They formed an overall plan and began to encourage personal initiative from the people who worked there.

Harry would be Kara's immediate supervisor, and Ben Jergens came down to brief him. He told Harry that his job would be to take Kara down a peg, and Harry assumed he was getting a spoiled junior officer. He was predisposed to believe Ben because of his first meeting with Kara.

Harry related that when he arrived at the squadron in April 1991, it had been Kara's responsibility as public affairs officer to get his photograph. She appeared at his desk one morning, without an appointment, introduced herself, and asked to take his picture. He was swamped with paper and he told her to come back. She did—that afternoon. Without a "Sorry to bother you, Sir, I know you're busy," or "Welcome to VAQ-33," she asked if now would be convenient for him. At that time she was a lieutenant junior grade and Harry was a lieutenant commander. He gave her his best scowl and attempted to brush her off soundlessly, bending over his desk.

When he glanced up after a while, she was still there calmly waiting. Harry prided himself on his talent for intimidation and couldn't figure out how she dared remain in his doorway observing him as he worked. Grudgingly, he got up and followed her out onto the runway and she took his picture. Then, without a "Thank you, Sir," she turned on her heel and walked away, leaving him standing there on the tarmac. He just shook his head and wondered who the hell she thought she was.

Harry had started out in the enlisted ranks at twenty years old. When he arrived at Key West he had had twenty-four years in the navy beginning as an aviation electronics technician. In 1979 he had been commissioned as a limited duty officer (LDO). He was a "Mustang," a handle given to those who earned their commissions from the ranks without a college education. The college-educated officers said LDO stood for Loud, Dumb, and Obnoxious.

Most of the LDOs were smugly content with that description. Their promotions had been earned by hands-on competence. The young newly commissioned officers, pipsqueaks to them, ignored them at their peril.

Harry was a no-nonsense person who knew what he was doing. As time went on, Kara developed a tremendous respect for him. She trusted him and that trust became very important to her. As far as Kara was concerned, Harry had only one flaw. He smoked. You weren't supposed to smoke in the hangar, but Harry told the commanding officer he would either smoke in his office or sit outside on a bench most of the day. The subject was dropped. Harry always kept his door closed because of the smoking, and Kara said when she opened the door she would have to peer through a veil of blue smoke to find him.

Wayne Lockley had become the maintenance officer in June 1991. An A-6 pilot with a great deal of experience, he was respected as an expert in the tactical possibilities and technical parameters of the electronic warfare area. Also, he had a computer background. He had arrived at the squadron around the first of the year and shown himself to be the strongest leader and the most competent by far of the lieutenant commanders. His reputation among his peers was as a highly professional and skilled pilot. Wayne was black, but he never made an issue of it. Like Kara, he didn't expect being a minority would be a factor one way or another.

Having served time on the second floor, in the purgatory of public affairs, Kara may have expected downstairs in maintenance to be hell. If so, she was surprised. Wayne and Harry had a well-developed sense of right and wrong, and they didn't think Kara was getting a fair deal.

Because Kara was one of his division officers, Wayne's professional duty was to mentor her, and he did. If she made a mistake, Wayne was the first to point it out to her in a professional not a personal manner, and she could accept that. He liked her and developed respect for her because she was a good officer—and he became one of her staunchest supporters. It was a natural liaison between two positive people.

Because she was able to open up and listen, Kara began to gain experience in dealing with people senior and less senior. She threw her energy into working for her people. She discovered there were more important things to worry about in the navy than whether or not Lieutenant Commander Jergens liked you or what he could do to hurt you. Life became more interesting for her. She was busy and had a sense of purpose.

All the hardships of the past year had tempered her, made her aware of how people with power could affect those who depended on them. Kara's background growing up had not prepared her to deal with people who were intemperate in their use of power.

She had learned how not to be a supervisor from Ben Jergens. Wayne and Harry, on the other hand, were giving their fledgling constructive advice and training, and Kara began to see positive things happening. Her past experiences with Ben served to make her empathetic to people who worked for her. This new understanding, the good and bad examples she had been exposed to, and her natural ability and enthusiasm allowed her to translate the lessons she had learned into her own style as she took her first tentative steps into the serious business of leadership.

It was satisfying to have a job she liked that was important to the squadron. It felt good to respect her bosses and feel that they respected her. Wayne Lockley and Harry Ennis began to support Kara when the Ready Room Commandos took shots at her.

Chapter 23 ❋ *Tailhook*
5 September 1991

"I'll find out if I made LT next week," Kara wrote Suzanne Parker on 11 August 1991. "Since I still have a pulse and I can fog a mirror, I can't see not making it. More moola to spend frivolously. Life is way too short not to have fun, I always say."

Kara did make lieutenant and carried her new rank to the convention for the members of the Tailhook Association in Las Vegas, Nevada, on Thursday, 5 September 1991. She, Sue, and Pam flew in from Key West in the tube of a P-3 along with other members of their squadron. The convention was to be held at the Hilton, but because it was full the women had to stay at another hotel.

Pilots and aircrew who have landed on a carrier are qualified to be regular members of the Tailhook Association, although anyone who supports naval aviation may join, and anyone who is affiliated with naval aviation may attend the Tailhook convention. Pam went that year because she had officially requested pilot transition and wanted to make contacts that would help get her request approved. It was a great opportunity to mingle with senior aviation officers so that when they saw her paperwork, they could put a face to it.

After they unpacked, Sue went to pick up a friend at the airport and Pam went with another group of friends from an F-14 squadron that routinely trained in Key West. Kara wanted to see her friends from AOCS and flight school and went to the now-infamous third floor of the Hilton to look for them in the various hospitality suites. She had on a black miniskirt, dagger heels that elevated her above the six-foot mark, a black lace camisole that was almost covered by a double-breasted, fitted tuxedo jacket, and dangling earrings. With her devilish smile, Kara was always larger than life, and she was especially so in four-inch heels. Her hair was Texas big; her lips were cheerleader red.

When she got off the elevator, the reaction was what could be expected when an imposing, beautiful, dressed-to-kill (or at least seriously injure) woman appeared in the midst of a tribal gathering of warriors in war paint. Victorious warriors at that, having only six months before secured the world for freedom in the Iraqi desert.

Some of the descriptions of in-flight heroics, complete with hand demonstrations of near misses and dodging enemy missiles, halted abruptly as the latest, most majestic of potential conquests stepped forth. The observers tried to decide what the price might be for a close encounter of the Kara kind. Then a captain who knew her from VAQ-33 said, referring to the label "hooker" attached to anyone who has caught a wire with their jet's tailhook while landing on an aircraft carrier, "Watch it, she's a hooker all right, but not the kind you think. That is an A-6 pilot."

The few people in that particular circle who heard the comment didn't entirely believe it. The rest continued to stare and make remarks. It was early in the evening and Kara found a friend in the crowd and joined his group.

The topic was aviation—they covered what they had been doing since they had last seen each other and what their current assignments were. Deference was shown to aviators who had flown missions in the Persian Gulf and their stories consumed the majority of the conversation. Of course, Kara lamented that she had not been given the opportunity to participate in the war and that with burgeoning world peace, it might be her last opportunity. She was sorry she didn't have a war story of her own to tell.

Somewhere amid this conversation, Kara felt a sensation, a groping beneath her miniskirt. She made a swatting motion with her hand, the one that wasn't holding her beer, and moved a little aside. She continued talking about her most passionate interests, flying and the injustice of her exclusion from flying carrier-based aircraft. She felt she might have lost her last chance to get the ultimate credential, the supreme status symbol among her peers—a warrior who has actually warred.

The presence of the hand was felt once again, and she looked down to see this man precariously crouching behind her with a sort of glazed expression, the kind she had seen before on people working on their tenth beer. According to the summary of Tailhook testimony in the inspector general's report, Kara, who was identified as Victim Number 5 (she hated being described as a "victim") "grabbed the man by the collar and slammed him into a wall."

"I'm a navy officer and an aviator," she said, right in his face. "Don't you touch me again."

He stared at her vacantly and slumped against the wall. Kara turned back to her friends. She was around men all the time and had seen some get pretty drunk and obnoxious before. Most of the time, she just deflected outrageous behavior with a joke. It took a lot to upset her. This man accomplished it, however, by biting her right buttock a few minutes later. She couldn't believe that anyone would have the audacity to bite her on the bottom after she identified herself as an A-6 driver.

"Here, hold my beer," she said to the pilot she was talking to. Then she smashed her elbow into the man still on his knees behind her, throwing all her weight into it. Her Viking blood was singing.

He fell to the ground, and when he recovered sufficiently, he crawled out the suite door into the hallway.

"Now where were we?" she said, taking back her beer.

"Wow, that was cool," said her friend, impressed. "That guy was an asshole."

When Fred Francis interviewed Kara for *America Close-Up* in the spring of 1993, he asked her if she was assaulted at Tailhook. Kara's answer was, "No, I was not assaulted. What happened to Paula [Coughlin] was criminal, malicious misconduct. What happened to me was irritating, and easily handled, and then blown out of proportion. The vast majority of my peers never have and never will require sexual harassment training. They were taught by their parents to treat people with dignity, good manners, and respect."

The Tailhook questions made her uncomfortable. She didn't want to sound "like a macho bitch that ran around beating men up."

Fred Francis continued: "This guy actually grabbed you?" She answered, "One person who had a lot to drink thought he was being clever, witty, and charming. I made it clear that his advances were unwelcome. I told him I'm an officer and an aviator, touch me again and I'll kill ya. When he came back he had obviously only heard the touch me again part and interpreted that as an invitation. So I decked him. He crawled away, and we all commented that he was an idiot."

"And none of the men around you jumped to your defense?" asked Francis.

"It wasn't necessary. I took care of it myself. I didn't need any help. Had someone been trying to maliciously and violently overpower me, there is no doubt in my mind that everyone would have rushed to my aid. I didn't need it."

Kara described the man as having an accent that she believed to be Australian, around six feet tall and sort of dumpy, weighing between 175 to 200 pounds, with light brown hair. Similarly identified by other victims, he came to be known as the Australian butt-biter.

She thankfully missed the Friday night fireworks on the third floor of the Las Vegas Hilton, the night of the infamous gauntlet. Early in the evening she had found her friend Mike Barger, and they had gone out to dinner.

On Saturday morning, nine admirals sat on what was called a Flag Panel in front of a packed house. It was a unique opportunity for the aviators because the admirals pledged to answer questions from anyone on any subject. The victories in the Gulf War six months before were still fresh, but talk of budget cuts had begun in earnest and the navy officers were worried about their futures.

Kara had her question about the future of the women aviators ready, but before she could ask it, a female C-2 pilot, Lt. Monica Rivadeneira, stood up. Lieutenant Rivadeneira's testimony before the Presidential Commission on Assignment of Women in the Armed Forces in Los Angeles was that the exclusion of women from ships and carriers contributed to bad morale in the navy for the men since it prevented them from rotating to shore duty. At Tailhook, she asked the admiral's panel when the policy would change to allow women to fly combat airplanes.

The men were worried enough about themselves. They certainly didn't want to hear anything about "female troubles." The audience booed and hooted. Vice Adm. Richard M. Dunleavy, the deputy chief of naval operations for air warfare, just said something about how the navy would comply with the law and left it at that. The jeers and catcalls continued and not one of the nine admirals sitting on the dais sought to quell the crowd. To Kara and the rest of the female aviators, that was the second gauntlet thrown at the women at the 1991 Tail-hook Convention.

"So what have you heard about the whole Tailhook fiasco? I was there," Kara wrote on 1 November 1991, to Paula Coleman, an A-4 pilot who had shared a house with her when they were training in Beeville. "I think it's really sad about what happened to all those women. I'm glad that my ESM started going off at about 2000 and I got out of there." ESM stands for electronic surveillance measures. Kara meant her "surveillance antennas" were warning her of enemy radar.

Kara's letter continued:

I don't want to disgust you with any details that you might not know. But about 10 or more female officers filed charges with the Las Vegas Police Department that night. We are not talking about sexual harassment. What they did is against the law—it's pathetic. It's kind of neat that these guys are so concerned about women getting raped as POWs but they are the ones assaulting us at our own professional symposium. What a joke. The worst part is the attitude that is so prevalent, "we wouldn't have this problem if they didn't let women in the navy." Wrong answer. I don't think we would have this problem if we didn't have men in the navy either.

Chapter 24   *Norway*

Kara was really excited about the detachment to Norway that was to leave a few days after she got back from the Tailhook Convention in Las Vegas. She had always wanted to visit Norway. After all, she was one-half Norwegian. Tor hadn't gotten around to taking his daughters there, nor had he taught them any Norwegian, his explanation being that it would be useless to learn a language spoken by fewer than 3 million people. The extent of Kara's Norwegian was *tusen tak,* meaning a thousand thanks, and *goddag,* meaning hello or good day.

The squadron's destination was an island that was nowhere near Drammen where her father was born, but Kara looked in the phone book and found a Tore Hultgren listed. His name wasn't spelled exactly the same as hers, but she called him anyway, and not only did he speak English he also turned out to have been in the Norwegian air force. They may or may not have been distant relatives but they had lots to talk about, and he had to have been impressed that a female American navy jet pilot named Hultgreen had called "out of the blue" to say hello.

Kara wrote Monique from Norway on 15 September 1991.

> I know I should have sent a beautiful postcard picturing a Fjord—but I'm freezing my butt off—above the Arctic circle—on an island called Andøya. Andøya, according to the Norwegians, means the armpit of Norway. Visualize frozen tundra interrupted by huge rocks (mountains). Actually it is really stunning and zorching thru the Fjords is amazing! The first quaint bistro I picked in the *tiny* fishing village turned out to be Chinese food—what a riot—it was excellent. I suppose I'll have to go to Hong Kong to find authentic Norwegian food.

She radiated her delight with the flying in a letter to Suzanne Parker: "I like this Norway DET! The flying is phenomenal. Someone had me and a jet in mind when they designed the Fjords. We even get to do 'Airfield Attacks' to train the Hawk Missile Sites. It's clearance to fly *low* and *fast* (two of my favorite things) right over the airfield. The troops like it almost as much as we do."

She told Paula Coleman reverently, "Norway was fantastic. I had a few flights that afterwards I felt like, 'I can die now—I have truly lived.'"

Heading home to Key West after completing the mission in Andøya, Kara was part of a section of three planes. Sue Still's A-6 had the lead. Sue was refueling during the flight from a big tanker aircraft that had dropped a hose with a basket on the end. The "drogue basket," which looked as if it were made of loose woven straw, had attached to the hooked snout protruding from the nose of Sue's A-6 and was delivering fuel when the hose fell away, leaving the basket attached to the probe of her plane.

Kara told Paula what happened: "Evidently the hose reel retract mechanism didn't work properly. It looked hilarious from my vantage point but the big spring, which was still attached to the basket, which was still attached to the probe, looked like a slinky in the airstream and it almost went through the canopy. That would have ruined our day for sure. It could have been worse though—nothing fodded the engines."

"Fod" is debris. If it finds its way into the jet engine, it could put it out of commission or cause a fire or other terrible crisis.

The hose or basket or both had cracked the windscreen on Sue's plane and she had to declare an emergency. The three planes diverted to Orland, Norway. Sue couldn't see very well out of her front window so Kara descended with Sue, leading her down to the field. An arresting wire was rigged on the field and Sue had to take a trap, meaning she had to catch a wire strung across the runway just as she would if she were landing on a carrier.

After Sue landed, her plane had to be untangled from the field arresting equipment. Meanwhile, Kara was circling around overhead. Since the refueling basket had been lost on Sue's plane, Kara wasn't able to refuel from the tanker and she was getting low on gas. The third plane had stayed at altitude, so it didn't have a fuel problem. Kara asked for clearance to land from the tower and was told she could either divert to another airport about three hundred miles away or land on the alternate runway.

She might have coaxed another three hundred miles from her dwindling fuel supply if everything went perfectly, but the weather was getting iffy and she decided it would be safer to land on the alternate runway. The tower cleared her to use it.

The alternate runway also was used as a taxiway. In the United States, taxiways are not the same as runways. They are narrower and aren't built to withstand the stress of landing an airplane, kind of like the difference between a road and a driveway. But in Europe, space is at a premium and taxiways are built to higher specifications because of their dual function. Landing on the taxiway—stressed and marked as a runway—was a perfect decision, and the lieutenant commander in Kara's right seat concurred.

The telephone lines immediately buzzed back to Key West with the misfortunes of the female pilots. Whether the Ready Room Commandos understood the difference between U.S. and European standards or not, it made a better story that Kara had landed on a taxiway, and they chose to make it a big joke.

Ben Jergens had left the squadron soon after Kara had turned over the PAO job, and Phil "Weasel" Mansfield was also gone, but other members of the O-4 Brute Squad remained in the squadron. Keith "Frog" Dustin had taken up "Weasel's" spot, and his version of the story left out the part about the tower asking her if she wanted to land on the taxiway and the fact that it was a legal alternate runway. The actual circumstances didn't interest him at all.

Kara's letter to Paula continued:

Anyway, the lead jet [Sue's] took a trap and it took forever to get them out of the gear. I was circling overhead waiting and waiting and a big rainstorm was closing in from the fjord and my nearest bingo was about 300 miles away. I was getting a little scosh on gas and ended up landing on the alternate runway (aka taxiway) and catching a lot of shit from certain O-4s at home. I still think it was the right decision and I would do it again. Fortunately the two O-4s that were dead set on seeing me FNAEBd are gone from the squadron. This last year has sucked. I haven't even gotten my section lead qual.

Kara was more active, more vocal, and getting more attention than ever in her fight for the repeal of the combat exclusion laws and that continued to irritate certain of the lieutenant commanders. The fact that it looked like she was going to win made them even more unhappy. She was still a target.

Sue had to remain in Norway with her broken jet. Kara flew on to Spain with Chuck "Swampthang" Gardner, one of the original card-carrying O-4 Brute Squad members, in the right seat. Harry Ennis confirmed that Gardner had been one of the first to relay the "taxiway" incident to his friends in the squadron back in Key West.

"Did I tell you this whole story?" Kara continued in her letter to Paula Coleman. "There is more."

> We left the broken jet in Norway and two of us flew to Spain without tanker support. We landed in Rota after an absolutely beautiful flight over France and the Pyrenees mountains at sunset. My navigator [Chuck Gardner], don't ask me why, decided to fold our wings after clearing the runway. We rarely fold our wings in this squadron—I've done it maybe twice in 18 months. Needless to say he didn't ask my permission or go through the appropriate checklist and all of a sudden I hear, "movin' on the right." I looked out the left and said, "NO! Put them back! Put them back!" Too late— he had initiated the fold with the wings dirty and of course our jets are so old that the idiot proofing doesn't work and the inboard slats were crunched. This is all I need—NOT! Of course it was deemed my fault because I signed for the jet. When I got back to Key West, the Safety Department wanted to do a Human Factors Board on me to document the incident. Fortunately my navigator got up in front of the Ready Room and took full responsibility. Also, fortunately, my Skipper [Commander Nottke] had no intention of doing a Board. Of course, no one ever came and told me they weren't going to—I had to confront the Skipper.

Before folding their wings, the pilot and navigator go through a checklist to make sure that all moving parts are in proper position. When Kara said that Chuck had initiated the fold with wings dirty, she meant the flaps were still down. They have to be raised before the wings can be folded or damage will occur to the aircraft.

A fully functioning aircraft has an idiot-proof safety mechanism that prevents the wings being folded when the flaps are down but that safety feature was inoperative on this particular jet. Also, it was not VAQ-33 standard operating procedure to fold the wings. Since neither of them had initiated the checklist procedure for folding the wings and since there was no apparent necessity to fold them at Rota, Chuck's action came as a complete surprise to Kara.

The carrier pigeon network was working fine. Before she got back to Key West, everyone was talking about the latest Kara screwup. The story of the wing fold back at the squadron was about Kara, not Chuck. He wasn't even mentioned. Only because maintenance investigated the matter was Chuck forced to take full responsibility for the mistake in front of the Ready Room.

Kara said in her letter to Paula:

I just think to myself, "Rise above it." I recommend two inspirational books. The first is called *Those Wonderful Women and Their Flying Machines* by Sally Van Wagenen Keil. It has a goofy title but it's a great book. The other one is called *Rising Above It: An Autobiography* by Edna Gardner Whyte with Ann L. Cooper. It's not quite as good but it is scary how much things haven't changed. Men are pigs, oh there's a news flash, grass is green, sky is blue, fire is hot too. I crack myself up. Whenever we have an AOM, the question is always raised at the end by the XO ["Billy Ray" Puckett] "ANY QUESTIONS?" and I always say to myself, "Yeah XO, I got a question . . . How do I get out of this chicken shit outfit?" It pretty much makes my day.

Chapter 25 ❈ *Transition Blues*

Commander Puckett, Kara's XO, was alternately encouraging and deflating. He seemed to think she was competent, even if she did need maturing and a little guidance, and he told her he would help her transition to F/A-18s. He changed his mind when it dawned on him that no more A-6 pilots were being trained and when he became the commanding officer he would need every A-6 pilot he had.

Kara complained bitterly about him in her letter to Paula Coleman:

> My XO is another story for my memoirs. The guy tells me in August that if the law changes that the placement officer has already penciled me in for F/A-18s and I could see orders within a few months. So in October [1991] it is really looking like the law will change so I call the XO and say, "When you go to D.C. make sure they still have us (me and Sue Still) going Hornets, and I'm ready to leave yesterday."
>
> Well all of a sudden CDR Selective Memory, CDR Inconsistent, CDR Nutcase is on the other end of the phone saying, "I refuse to let you leave early! You'll just have to get used to EA-6As because I need to keep my good JOs [junior officers] right here, and when I become Skipper in February . . . Blahh Blahh Blahh." So then I tell him that I was planning to call my detailer, and send in an officer preference card—big mistake. He then turns into CDR Unlawful Order and tells me, "I forbid you to call your detailer, and don't send a preference card until I get back."
>
> "It was great talking to you XO," and then under my breath, "NOT!"

Every few months, Kara submitted an Officer Preference and Personal Information Card stating her next duty preferences. She turned twenty-six on 5 October 1991, as good an occasion as any for submitting another preference card. Kara listed F/A-18s as her first three choices. She would go anywhere those squadrons were located. Her fourth choice was to fly F-16s in Norway. The two requisites were to get into a fighter and out of VAQ-33.

Under remarks, she said, "Send me to a combat squadron as soon as the law allows! I prefer to fly a single-seat jet and will go anywhere in the world as an exchange pilot."

The detailers, the people responsible for assigning pilots' jobs, kept telling Kara that even if the combat exclusion laws were repealed and women were allowed to fly in fleet squadrons, her logical next assignment would be EA-6B Prowlers.

Kara's letter to Paula continued:

Needless to say I called my detailer anyway. And that was no slice of sunshine conversation either. Basically he said that I would most likely have to go EA-6Bs and if I expected any hope of a transition I would have to break out in the top 5 on my first LT fitrep. (I made lieutenant by the way—cool eh?) So figure the odds of being in the top 5 of 30 LT's after being a LT for a month, especially when you are tagged by all the LCDRs as dangerous and untrainable. Did I tell you when I got blamed for overstressing a jet? I didn't do it— ask any of the maintenance chiefs—look at the ADBs—but according to the O-4 brute squad they talked about it at every Aircrew qual board as if I did.

They also say I did an aileron roll at 1000 feet with a navigator that is no longer here a year and a half ago—I never did that either. It's funny how things get talked about and perceptions are built on lies and it is so damaging. I don't think I made any friends by being so vocal about the women's issues, writing senators, getting NBC Nightly News to the squadron, doing articles in papers, traveling up to D.C. to lobby. etc.

Kara was offered the opportunity to become the first woman to fly the EA-6B Prowler, but she turned it down. She had been tempted because it would have allowed her to get out of VAQ-33, but she was determined to hold out for the F/A-18. Linda accepted an assignment to fly in the right seat of the Prowler on 18 October 1991. She would train and then be assigned to a VAQ squadron unless and until the law changed. If and when it did, she would be in position to complete the full syllabus and transition to a fleet squadron.

"I hope she does well in the Prowler RAG," Kara wrote on her new laptop computer. "To think I could be there now. Ick. I don't want to fly Prowlers."

Kara summed up her year in a letter she wrote to Molly Gairdner on 11 November 1991. Kara's father had married Sue Gairdner on 13 September in Appleton, Wisconsin. Molly was Sue's daughter. Kara had been on detachment in Norway and hadn't been able to go to the wedding.

> This last year has been the worst year of my life in a lot of ways but it has also been filled with some great memories too. Norway was incredible! I hated to miss the wedding, but I wouldn't have missed the experience, not that I had a choice. The flying was phenomenal. The fjords were absolutely beautiful. We had to emergency divert into Orland Norway on the way home after the refueling basket came off on Sue Still's jet (she is the other female A-6 pilot in the world). Then I got stuck in Spain for a week. It was great. I visited Marbella and saw Gibraltar, and you could see Africa—it was too cool. . . .
>
> So you think my career is going gangbusters eh? Well that's been the part that's been the worst this year. Unfortunately I'm in a squadron full of insecure losers that can't stand to see anyone else succeed where they have failed. I have also been fairly active politically trying to get the combat exclusion laws repealed. I actually went to D.C. and "educated" Senators—that is an interesting story in itself but I won't get into it. Let's just say I haven't been making a lot of friends by being so vocal. I was even on NBC Nightly News. If the President signs the defense authorization act it will have all been worth it. Hopefully I didn't sacrifice my career, but only time will tell.

The defense authorization act did not actually require that women be placed in the cockpits of combat aircraft; it allowed the military to make its own policy. And it contained a provision allowing George Bush to form a presidential commission that would study the subject. Bush signed the bill, but it was understood that the service chiefs would have to wait until the commission made its recommendations before taking any action. The long-awaited repeal of the combat exclusion laws was something of an anticlimax for Kara and the other women aviators who had lobbied so hard for it.

Her letter to Molly concluded: "How am I inside? Well, that's pretty closely linked to how I am professionally. And I'm not challenged in this platform. I want to fly F/A-18s in a combat squadron. So I am a one-day-at-a-time kind of gal. I'm just waiting to see what happens. I will either be in on the ground floor or too late, too bad, so sad."

Since Kara had made that one big mistake in the beginning of the year, when she nearly crashed her plane landing at Cecil Field, everything had backfired on her. She had escaped with her life but was beginning to wonder if her career had any future.

To top off 1991, Kara let her swimming and physical fitness qualification lapse and couldn't fly again until she requalified. She had made mistakes before, but she really hated making a careless one like that. She didn't find out about it until right before she was scheduled to leave on detachment. It prevented her from going, causing her to miss an assignment she wanted and creating a problem for the squadron. Not a good thing for someone already under the gun.

Chapter 26 ❈ *Christmas 1991*

Kara spent Christmas 1991 in San Antonio with her mother and sisters. She wrote in her diary on 28 December, "I had a terrific Christmas. But we all missed my Dad." For the first Christmas since her parents separated in 1976, Tor hadn't spent Christmas with Dagny, Kirsten, Kara, and Sally, together as a family.

In Kara's letter to Molly in November, she had written: "It was very strange looking at the wedding pictures and not being in them. I would have loved to see you and Jimmy [Molly's brother]. I missed seeing Dagny and Kirsten too. I'll see them at Christmas though. I won't be coming to Appleton. . . . There is no way I would leave my mother alone at Christmas. I guess this is the first year I'll feel like I'm from a broken home. It's too bad."

Tor, the reserved Norwegian, was Santa incarnate at Christmas. Since 1981 when Sally and Kara moved back to Texas, the procedure had been for everyone to gather in San Antonio. Then they all went shopping, but Tor did most of the buying. The girls were also generous with each other and with their father and mother.

The Christmases developed themes. One year it was electronics. Stereos, speakers, boom boxes, and CDs surrounded the tree. Kara and Tor arrived in San Antonio in the morning. Dagny and Kirsten were to come in later that afternoon. Tor, Kara, and her mother got a head start shopping. Kara and her dad were cracking jokes, more than a few at Sally's expense. By the time they had been to several stores, Sally was hungry and annoyed with both of them.

She snapped, "You know, Tor, your plane just landed three hours ago and I am as irritated with you after three hours as I usually am after you have been here three days."

Kara lifted her eyebrows and with her innocent little smile, shrugged and said, "See, Dad? You're getting more efficient."

The year before, the girls had dragged their father into Victoria's

Secret. He stood stoically by a counter as saleswomen paraded by him carrying lingerie into dressing rooms where his three grown, beautiful daughters were trying on push-up bras, skimpy panties, and lacy teddies.

They all missed him that Christmas of 1991.

Still, Kara felt better than she had in a long time. She was home for the holidays with her family, and since the lapse of her swimming and physical fitness qualification, nothing else terrible had happened. She began to think that her time of tribulation had been a fluke, a mere detour. "Suffering builds character," was her Grandmother Hultgreen's favorite saying. "I have suffered. I am officially a character," said Kara, but she felt more upbeat, thinking that possibly she just might have ridden out the difficult times.

On 31 December 1991, she wrote Monique:

I had a great holiday (of course the highlight was seeing you again). It was really fun to just hang out with Dagny & Kirsten.

I think next year we are planning to go to Appleton and visit Santa [referring to her father's legendary generosity at Christmas]. I haven't seen a white Christmas since it snowed in San Antonio that year. So I've got that goin' for me.

I have a great feeling about 1992. It's going to be the best year yet.

She was wrong.

Chapter 27 *Pamela*

"I think Miss Pamela decided she doesn't like me anymore," Kara wrote in her diary after the holidays. "I don't know why or what I did. Dagny and Kirsten think I should ask her. This is kind of awkward. . . . 'So Pamela—did I do something to piss you off or what?'"

Two days later, she wrote:

> I had the duty yesterday. Called Pamela. She said she was sleeping and would call me back. She called me back this morning. Hmmm . . .
>
> I think Pam hasn't treated me well. She made a comment about how she hadn't talked to her "good friend, Kara," in a while—so I said "Yeah, I was beginning to think I'd done something to piss you off." She said "No, no, not at all." And then she said, "I've got to go. We [Pam and Sue] are going to Camilles for breakfast." Well, I'm so glad she called. . . . Not. If I haven't done anything to piss her off, she has pissed me off. So much for good friends, eh? I would say that in my life, Joanie [Kara's best friend from Canada] and Monique have truly been good friends. And Dagny and Kirsten and Mother.
>
> I do not consider Sue to be a good friend and I consider Pamela to be a disappointment. Misjudged. It really ticks me off.

On Sunday, 12 January 1992, Kara wrote,

> Surprise, surprise, Pamela called and wanted to go to dinner. Went to Duval Deli . . . I just don't see the point . . . I feel very uncomfortable around her.

Her journal entry for 20 January said, "Pam is acting like we are best buddies, but I think that something is lost."

The squadron hosted a Hail and Farewell party for Dave Kidder on Friday night before the Super Bowl. A Hail and Farewell is a party to welcome new members into the squadron and tell old friends goodbye. Kara wore a black blazer over a skirt made from a fringed suede shawl tied around her waist, black hose, and black heels. Marc, a lieu-tenant relatively new to the squadron, told Kara that she looked "crazy, stupid, hot."

She had been taught well by Dagny, who had spent a year in New York and Tokyo as a model and was always up on the latest fashion trends—if she wasn't setting them herself. Miniskirts were in style and they were made for Kara and her sisters, who all had long beautiful legs. Their Uncle Jimmy said the women in his family had great "wheels."

"I felt good about the outfit," Kara wrote in her journal, but she learned later that a few of the officers and their wives attending the Hail and Farewell were very disapproving. Marc told her that Harry Ennis said, "My outfit gave credence to the rumors he had heard about me and some guy out in town locking lips" and that "Pam and Sue didn't contest it or stick up for me because it was true!! Oh fuck-ing spare me. That was about a year ago. I am beyond being hurt . . . I'm disgusted. Marc said they went out last night and he asked, 'Where's Kara?' and they both just scoffed and said, 'Who cares?'"

Kara knew Marc was capable of making up a story just to get a reaction, and he wouldn't have denied it. She once wrote him, "I really miss having you around to talk with. I miss your point of view, and insight, and most of all I miss your exaggeration, flattery and outright lies—the very core of any lasting friendship." But because Pam had been so distant since Christmas, she believed him. She told her father that she was "being shunned by my friends."

Her narrative continued on 27 January:

Sunday night Super Bowl party . . . Monday . . . Junior Officers vs. O-4s softball game. I batted in the winning run so that was good. I dropped off Sue then Pamela. Went in to help Pam unload new tile for bathroom.

I was telling Pam about Saturday night conversation with Dagny about seeing a therapist this Tuesday. She's going to find out if she is angry with her mother or father. . . . Pam said, "you are just like your mother—you are very judgmental." She also pointed out that Sue's motivation was to please her father and mine was/is to win. "To win at what," I asked. . . . "At everything." So I'm judgmental and competitive. Sue agrees. . . . Actually, I think I'm fine the way I am. Yes I am competitive and yes I am confident and I have strong beliefs. . . . My judgmental mother said . . . "People are flawed—don't take it personally."

I let Pamela borrow my book *Confessions of a Failed Southern Lady.* I want it back. Fair weather friend. I am angry with her—for free, said it, there.

I haven't had anything nice to say about Pam or Sue since Christmas leave.

Petty Officer Schwarz stopped Kara in the hangar and told her, "I finally figured it out. It has bothered me since the first time I laid eyes on you. . . . Mrs. Peel—You look like Mrs. Peel from the *Avengers!*"

"It made my day," Kara wrote.

> I watched the *Avengers* tonight and I'm quite flattered. Luke Koeller said that too about a year ago—so it *must* be true! I'm thinking I would get gonged on *Body Double* if I said it on "E" ["E" Entertainment Television]. Maybe it's the whole personality package. I told Kirsten and she said someone told her she looked like Linda Carter. Wonder Woman (We started singing) hmm hmm hmm . . . You're a wonder, Wonder Woman. And we thought (a simo [simultaneous] thought) that I look just like Kirsten so I must look like Wonder Woman too! How could it be?—Linda Carter with no lips or boobs. I'd rather be Mrs. Peel than Wonder Woman anyway.

Kara told her father that she was dieting and going to be "as skinny as Kirsten." Kirsten had been running her own fitness business in Austin since she graduated from the University of Texas in 1986. She taught an aerobics class or two each day and was always in fantastic shape.

Tor said, "Too skinny—you don't need to diet."

"Well I think the PRT measurements speak for themselves," Kara wrote. "Way too much body fat."

She was five feet, ten inches tall and looked fresh and healthy, like she belonged in an advertisement for an Aspen ski vacation. But like most women, she always wanted to be thinner. To put her concerns in perspective, the average woman has about 25 percent body fat while a nationally ranked female runner might have 12 percent. Kara's percentage was anywhere between 16 percent and 19 percent, which was very good but didn't satisfy her. She was shooting for about 15 percent.

"Of course," she said, "I need to stop eating cookies too. Damn. It'll be worth it. No more fat body!!"

"Just talked to Mom," she wrote. "I'm so lucky to have my mother. We are in a race to 150 pounds. I'm 155 pounds now. I think I'm going to lose 15–20 pounds and make Pam and Sue so damn jealous they won't be able to stand it."

"The DET was great!" Kara wrote on 9 February 1992 about the squadron detachment to Puerto Rico. She continued:

It could probably be attributed to the fact that Sue didn't go. I love going to Puerto Rico. The first night I went to the Club and saw many old friends. Mike Barger was there playing that game where you slide the pucks down a table—kind of like shuffle board on a table. So I played that and won many games. (There goes that competitive spirit again.) I drank many Coronas. Mike "Scally" Scavone, A-6 Pilot—CAG 8 LSO—old RAG instructor—was there too. So I hung out with Scally. A few Coronas later—just before the bar closed, the Skippers of VF-84 and VA-36 came over to meet the best looking (translation—only) woman in the Roosey Club.

Their tone changed considerably when Scally told them I was an A-6 pilot at VAQ-33. They *had* to offer their views on women in combat. The short RIO brought up *all* the legitimate arguments concerning the integration of women on carriers.

Teamwork/bonding/fraternization/rape/berthing/etc. . . . all the things that will make being a Skipper more challenging. Why change if we don't have to? I can deal with those questions and I can't deny that it will be a difficult transition. The big fat Nebraska Linebacker A-6 pilot, however, started saying bullshit like "There is no *way* a woman could do the same job I do!" I informed him that I was not the average woman. (I'm in the top 1 percent of my peer group—wasn't he?)

He asked, "Have you ever been so scared that you could barely move? There is no way you could handle the ship at night." Well to make a long story short, he really pissed me off and I think I asked him why he was so threatened by me or was it women in general after he said women had no business in his Navy or in Navy aircraft. I also insulted his mother (for being incompetent, foolish, and worthless); I told him he would never make CAG, that his obvious lack of support for equal opportunity in the Navy was pathetic and indicative of a poor leader. I said I hoped I was never in his squadron—there is nothing worse than a bad Skipper. . . .

Scally finally stepped in and dragged me out of the Club as I was pointing my finger saying, "And another thing, Pal! . . ."

Scally gave me a lecture about how that's a bad way to get a transition and mouthing off to superiors—especially when they are drunk—is not smart. "All he is going to remember is, 'That little Bitch.'" Oh well, so much for my career.

"So how am I supposed to handle those assholes?" she asked "Scally" later.

"Well," he said, "you excuse yourself to go to the head, and then you don't come back."

And that's what she did from then on. Of course, she added a Kara twist. When the discussion got heated, she would say that her detailers told her "confidentially" that they had been advised that the policy was going to change right away, and she could expect orders any day.

"They tell me I have a very good chance of being assigned to your air wing," she would advise them, and as they began to stammer, she would say, "Excuse me, but I have to go to the ladies room. Would you hold my beer a sec?"

And she would leave and not go back.

"The three best quotes of the DET were by, towards or about me," Kara continued in her journal.

> By: "And another thing, Pal!"
> Towards: "No way a woman could do my job!"
> About: Putt came up with this one . . . "I think Kara likes flying more than sex!" I laughed when they told me that one and I wouldn't validate the comment either way. I said I preferred to keep the mystery alive but everyone could be sure Putt would never know—his "Do-me factor" is zero at best. We all laughed at Putt's expense for quite a while.
>
> Today while we were putting on our flight gear, Putt walked up and I was smiling about something (unrelated). Putt got all defensive and said, "What? . . . What's so funny? You have that look." And I said, "Oh nothing, Putt, I just *love* to fly." And Putt said, "And it shows."

And I said, "Yeah, I probably love to fly more than anything in the whole world!" and Putt turned bright red and said, "Oh no, you heard! Who told you?"

"No, Putt," I said, "The question is who told *you?*"

We all laughed so hard.

I didn't want to come home.

Kara was devastated by the loss of Pam's friendship. She missed their easy companionship and couldn't think what she had done to offend Pam. Though Kara was outgoing and personable, she didn't allow many people to get close. She loved Pam and had trusted her; now she felt betrayed and hurt.

Kara admired Pam because she was smart and a good athlete; she had encouraged Pam to apply for pilot training. The possibility had never occurred to Pam; certainly the navy recruiter hadn't suggested aviation as a career path. Pam first became aware of the extensive opportunities for women when she met Kara and Sue.

But times were tough. Military budgets were shrinking. At age twenty-five, Pam was already a naval officer and didn't have any leverage. Kara was promised an aviation slot when she signed up to join the navy in her senior year in college; she was only twenty-two when she began her aviation training. Eventually, Pam was offered the opportunity to train as an NFO. But she'd been hanging around with pilots—Kara, Sue, her fiancé, Peter. She decided that if she were going to take the risks associated with aviation, she wanted to be in charge, rather than place her life in someone else's hands.

Pam accepted that she had little hope for pilot training. As for Kara, giving up a goal, even when the percentages were against you, was not a concept she understood. She assumed Pam had a soul-searing desire to fly and was as motivated as Kara was to remove the restrictions on women in combat aviation. Kara was totally focused on her mission, and she couldn't see that Pam was not as driven as she was. Her determination to achieve her goals enabled her to persevere when others might give up, but that determination was sometimes hard on her friends.

Kara had become so immersed in the cause of women in combat aviation, she could talk of little else. Pam knew Kara wasn't doing herself any good within the squadron, and she found it difficult to watch

Kara make what seemed to her to be the same mistakes over and over. She tried to tell Kara to tone down her reactions or just to keep quiet about it like Sue, but Kara couldn't accept that. She was willing to endure the adverse reactions of some of the senior officers; her dream was at stake and she didn't have the luxury of standing on the sidelines.

But Kara's dream wasn't Pam's. Pam wasn't an aviator; she had nothing to gain and a lot to lose by being associated with Kara's cause. And like most of the men in the squadron, she was tired of hearing about it. She just wanted to do her job and be ranked number one, and she worried that the enmity directed toward Kara would spill over to her.

Pam was a general unrestricted line officer, a category created by the navy when the military became all volunteer and actually wanted to attract women. No "warfare specialty" was associated with the job, but it allowed women to attain equivalent rank with men. Until that time, with a few special exceptions, the only female line officers were nurses.

Pam saw that once women could fly Hornets, Tomcats, Intruders, Prowlers, and every other kind of aircraft in the fleet, when all the options were open, there would be no reason to have line officer positions reserved for women. She would have to find a new job in the navy or just go away. There was no room in Kara's dream for Pam.

"I felt like I was going to be left behind," Pam said. "I wasn't going to be part of what Kara was trying to make happen. The very thing she was lobbying for would have done away with my job. And essentially it did; the community went away."

Whether Pam couldn't articulate how she felt or Kara didn't listen, Kara never understood what made Pam distance herself from her. Inability to communicate has caused more than one friendship to suffer.

Chapter 28 ✻ *Billy Ray*

W. R. "Billy Ray" Puckett became the commanding officer of the squadron on 13 February 1992. Executive officer since December 1990, he had been present during the grand inquisition of Kara at the All Officers Meeting in the winter of 1991 and had not intervened to temper the hostile atmosphere. He was XO when Kara was accused of overstressing her jet landing at Whidbey Island, but denied he knew about the gossip. He had made the decision that Sue, not Kara, would fly the NBC news photographer. And he had withdrawn his support of Kara's request to transition to fly F/A-18s after he realized that when he became the CO, it would be in his best interest for her to remain in the squadron as an A-6 pilot.

Even though he had been a commander, an O-5, during his time in the squadron, "Billy Ray" had been an honorary member of Ben Jergen's O-4 Brute Squad, listening to Ben's assessment of Kara as an insubordinate junior officer who thought she was so great. He also believed, rightly or wrongly, that navy higher-ups considered Kara something special. This perception was reinforced because Don Foulk, the CO in 1990 when Kara first arrived, would call him from time to time to find out how she was doing and to make suggestions about her career progress. Don Foulk and his wife, Pattie, were very fond of Kara, and Foulk, then a captain based at the Pentagon, acted as her mentor, supporting her throughout her career.

Commander Puckett made comments to some of his department heads that he thought Foulk was out of line and that he resented the interference. His reaction might have been a natural one, but he acted as if Kara were responsible for Captain Foulk's action.

"Billy Ray" was a born-again Christian, zealous in the practice of his religion. For example, every year the navy supported the charitable contribution program called Combined Federal Campaign. The campaign supported a long list of causes from asthma cures, to homeless shelters, to Alzheimer research. Kara told her mother that "Billy Ray" didn't want anyone in his squadron to contribute to any organizations that condoned abortions because that was against the Bible, and if any officer in his command wanted to contribute to any of these organizations, he or she would have to come to his office and explain it to him first. Kara was incredulous and thought he was totally out of line. She called him the raving righteous one.

"Billy Ray" flew as an electronic warfare officer in the tube of a P-3, a large turboprop aircraft with four propellers. The tube is all of the area behind the cockpit, which in a large aircraft is huge, like the passenger section of a civilian aircraft, and there are no ejection seats in the tube. The P-3 is never carrier based. Its mission was electronic surveillance—listening to all kinds of electronic emissions from across the radio frequency spectrum, analyzing, locating, and recording.

The P-3 has two pilots, and there could be as many as ten in the crew, which would include enlisted personnel, some of whom would be operating the electronic warfare equipment. The majority of flight officers in the back have no duties involving actual flying. Some pilots have the attitude that NFOs, even in a two-position aircraft, are just along for the ride anyway. The navy promotes the crew concept—the NFO makes the same amount of money as the pilot, for example—but the pilot is the person in charge of the aircraft, regardless of the seniority of the naval flight officer. For example, Kara might be a junior officer, but as the pilot she would be in charge of her airplane even if she were taking the base commanding officer flying. On the other hand, an NFO can be in command of an overall mission.

The pilot superiority complex of all the P-3 pilots to the aircrew in the fuselage is the worst. It's "to the back of the bus, please, you second-class citizen you," as if the pilots were better than anybody else in the world. Few words are ever spoken with more condescension than a naval aviator describing an NFO as a "P-3 tube guy." The standard joke goes: "Why is it good to have an NFO if you have a crash?" The answer: "Because you'll have a hundred pounds of meat and their glasses to start a fire." The usual physical reason people are disqualified from pilot training is their eyesight is less than perfect.

The new executive officer was Cdr. Milton Shadowtree, who had come to the squadron in December 1991. He was a fleet air reconnaissance (VQ) veteran who had more than three thousand hours as a naval flight officer (NFO) in EP-3s. The fact that both the commanding and executive officers of VAQ-33 were lowly "tube guys" caused snickering both inside and out of the squadron.

By the time Puckett assumed command in February 1992, the maintenance department, under the supervision of Wayne Lockley and Harry Ennis, had vastly improved. Four of the older nonrecap A-6s were cocooned, which allowed maintenance to concentrate on the four recaps and the five nonrecaps that remained. Now at least six of the nine A-6s were on the flight line every day, available to fly training missions and, sometimes, amazingly, even cross-country flights.

At some point in 1992, the squadron learned it would not be in line to receive the prized F/A-18s after all. The F/A-18s were not suitable for carrying all the expensive electronic warfare pods. Kara was crushed. The fact that she would not be flying an F/A-18 was the biggest disappointment she suffered in her navy career.

Instead, the remaining five nonrecap A-6s would be modified to be EA-6As; they would take over the A-3 mission. By the time the A-3s were retired in October 1992, the squadron had nine recap EA-6As. Nine planes were enough not only to pick up the mission of the A-3, as far as it was possible for the A-6 to do, but also to begin working with the F-14 and F-18 training squadrons in providing airborne electronic warfare training to the fighter community.

The upside of these changes was that the junior EA-6A pilots and navigators now would be able to get the flight hours they needed to maintain and improve their skills. Kara reasoned that if expensive gas were to be burned, why not burn it going somewhere fun? Kara and Amy put in for cross-country trips. They were both adventuresome and single; their weekends were free; and for a while "Billy Ray" approved those trips. When there was money in the budget, no commanding officer worth his command would spend less than all of it for fear of being cut back the next quarter.

Chapter 29 ❀ *Hot Brakes*

"The last two weekends have been outstanding!" Kara wrote in her diary on 2 March 1992. The first weekend, she and Amy had gone to Denver, Colorado. Skiing at Copper Mountain— "met Bob Williamson, Very cute—nice smile"—had been a great way to spend the time between landing at Buckley Air Force Base and taking back off for Key West.

Only one thing happened to mar an otherwise perfect weekend, and it became the first event since the wing fold mix-up in Spain the past September that Kara would have to explain. Used to sea level landings, Kara didn't take into account the thinner atmosphere in the mountains. She came in for her landing too fast and had to hit her brakes hard in order to stop, ruining the brake and the tire. Her diary notation was, "Hot brake—flat tire—stuck."

It was no surprise to the plane handlers in Colorado when navy pilots came in too fast trying to land in the thin air of the mountains. Whenever a navy plane was about to land, the ground crew would place bets among themselves about whether or not they would soon be replacing brakes and tires, but it happened so consistently no one would take the other side of the bet anymore. A commonplace mistake or not, it was embarrassing to Kara, and she was mortified to have to call her CO and admit she had burned out her brake and blown out her tire—especially since, as far as she knew, she was still under double super secret probation.

Of course, there was no supply of navy A-6 tires at the air force base so one had to be flown out from Key West. The squadron sent a P-3 with a new tire on Sunday, but because communications were faulty between the duty officer who took the call and the operations and maintenance departments, they neglected to bring a new brake. On Monday, another flight crew, "Wedge" and "Herman," in an A-6 this time, had to bring a new brake in a blivet, which is a storage-baggage pod hung on the wing.

Kara, Amy, "Wedge," and "Herman" went to the Grizzly Rose that night. They were "stuck in Ohio" on Tuesday and stayed at "Wedge's" mom's house. Wednesday they flew back to Key West.

After she got back home, Kara sent the transient services crew at Buckley a care package (pictures, patches, and homemade cookies) in appreciation for their help. She knew how important the people who serviced the plane were, and she always showed her appreciation to the ground crews—and to anyone else who did something nice for her. Jim Freeland, one of the Buckley AFB plane captains, wrote her a thank-you note and related the latest "hot brakes" incidents:

> The next weekend after you left, VA-75 came in with 4 A6s. Two had cherry red brakes. The tires stayed up but we had to change a brake because it started leaking real bad. Another one ran fuel out of the top of the fuselage so bad (twice) we had two major fuel spills.
>
> Also, now we have an EA-6B from Whidbey Island that had hot brakes and the left main tire went flat. Some of the guys said they remembered you. Their last names are McCawley, Lany, and Monroe.
>
> I hope you can make it to Buckley again. Say Hi to Amy.

She and Amy went to Memphis, Tennessee, the next weekend. "The Road Hounds!" she wrote. "Walking with our feet ten feet off of beach. Rum Boogie Cafe—red beans and rice. B. B. King—Ruby Wilson—awesome voice. Met Harold from Kentucky and Jan from Ohio. Sunday went to Graceland with Harold—Fun. Life is good . . . where to next weekend? An air show or Phoenix to see Bob?"

Kara wrote her mother a postcard on 7 March with a picture of a skier going down an unblemished snowy slope against a background of frosted pine trees, blue Lake Tahoe, icy mountains, and azure sky.

Well Mom—

What can I say? Life is Great! Tahoe is absolutely *breathtaking!* The skiing is fantastic—but a tad short of Colorado. This was a long trip from Key West for one day of skiing—but very much worth it!

We want to go back to Denver next weekend, of course, we've never skied Utah . . . Hmm . . . or New Mexico . . . The continent is our oyster.

The trip hadn't been without incident, however. She and Amy were flying from Key West to Sacramento and they had to stop for gas midway. Kelly Air Force Base in San Antonio was always convenient, even though this time Kara didn't plan to see her mother. She told Sally not to bother to meet her at Kelly because she wouldn't be there any longer than it took them to refill her tank and get back in the air.

"Went to Sacramento, CA, Mather AFB on our cross-country," Kara wrote in her diary on 11 March 1992. "Didn't get a PPR [prior permission request] for gas & go at Kelly—it was NOTAMed."

NOTAM stood for "Notice to Airmen" and was sent via electronic means to base operations across the country. It meant that for some reason Kelly was going to be closed for transient flights and you would have to get prior permission to land there. Usually, Kelly didn't require pilots to submit a PPR.

"XO spooled up to the moon," Kara wrote. "They almost made us fly home from Kelly Friday night."

It was a minor infraction and there was no reason for Commander Shadowtree to overreact, but he had to be talked out of bringing them home by some of the other officers in Key West. Kara swore she had read the NOTAMs and one from Kelly hadn't been there. Janet Marnane, an NFO who was a good friend of Kara's, later talked to Kelly Base Operations and they weren't concerned that a PPR hadn't been filed.

"Oh well." Kara was accustomed to weird reactions by now. "Home on Sunday night. Duty Monday. XO lectured us on perceptions—I think I know too much about perceptions."

Chapter 30 *The Journal*

Kara loved those cross-country trips. The exuberant tone was back in her voice. She wrote Monique:

> Mo Mo Mo *Mo*tivation!
>
> How in the hell are ya Mo? So when are you going to visit Key West? Not that I'm ever here. I've been a cross-country hound for the last few months. Denver, Tahoe, Memphis, Austin, D.C., Pensacola—It's been fabulous. Next weekend my roommate (Miss Amy) and I are going to an air show in Tampa—no doubt we'll be the most popular plane at the party!

Kara would stand by her plane at air shows and explain patiently to all the little kids hour after hour how great it was to fly jets in the navy. One time when she was still in jet training, a little boy about six or seven was staring in awe at her plane. The A-4F Skyhawk has a very long straight refueling probe running along one side of its nose that sticks out several feet in front of the plane.

"What's that?" he asked, stepping away from his father and pointing at the probe.

She bent down to talk to him. "I'm not allowed to say," she said. Then she appeared to reconsider. "If I tell you, you'll have to promise not to tell anyone."

"I promise," he agreed earnestly.

"I mean it," Kara repeated, her voice low and conspiratorial so no one else could hear. "You have to give me your solemn word you won't tell a soul."

The little boy's eyes grew large and he crossed his heart.

She whispered, "It's a super secret death ray."

He was so excited as he ran toward his father he almost tripped. They had been gone just a few minutes when she saw the father striding back toward her practically dragging the little boy, who was ducking his head sheepishly. She thought she was really in trouble as he confronted her.

"Did you tell my son that was a super secret death ray?" he asked, pointing at the refueling probe.

"Uh, yes sir, I did," admitted Kara.

"I knew we had that shit!" he exclaimed.

But in between cross-country trips, Kara had to come back to Key West, and the time she spent there was, for the most part, depressing. Journal entry—11 March 1992:

> Tues. night went to sushi with Pam. I started the dreaded conversation about why had she been such a bitch.
>
> So what had I done to deserve the cold shoulder after Christmas? Well, it was interesting that she felt like I was the one blowing her off. . . . I don't know. I said I really felt at a loss. She had been my best friend and she treated me like shit. Some of it I can see. . . . But I think it's kind of pointless now—almost too late to salvage anything. I went over to see the dogs today and went to Pancho & Lefty's with Pam. It was a little strange. A tad strained. It's too bad.

Journal entry—25 March 1992: "Lots of things happening . . . Pensacola trip—very fun—ego boost. Paul Slajus is very cute . . . Hash House Harriers Run . . . Too far but fun. A drinking club with a running problem."

Kara kept getting reports from various guys that there was a stripper in Key West named Candace who looked just like her. "Went to see my twin—the stripper . . . at the Peek-a-Boo Club. She wasn't working. Marc and I had a good time—He is so sweet. We were propositioned by a stripper—she was definitely interested in me . . . very strange. I wish I could have seen Candace."

Kara had bought a handwriting analysis book and she was analyzing everyone's handwriting, including her own. She was searching for any clue as to why her life had been so jumbled that past year. On 11 April 1992, she wrote Monique, "I started this letter writing in cursive and I couldn't read it the next day. When someone prints all the time and their cursive is legible, it means they are trying to reveal little about themselves. After analyzing my own writing, I realize that I prefer no one realize that I am a psychotic and extremely unstable individual with erratic mood swings . . . so I print for legibility."

Then she proceeded to analyze Monique's handwriting, and Monique didn't come out much better than Kara.

Journal entry—10 April 1992:

Amy & I were supposed to be at the MacDill [MacDill Air Force Base] air show in Tampa this weekend. This hasn't been my day. A duty night from hell. Starting at midnight PR3 Nalley needed to go on emergency leave. No sooner do I get home than AEAN Frable is arrested. Duty driver picked him up at security, took him back to the barracks with orders to report to SDO [squadron duty officer] at 0630. Well the little asshole went back in town and was arrested again. DUI [driving under the influence]. Super. I had to go get him at security at 0330—didn't get back home until 0530. Then the idiot is 40 minutes late mustering this morning. Unbelievable—he overslept. I, on the other hand, got no sleep. Thank you very much.

To top off the morning—maintenance couldn't provide a jet for the air show. I secured early and slept all afternoon.

I'm still trying to figure out what to put on Pam's birthday card. Do I write something heartfelt? Or do I keep it distanced and aloof. Or maybe simple like . . . "Happy Birthday." I feel like she's been making an effort to be nice lately. Too little, too late.

Journal entry—Saturday, 11 April 1992: "Bought Kirsten two belts. A wedding gift for Joanie—jewel stone vase. A B-day gift for Pam— a formal silver glitter clutch type purse. I kept the card fairly simple— what can I say?"

Journal entry—Sunday, 12 April 1992: "Rented 3 movies: *Dead Again, Goodfellas* and *Mr. Destiny*. Liked 'em all."

Journal entry—9 May 1992:

Well, I haven't written in my diary here in quite a while. What would I like to remember about the last month of my life. Not much. The morale low light has been on steady for quite a while. I figure I would rather not remember the time that I was unhappy. I'll be glad when Pam & Sue leave.

Dagny was not hurt during the riots in L.A. last week—She went to Pasadena. They shut down the Studio at E! for a few days. Dagny is angry with her mother. This therapy thing is making Dagny evaluate her whole childhood. She wants to know why she always gets into relationships that aren't going anywhere. She sees her friends getting married and sees herself ending up like mother. She doesn't want to be alone for the rest of her life—she doesn't think mother is really happy. She wants to find someone that she can build a home with—a life with.

This whole thing has me very depressed. I don't think I am ready to hash through my miserable childhood. I hated being a kid. I promised myself that I wouldn't have kids and put anyone through it. Like I said, I prefer to forget the times that I was unhappy. So why the hell am I writing in a journal now? This is most definitely a low point in my life. No wonder my handwriting has always been so bad. I went to sleep last night at 1930 and slept for 12 hours. I feel completely unsociable.

I went to Joanie's wedding a couple of weekends ago. It was fun to see her family again. Joanie and I don't have much in common anymore. I drove 7 ½ hours each way. I had the top down and I got burned on the way there. I had a ridiculous tan line in my dress. I didn't really have that much to say. I'm not too pleased with my life lately. So I had to lie and talk about the good stuff. Be entertaining. What is the fucking point anyway?

I wasn't envious of anyone else's life. So many people are so screwed up. Including me. I don't even know what is important to me anymore. I have been on a professional and personal roller coaster for a year and a half. Do I still want to be an astronaut? An F/A-18 pilot? A Blue Angel? Do I want to be famous? Why? Why do I always try and be the center of attention? Why do I want to break barriers? Do I? I used to be so goal oriented and it was so easy. I kept so busy. I don't think I care anymore.

Life is pain highness. I am too sensitive. I have created walls to keep from being hurt. I avoid relationships that have any future. I'm in a dangerous and inconvenient job that requires a lot of travel and is perfect for not building a relationship. Just about everyone I've ever trusted has disappointed me. I don't date—I'm not even interested in dating. What would be the point. Children? I can't imagine having the energy, patience, or inclination to deal with kids. I wouldn't want a sensitive kid, a marshmallow—I can't even stand to think about my childhood. I don't like people. I don't want to work. I don't want to live in San Antonio.

If my cross-countries hadn't all been disapproved lately, I wouldn't be sitting here thinking about this.

Chapter 31   *VIP Scare*

Fortunately for her frame of mind, it wasn't long before Kara was off on another detachment. Her mood soared with her airplane as she took off from Key West bound for Hawaii. She was flying with Janet "Maniac" Marnane. They flew to Point Magu Naval Air Weapons Station in California the weekend of 20 June 1992, rented a car, and drove to Los Angeles to visit Dagny. Then they would be off to Hawaii.

Journal entry—15 August 1992:

> Dagny was super! She took us to Spago with some of her friends from E! Holly ("It's a career") from U.T. She had been kicked out of Alpha Chi Omega. Alpha Chi Omega is a Christian Sorority and she was on the street when they found out she was Jewish. She didn't know. Who would? She was entertaining. We also met a soap star, Robert Kelly-Kirker or something, from *Days of Our Lives*, I think. Dagny took us shopping—her favorite exercise—I think she could make it an Olympic Event—bought Bullet Boob Bras.
>
> Monday, June 22nd we flew a low level to Miramar. Wednesday we tanked to Hawaii with 5 EA-6As. No problems—it was fun. 5 jet break at Barbers. Ferris out of position, "We can both get critical—so just Buzz Off!" What a geek. Hawaii was gorgeous—flew every day—lots of VFR island cruises—best cloud chasing ever. Super beaches. Hanauma Bay, Wiamea Bay, Sandy Beach with the killer shore break. Played Hackey Sack. I flew my butt off in Hawaii and still got a great tan. It was gorgeous, but I have no desire to move there.
>
> Watched the Tailhook Sex Scandal on T.V. Learned a love song for the "alternate lifestyle"—(to the tune of "My Girl") "I've got sunshine on a cloudy day; I've got a girlfriend and she's a little strange; Yes she likes men it's true; but she also digs chicks too, Bi-girl, Talkin' 'bout Bi-girl...." Hilarious. Karaoke, the Monkey Bar, Chinese pizza. Back home yesterday with messages from NBC and ABC and Skipper Mariner.

Kara wrote Monique a postcard dated 23 July 1992: "Yo Babe—You sweet cakes foxy Mama. I'm a Tailhook aviator and I'll sexually harass you if I please. I'm back from Hawaii—a fabulous experience. I'm so tan—I'm too sexy for this tan. I'm back to San Diego next week. Life is good. I'm so proud to be part of Naval Aviation."

Kara loved to fly with Janet Marnane because she was a lot of fun. On the way back from Hawaii, they played hangman and whoever won got to do a flaperon roll. In the A-6 it's possible for the right-seater to reach the stick. They were in a loose formation over the ocean with the tanker and other A-6s. Troops riding in the tanker were thrilled at the "air show" and greeted Kara enthusiastically on deck when they landed back in California at March Air Force Base.

Two days after she got back to Key West from Hawaii, Kara was asked to take the commanding officer of NAS Key West, Capt. Mike Currie, to Norfolk, Virginia, for a commander's conference. The captain was a BN (bombardier-navigator) from the fleet A-6 community. She considered it a great honor and was very excited about the trip.

The captain talked to Kara about how he missed the action and Kara suggested they go into the break on landing at Oceana Naval Air Station in Virginia Beach, Virginia. That meant that instead of coming on to the runway straight and level like air force and commercial pilots, they would approach the field as if they were landing on a carrier, taking a hard turn to bleed off airspeed. They thoroughly briefed the flight, including going into the break. The only unplanned thing that happened was that the call from the controller to descend was late, and Kara did a roll to get down to altitude.

After they landed, Captain Currie told her he had had a great time; he hadn't had so much fun since he was junior officer and flying all the time. Kara was elated that the flight had gone so well. She dropped the captain in Oceana and flew on to Cecil Naval Air Station, which is about fourteen miles west of Jacksonville, Florida. She returned to Key West on Saturday, and on Monday, she left for San Diego.

Kara described what followed in her August journal entry: "The good news was that the Aircrew Qual Board decided I was not only ready for my FCF but also I would be leading the division to SOCAL [an acronym for Southern California]. Well I guess I'm out of Double Super Secret Probation. Cool! Not so fast."

FCF stands for functional check flight and it's an important qualification. The pilot has to ask for it and the request has to be approved by operations, safety, and maintenance. Having the FCF qualification allows the pilot to fly a check or acceptance hop on an airplane just up from having major maintenance performed on it. Pilots continually compete for flight time and when airplanes have been down for maintenance and one finally comes up on the flight line, the pilot who has the FCF qualification will get to fly it. A pilot has to have a certain number of flight hours before he or she can be nominated, and the skipper of the squadron has to sign off on it.

"Backtrack to Capt. Currie . . . Evidently the Skipper ["Billy Ray" Puckett] was extremely upset that I had done a roll out of altitude and I had pulled excessive 'Gs' in the break. The XO [Shadowtree] called me into the Skipper's office as I was walking to my division lead brief."

Both Puckett and Shadowtree were waiting to talk to Kara.

I thought he [Puckett] was joking when he started on a long drawn out story about Capt. Currie seeing him at a wedding reception over the weekend and relaying a story about some A-6 pilot that had ejected on a cat shot and then was too conservative until he did a low transition and departed the jet and killed himself and an NFO. I'm thinking to myself, "Sir is this going to take long? I'm now officially late for my brief." Well what was his point? Capt. Currie thinks I might be lacking in maturity and judgment. OH. Is that it?

Bottom line is that I'm back on probation. I got a formal letter of counseling from the Skipper when I got back from SOCAL. I think I'll have it framed. It says that I rolled 180 degrees and pulled through an unusual attitude on an IFR clearance blahh blahh blah exceeded 250 KIAS below 10K by going into the break at 400 KIAS. EXSQUEEZE ME?

I wonder, "How did I get myself into this mess?" I suppose it's a combination of my personality and something else. I've made my share of mistakes.

Kara was shocked that Captain Currie would complain to the Skipper about their flight and believed that whatever Captain Currie said, he didn't mean it as criticism or to get her in trouble. She was sure "Billy Ray" had misunderstood the message. She thought probably that Captain Currie had made the sort of joking comment that guys make at parties, exaggerating the fun, fear, or feat, whatever it was.

She wanted to ask Captain Currie just what he had said, but she couldn't do that because it would appear that she doubted her commanding officer. Her boss in maintenance, Wayne Lockley, told her she should tell her CO she knew she had violated the strict NATOPS procedures and promise she wouldn't do it again.

It came as a surprise to Kara that the CO would take such a hard line against her, regardless of how it was presented to him by Captain Currie. Janet told Commander Puckett she thought a letter was uncalled for, but he would hear none of it. He also put her FCF qualification on hold for thirty days.

If it had been any of the other pilots, Kara guessed that "Billy Ray" would have clapped him on the shoulder in clan camaraderie. Whenever anything happened while she was flying, no matter how unremarkable, it was commented upon and added to the informal list of errors kept on her.

"I must fly a single-seat jet to be truly happy," she wrote in her diary on 27 July 1992. "I am sick of back-stabbing NFOs."

Chapter 32 ❧ *Mom*

Pam and Sue completed their three-year tours in the squadron the summer of 1992. Kara's tour wouldn't be over until the spring of 1993. Pam was assigned to the public affairs staff of the commander in chief U.S. Atlantic Fleet in Norfolk, Virginia. Sue received a coveted assignment to test pilot school at Pax River in Patuxent, Maryland, which was a preferred avenue to the astronaut program.

Kara would have given anything to go to test pilot school when her current tour was over, but she would have been too junior. Although she still wanted to be an astronaut someday, what she wanted to do first, above everything else and with all her soul, was to fly the F/A-18. Her quest was a berth on a carrier, because that was where the fighter planes lived. Noncarrier-based F/A-18 pilot opportunities were few.

She was looking forward to going on leave the first week of August 1992 and excited about meeting her sisters in San Antonio. The three sisters always planned their trips so they would be home at the same time. All of them had full lives and they lived far apart, but they put a lot of effort into being together—always at Christmas and otherwise as often as possible.

The whole family gathered for dinner on the deck of Sally's house on a surprisingly mild Texas evening. Uncle Jimmy was in charge of barbecuing the specialty he called "4-Plex Chicken." Kara's grandmother, Uncle Tommy, Aunt Carol, her daughter, Blakely, Dagny, Kirsten, and Sally were also there.

As usual, it was Kara's show and she had enthusiastic listeners. She was revved, even more animated than usual, as she regaled the group with tales of her travels. Never cool when she was talking about flying, she used her hands to trace take offs and landings and aileron rolls and she created sound effects, roars, screeches, plops, pops, whoops, radio static, like a little kid. She told story after story about the goings-on in VAQ-33. Kara could describe her trials and tribulations with such wit and humor that you would never guess she was truly hurt by some of the conduct toward her.

Though the combat exclusion laws had been repealed in October 1991, almost a year before, the services still had policies against assigning women to fly combat aircraft, and the presidential commission appointed by George Bush was still "studying" the matter. Kara didn't have much hope that anything would happen until after the presidential election in November. To make matters bleaker, budgets were tight for the military. Pensacola, Florida, the home of naval aviation, was looking like a ghost town. Aviation Officer Candidate School was graduating only about five people per class that fall.

Kara was upset on both a general and a personal level. The continuing delay offended her sense of justice, and it kept the friction active between her and the men she flew with. The constant battle was wearing on her.

Suzanne Parker joined the group later. She was on her way to San Diego to fly helicopters. Now that there was someone in the audience who really understood what she was saying, Kara was no longer telling her stories to entertain. Her smile was gone and her face was taunt and strained as she told Suzanne how alone she felt sometimes in the tropic of VAQ-33. The way she held herself and the tone of her voice betrayed her anger, hurt, and frustration, and the stress she'd been under.

As the evening went on, Sally began to spend more and more time in the kitchen and Dagny and Kirsten drifted upstairs. They loved Kara and were interested in what she was doing, but after awhile, they wanted to talk about something—anything—else.

The next day, Dagny, Kirsten, Kara, and their mother were off to Tuesday Morning, their favorite discount store. It was a ritual visit when the girls came to San Antonio. They piled into Sally's car and were hardly out of the driveway when Kara began talking again about her campaign to fly fighter aircraft and her problems in the squadron. Dagny and Kirsten looked out the windows, not wanting to cut Kara off or hurt her feelings, but not interested in what she was saying either. Halfway to their destination, Sally finally said, "Kara, that's enough. Talk about something else. We can't listen anymore this trip to anything having to do with airplanes."

"Amen," said Dagny and Kirsten.

Kara's cheeks became two bright red circles on blanched white skin. She looked as if her mother had struck her. In a way she had. Kara felt she had to fight the whole world and now she couldn't even rely on her own family for support. She was immediately silent, furious with her mother. Sally felt terrible for having said anything—but not terrible enough to take it back. Even though she knew how tough things had been for Kara, they were all really sick of the subject of women flying combat aircraft.

Neither her mother nor her sisters could recognize one plane from another anyway. The unfortunate truth was that what she was doing was so foreign to the people who loved her they really couldn't understand all the things that were happening to her. Until Kara joined the navy, they hadn't been a military family. Everything was new to them. The navy spoke in acronyms and other strange words. They couldn't relate to how it felt to command a jet airplane into the sky or jump the clouds.

Kara tried so hard to bring them into it. She would tell them about her experiences, lovingly describing the thrill of flight and exulting in her accomplishments. She was equally candid about her mistakes and disappointments. They tried to listen and comprehend, but she might as well have been speaking Russian. Still, she talked to her mother and her sisters and her father and they tried to empathize with her as best they could. They all loved each other dearly.

But that morning was spoiled, and Kara hardly spoke the rest of the time they spent shopping. She packed and left for Key West when they got home.

Her mother thought a lot about what had happened, and then decided she might as well go ahead and make things worse. She wrote Kara a letter on 10 August 1992.

Dearest Kara,

I know you are upset with me. You are going to be even more upset as you read this letter, but I am going to write it anyway.

When I said I was tired of hearing you talk about the problems of women in the Navy I was referring to your delivery rather than the content.

At the Wednesday night barbecue, as I was standing at the sink in the kitchen for hours, I heard you talk non-stop. When I turned to look at you, I saw your pretty face scrunched into a scowl, your fingers crooked and stiffened into a claw jabbing emphatically and your shoulders hunched intensely as you leaned into your subject.

The next morning as we drove off to shop at Tuesday Morning you began again.

In any event, if you decide to become a martyr to this cause you should do the following:

1. Keep your lectures to 5 minutes or less. Even the eyes of disciples begin to glaze over after that amount of time.

2. Cut out the sound effects when describing jets. You are not a 13-year-old boy. You may, however, use sound effects when you are talking to 13-year-old or under boys if you like.

3. Keep your hands and fingers relaxed and use them gracefully and sparingly.

4. Vary the inflection in your voice and lighten up. Humor and grace sell much better than stridency.

5. Never complain about the treatment you receive personally unless you do it formally and pursuant to Navy procedure.

Otherwise you are perfect. I love you.

Kara wrote her back the following on a postcard from Miami on 15 August: "Sounds like good advice. I'm not upset with you. I just hate my job, my life, my uniform pants and my lips (when found.) Otherwise I'm perfect."

She was more open in her letter to Monique on 27 August:

Remember how we talked about 1992 being a really good year? I think we jinxed it because this year has been less than stellar. How's yours going?

I haven't written much at all or called because I have no good news. I'm turning into one of those bitter women I always hated. I was in San Antonio on leave with my sisters and my mother ticked me off so much I don't know if I'll ever go back. I'm serious. What really irritates me is when I know she's right but the truth really isn't what I'm after.

On 15 September 1992, Kara wrote her mother:

Howdy Mom—

I'm Med down in Oceana with an ear infection. So instead of feasting on flight time I have the duty in a smoke-filled room.

I met the new female A-6 pilot—she started the RAG today. Her name is Nancy Nichols—she's short, cute, and seems nice. I'm being so positive about Key West/VAQ-33 I know it would make you proud.

Chapter 33 ❀ *Babies*

"XO [Shadowtree] talked to me today," Kara wrote in her journal on 26 August 1992. "Capt. Foulk told him that I had said that he suggested I get out of the Navy and have babies. He assured me that he was supportive of women in the Navy. I was very embarrassed. I shouldn't have repeated that to anyone."

Kara's conversation with Shadowtree had been in the context of what kind of career she could have if the policy toward women flying combat aircraft was not changed. There was no longer a Soviet threat and therefore no future for the electronic warfare training mission. The support squadrons, electronic warfare training and aggressor squadrons, were scheduled to be decommissioned. Without the electronic warfare support training squadrons, there would be few places left in the navy for women jet pilots.

The presidential election would probably decide things one way or another. Kara wrote Monique on 27 August: "Part of the Republican Party Platform is no women in combat, 'We must protect our wives & daughters.' So if you vote for Bush I don't want to hear about it, OK?"

The recommendations of George Bush's presidential commission were due to be released soon and they were not expected to be favorable to women. The commission had been packed with far-right conservative members, the most vocal of whom was Elaine Donnelly, a protégée of Phyllis Schafly, the woman who led the opposition to the Equal Rights Amendment. Ms. Donnelly was president of the Center for Military Readiness, an organization she founded and operated out of the basement of her home in Livonia, Michigan. She lobbied hard against expanded roles for women in the armed services.

Also on the presidential commission were a vice president of the Heritage Foundation, a female master sergeant in the air force who was affiliated with the ultraconservative Concerned Women for America, and a fundamentalist Christian who received his instructions directly from the Bible. They all urged that the ban on women flying combat aircraft be reinstated.

Senior male officers like Commander Shadowtree were also facing the possibility of premature career death as a result of the imminent demise of the electronic warfare squadrons, so they weren't sympathetic to the plight of the women. But whatever anxiety Shadowtree had about his own situation, it wasn't very sensitive or politically astute of him to make a light comment about Kara's bleak future in the navy, much less to suggest that motherhood was really the proper goal for her. He should have known better: his wife was a naval officer.

It was the kind of sexist remark that men made without thinking and Kara was used to it, except that coming from a man who was to be her commanding officer in a few months, it jolted her. In any event, she hadn't meant to make a sexual harassment issue of it with Don Foulk.

She told Pamela Kunze what had happened in a letter dated 4 October 1992. Pam, lonely in her new assignment in Norfolk, Virginia, had written Kara, and Kara was happy to hear from her. Though their friendship had been strained since Christmas 1991, Kara had missed Pam.

I had recently written a letter to Captain Foulk and mentioned that I didn't sense much support from the front office concerning my transition. The XO's career advice, "You should just get out and have babies," sort of worried me. Well, Dondo calls me and says, "Did he really say that? He must have been kidding! His wife's a Commander!"

I told him I didn't take it as a female slam—I took it personally. Dondo then took it upon himself to call Puckett and then Shadowtree. "What kind of show are you running telling Kara to have babies instead of pursuing a career as a naval officer?"

Yikes! The XO then calls me in to apologize and assure me that he was very pro women . . . his wife . . . yuk, yuk, yuk. . . .

I told him that I'm sure he is supportive of women but I had taken it personally and I was sorry that Skipper Foulk had misinterpreted my point. It was incredibly embarrassing. Thanks Skipper Foulk!

Chapter 34 ❧ *Hurricane Andrew*

"I've been thinkin' about you," Kara wrote in her 27 August 1992 letter to Monique and then she catalogued her recent travels:

> I've been to San Diego for 2 weeks, Hawaii (2 wks), Oceana, Jacksonville, Oceana again, went on leave, and came back to evacuate from Hurricane Andrew. We flew our jets to Atlanta and it was a blast!
>
> I'm still kind of dealing with my initial disappointment that Key West wasn't wiped off the map instead of Homestead. I would have lost everything—which in my case is almost nothing. We would have just moved to Atlanta. I wanted total devastation—is that so wrong? We came back on Tuesday and not one leaf was out of place—hardly a lesson for the fools that didn't evacuate the Keys. We are on electricity rationing (no A/C in the hangar at work—it's miserable at best).

In order to escape the predicted path of Hurricane Andrew, the squadron had flown all its jet airplanes to Atlanta. As it turned out, the hurricane completely missed Key West but devastated and demolished Homestead AFB instead. Kara's letter to Monique continued: "Atlanta was fun. Ron Lotz, Fossil, Amy Lyons, Amy Boyer, and Amy Kingston and moi went partying Monday night. Ron Lotz 'Gunny' is a riot. Something may be brewing between Scarlett & Gunny—she said she's ready for an affair. And he's only semi-married and he has a ski boat. Perfect. He is supposed to have a friend to set me up with."

The best thing that happened though was that when she got back, she received praise for her performance during the exercise from one of the senior chiefs. "Chief Kangelo told me I had chutzpa today. The Division had a post hurricane bitch session. It was very honest and informative. Anyway, a compliment from the Chief is worth a lot. He said, 'They told me we had a real Division Officer. I guess I know it's true now.' Is that cool or what?"

Commander Puckett had a "Hurevac" (navy for hurricane evacuation) debrief at Station Theater. Kara described it in a letter to Brenda Scheufele, an F/A-18 pilot in one of the West Coast electronic warfare squadrons, whom she had met on her last SOCAL det. "We had a squadron debrief about the whole hurricane fiasco. The Skipper got up and told the squadron that on Saturday night he wanted to cut loose the military 'men' that needed to take care of their 'wives.' He worried about all the wives on the road by themselves. He must have said 'men' and 'wives' about 3 times. Yes, we are in a leadership vacuum here in Key West."

Kara and several other women officers—Amy Lyons, Amy Boyer, Amy Kingston, and Janet Marnane—decided to let him know that next time he might want to think about the impact of his words on military women before he implied that all the "wives" needed manly protection.

So I thought maybe a group of senior women should go let the Skipper know that he alienated a whole group of individuals—mainly women—a lot of whom are single parents. . . . Maybe next time you could say military member and dependents? Schwwinnl—Bad idea. He got completely defensive and said he was talking from his experience and his main concern was that he didn't want his wife on the road alone.

Correct me if I'm wrong, Skipper—aren't these the same wives that manage alone for 6-month deployments? Your attitude just perpetuates the myth that women are incapable of taking care of themselves. It effectively destroys the progress that women in the shops have made—the respect they have *earned,* and it undermines my authority as a Division Officer. *We* all know what you meant and are not here to attack you but just to help you gain perspective on your audience. It's a simple matter of semantics and your choice of words was not politically correct.

I think the phrase "no tally, no visual, no clue" pretty much describes our Skipper.

Chapter 35   *Lester*

Kara hoped a Democrat would win the presidential election in the fall; then, the policy against women flying carrier-based aircraft almost surely would change by the time she was ready for a new assignment. Still, getting an F/A-18 Hornet transition wouldn't be a sure thing, even if women were allowed to go to the fleet. Her detailer gave her no encouragement that an F/A-18 slot would open up in the spring. Skipper Puckett assured her that he would endorse her transition package, but Shadowtree, the XO, cautioned her that a transition to Hornets would depend on how well she did in VAQ-33.

"I want Hornets," she wrote. "I must use positive mental imaging. Maybe I'll call a psychic." If she had to wait out another three-year tour flying A-6s, she would probably be considered too senior in rank to make the transition to fly F/A-18s. That she managed to find the humor in almost every situation helped her to keep some perspective in her life.

"I saw a bumper sticker that read, 'Lick Bush in '92,'" she wrote Monique. "It was a lesbian thing and unrelated to the election. So you were wondering why I wanted to move to Atlanta? I've got a blind date tomorrow. If he's nice and sensitive and thoughtful, it'll be a sure sign he already has a boyfriend. Yikes!"

Kara loved to tell the story about being with friends at an outdoor bar in Key West when a rainstorm suddenly came up, sheets of rain, pouring hard. She and everyone else ran for cover underneath the only awning around. She found herself wedged between two of the best-looking men she had ever seen and they were laughing and flirting, when one of them mentioned something about his being already attached to the guy plastered to her other side. "Couldn't you just think about it?" asked Kara, "I'm a navy jet pilot, after all. That's pretty macho for a chick."

A card to Suzanne Parker on 10 September 1992 pictured a beautiful brunette saying, "I don't believe it's true that blonds have more fun." Inside it said, "It's just that their attention span is so short, everything seems new and exciting." But in VAQ-33, incidents continued to occur in which even Kara couldn't find the humor.

One of the senior officers in the squadron, Lester Cook, was prone to making observations about female attributes. One working day as Kara walked across the hangar bay in her uniform skirt, Lester made a comment everyone could hear about what great legs she had.

A lot of enlisted people who worked for her were around and they all looked at him and then to her to see how she would react. It put Kara on the spot. Part of Kara's job as division officer in maintenance was to handle sexual harassment issues and she was very embarrassed that a fellow officer would act toward her in a way she would never have permitted the men she supervised to act toward the women they worked with.

Kara liked getting compliments from men and didn't overreact even if they were clumsy or suggestive. She was used to getting whistles because of her shapely legs, but Lester wasn't part of a crew ogling her as she walked by a construction site. They were on base and on duty, and he was a navy officer who should have known better than to make a sexist remark to a woman officer in front of her troops. She tried to explain to him later why his remarks were inappropriate, but Lester didn't understand what she meant.

Kara was talking to some friends in front of the bachelor officers quarters on detachment at Miramar when Lester came up behind her and ran his hand up her bare leg right to the hem of her running shorts. Incensed, she whirled around and told him never to touch her again. But he still didn't get the message that he was way out of line. And of course, Kara took a risk when she stood up for herself. After she challenged him, Lester had nothing good to say about her.

He was on the lieutenant ranking board and his opinion of her would influence not only what plane she flew but also the rest of her navy career. "I'm sure I did really well—NOT," Kara wrote Pam after the lieutenant ranking board met. "Lester went to bat for me no doubt—like a Mexican with a pinata."

Kara's 20 September 1992 journal entry illustrated how it worked.

Back from DET NTU—med down, ear infection. Lester asked, "Did she go to medical to *prove* she's med down?" Oh like I'm sure—Kara the Seagull loves to come on DET and not fly. What an ass-hole. Rider [Wayne Lockley] says to Lester, "What is that about?" And he says to Rider, "You're always sticking up for her."

Rider: "She happens to work for me, I think she's a good offi-cer, and I don't have any problems with her." Lester: "Well, I *do* have problems with her." So I wonder what his damn problem could be except that I wasn't interested in his sexual innuendo. Damn Damn Damn Son of a bitch. I'm so mad & frustrated.

Chapter 36 ❀ *Professor Rudolph Hensingmuller*

Kara found a reprint of a 1911 article by Prof. Rudolph Hensing-muller in which he stated the reasons why he believed women were better pilots than men. She circulated it as a big joke, but she soon stopped because most of the guys thought these reasons were about the best ones they had ever heard of for letting women in the cockpit. The reasons were

> because she has retained the primitive faculty of seeing with full retina; enforced modesty and flirting have caused this;
> because she has scattered attention instead of concentration; this is invaluable to an aviator who must notice many things at once;
> because she has the faculty of intuition—that quality of the mind which can take in a number of causes simultaneously and induce a conclusion—an essential in aviation;
> because her specific gravity is less than man's;
> because she needs less oxygen and therefore can better meet the suffocating rush of air; altitude effects [*sic*] her less than it does man;
> because her sneezes, in man an actual spasm, have been controlled by ages of polite repression;
> because she feels more quickly warning atmospheric changes;
> because she loves to speed.

Kara found no fault with the last reason, at least.

Brenda Scheufele gave Kara a copy of a memorandum sent by C. R. Rondestvedt, the commanding officer of F/A-18 Strike Fighter Squadron 22, to the commanding officer of Tactical Electronic Warfare Squadron 34 in San Diego, Brenda's squadron. The enclosure was "VFA-22 Junior Officer Questions Regarding Ready Room Female Pilot Integration." The CO requested that his wardroom meet with the VAQ-34 women pilots in a neutral site as a fitting conclusion to his squadron's sexual harassment training.

Of the thirty-nine questions, some of them were thoughtful such as, "Do you feel there will be sexual tension in close quarters aboard ship and how do you feel this will impact the work environment both in the air and the wardroom?"

A civilian would think some of the other questions were asked with tongue in cheek, but they voiced real concerns of the male fighter pilots. "With women on board the wardroom, should there be any restrictions on Saturday night video of Playboy's Wet & Wild, and/or will the Wife's Club Calendar be viewed as offensive?" and "What do you think of eating an olive out of a fat greased belly button (i.e., Shellback Initiation)? Do you expect Navy traditions such as this to change?"

By number twelve, the questions got more pointed. "Given that the vast majority of current Naval Aviators are vehemently opposed to the integration of women in fleet squadrons, how do you propose to successfully integrate into squadrons without simply declaring 'Here we are, learn to live with it?'"

And question number fourteen was downright insulting: "It is common knowledge that females are not subject to the same standards as male aviators in the training command RAGs. If you do not subject yourselves to the *EXACT SAME* standards, both physically and operationally, how do you feel you can arrive at a squadron with any credibility?"

Seven of the thirty-nine questions were about pregnancy. Number thirty asked, "Will women pilots have the option of getting pregnant at any time during a sea tour?" The mind-set was implicit in the follow-up question, "What will be the punishment?"

Only two questions involved hormones. Number twenty-six asked, "How will women['s] physical differences affect their ability to perform, i.e., menstural [*sic*] cycle?" Number thirty-four asked, "If you are a female that gets bad cramps and has a slight personality problem with the hormonal imbalance, are we going to have to schedule you around your cramps and menstrual cycle?"

In her letter to Brenda, Kara said: "I read them to my mother thinking they were really funny—she thought they were completely sexist and couldn't believe grown men would come up with them. I said, 'grown men? Who said anything about grown men? F-18 pilots came up with these.'"

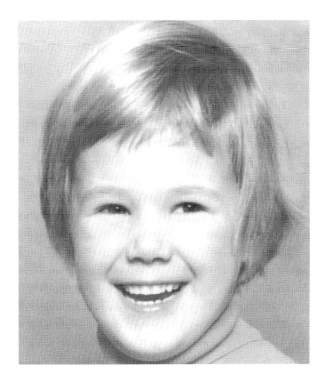

Kara, age 5.

Alamo Heights high school annual, senior picture, 1983.

Kara and Monique at Monique's house at Christmas.

Aviation Officer Candidate School, Honor Class, November 1987.

Kara's first salute from Gunnery Sergeant Snow.

Kara takes her parents to the Pensacola airport after being
commissioned, 1987.

Ensign Kara "Pancho" Hultgreen sitting on her T-2C Buckeye during jet training at Beeville, Texas, in 1988. A corrosion control technician stenciled Kara's name and call sign on the side of the Buckeye, although that wasn't normally done for student pilots. The call sign was for Pancho Barnes, one of the first and best female pilots, who won many air races and trained military pilots in World War II even though she was a civilian.

Kara on her Kawasaki 500 on the Corpus Christi freeway.

Kara's class at the winging ceremony at Beeville, August 1989.

Kara with her parents, Tor and Sally. Tor has just pinned Kara's wings on her.

Kirsten and Sally visit Kara in Key West, Thanksgiving 1989.

Kara, Pam Kunze, Don Foulk, Linda Heid *(left to right)*,
Chris Riposo *(front)*, January 1991.

Kara peeks out from under her EA-6A, November 1990.

Left to right: Pete Wilkens, Kara, and Gerry Walsh, enjoying a night out on the town.

Left to right: Sue Still, Kara, Pam Kunze; Tailhook, September 1991.

Kara with Pam's dog, Knuckle.

Kara in her flight suit; she is standing in front of her EA-6A.

Kara in front of her EA-6A during March 1991 interview with Marina Pisano of the *San Antonio Express-News*. *(Photo by Gloria Ferniz)*

Kara and maintenance crew beside Sue Still's plane in Orland, Norway. The drogue basket is still attached to the refueling probe.

Dagny, Tor, Kara *(left to right)*, Kirsten *(front)*; Christmas 1990 at Sally's house.

Returning to Key West from Colorado, Amy Boyer, Kara, "Wedge," and "Herman" stayed overnight with "Wedge's" mom at her house in Ohio.

Kara is about to read the oath of reinstatement. A sailor may ask any officer to administer the oath, and Kara was asked often. She always felt honored.

Kara, her NFO Ron Lotz, and the limping EA-6A after their one-wheel landing in Pensacola, October 1992.

Left to right: Kirsten, Dagny, and Kara at Dagny's wedding in Los Angeles on 31 July 1993. The next day Dagny left for her honeymoon and Kara left for Miramar to begin training to fly the F-14. *(Photo by Jack Caputo Photography, Beverly Hills)*

Kara taking pictures as part of her duties as public affairs officer of
VF-213.

Kara's F-14A, Lion 103, lying upside down on the deck of the barge after having been raised from 3,700 feet below the surface of the Pacific Ocean.

Funeral at Arlington, the caisson. *(Photo by Ernie Cox Jr.)*

Secretary of the Navy John Dalton presents the flag to Kara's mother, Sally. Kara's sisters, Kirsten and Dagny, are to Sally's right. *(Courtesy the Secretary of the Navy)*

Kara in front of the pointy nose of an F-14A. Kara sent both her parents a copy of the photo. They received the photo the day after she died. *(Photo by Rob Allen)*

Chapter 37   ❋   *Karash*

"Interesting program they showed on the ship's TV the other night," Kara's friend Mike "Scally" Scavone wrote from his cruise in the Adriatic; "—some female Navy pilot that's some kind of a hero for landing a gear-up EA-6A in Pensacola. I'll tell you this—she's gorgeous (a bit sturdy, but gorgeous just the same)."

It was a sunny hazy afternoon in the Florida panhandle on 10 October 1992, when Kara and Ron Lotz approached the Pensacola Naval Air Station to refuel. They were returning to Key West from a mission in San Diego and their flight plan called for a "gas and go" in Pensacola.

Kara loved flying with Ron. He was not only competent but also told great jokes, and that was a real plus. When they weren't busy at the controls, they mostly tried to one-up each other's stories. The flight had been routine. They were on schedule, and the old airplane was behaving itself as it entered the break, everything uneventful—until she lowered the landing gear. The nose wheel and the left landing gear came down, but the gear on the right did not. The tower confirmed that the right main gear was hung.

This wasn't a trivial problem. It was deadly serious. With no right wheel, the least of her problems would be that it would be impossible to steer the plane. The dilemma she faced was that at some point during the landing, the right wing would touch the ground, and if that happened at full landing speed, it could cause the aircraft to pitch over. Pieces would tear off as it careened along the concrete, causing extensive damage to the plane and maybe its occupants.

A frozen gear creates a much more dangerous situation on the A-6 than it would on most other aircraft because of the way its flight control surfaces operate. In the A-6 a wing can only have its lift spoiled. Kara would have to get her plane down on the left gear and then the nose gear, keeping up speed to maintain equilibrium. If the gearless right wing came down too soon, or wrong, or too hard— "I'll think about that tomorrow, when I can stand it," she told Ron, her favorite Scarlet O'Hara quote coming in handy once again.

While she soared around trying to see if the gear would magically deploy, she was trying to decide, if it didn't, whether to discard the $4-million electronics pod she had used during the San Diego training mission. It was strapped underneath her right wing, the wing over the jammed wheel.

A typical Kara quandary. If she ditched the 170 pod before she attempted to land and saved the plane, well, it was certainly justified by NATOPS procedures, but she would be criticized for abandoning a $4-million pod. If she didn't scrap it and lost both the plane and the electronic pod, that would be "max grief." They would say, "Bad head work, if you had jettisoned the stores, you would have saved the plane."

Thinking about the FA-18 squadron's questions concerning female hormone problems, Kara smiled to herself as she said, "Uh, Ron, I think I'm ovulating." Still striving to jiggle down the wheel, she added, "But don't worry. I'm days away from PMS."

"If I dick this up, they'll probably take away my wings and you will most likely die," she told him as she rolled on final. "If it works out *perfectly* maybe, just maybe, we'll both get letters of appreciation in 6 months or so . . . signed by the Skipper! . . . Don't forget to call the ball."

"He laughed," Kara wrote Pam later. "Ron is great."

They circled around the airfield in a twenty-six-hundred-foot delta pattern for forty-five minutes trying to shake the gear loose and also using up excess gasoline—they didn't want to keep fuel to feed the fire in case they crashed. They would have to make an "arrested" landing where Kara would lower the tailhook on her plane and try to catch the wire to bring her to a stop, just as if she were landing on a carrier.

The arresting wire across the runway was set up for a short field arrestment and an LSO (landing signal officer) was called on station. Fire trucks and emergency crews were alerted. Bringing in a huge airplane with only one main landing gear and the nose wheel was not a minor crisis.

She made one pass to get her bearings; the second one was for real. The emergency crews were in position. She hit the runway on the left wheel and caught the center of the wire. The nose wheel came down but because there was no weight on the right, it wasn't possible to steer the plane. She kept the plane on the runway by braking with the left wheel only. The wing over the jammed right main mount dipped, but before it touched the ground, she gunned the engines until she felt the pull of the arresting gear. The wing stayed up until the wire stopped the plane. Then the tip of the wing over the tucked up right wheel settled gently to the ground.

The plane made a half rotation around its grounded right wing before it came to a stop. It was a perfect landing. An ambulance and four fire trucks, sirens blaring, quickly surrounded the plane. The firemen all dressed in their protective yellow slickers jumped from their trucks and circled the plane checking for any sign of a fire. Ron climbed out of the cockpit and then Kara. A navy photographer for the Blue Angels got the whole thing on tape. You could hear the applause from the people standing out on the runway.

The plane flew back to Key West a few days later after having been thoroughly inspected. The forward main landing gear door had been jammed shut and blocked by the engine bay door. The emergency landing of the crippled aircraft had resulted in only minor cosmetic damage to the underside of the wing tip and the outboard flap. The total amount of the damage was $16.00. And the $4-million electronics pod was safe.

Kara told Monique all about it in her letter dated 24 October 1992:

Ron Lotz—Super ECMO (Electronic Counter Measures Officer)— and I flew to Pensacola FL where we were forced to crash land with a hung right main mount. Anyway, we are pretty much heroes for saving the 4 million dollar pod and sustaining only minor wing tip cosmetic damage. It worked out perfectly—we took a field arrestment and kept the jet on the runway. It's nice to have everyone telling me what a great job I did for a change.

We called our Skipper ["Billy Ray" Puckett] and his first question was, "How's the 170 pod?" Second question, "How's the jet?" His third comment, "You and Ron are fine? That's the important thing." Yeah I could tell we are the priority you asshole. Furthermore when Ron & I flew home commercially no one met us at the airport—and the Skipper has yet to say word one to me. I would think he would have called me and Ron in for a personal debrief. He's probably still trying to figure out how I did this on purpose so that I could prove something—because I'm a girl.

What is really cool is that a fleet A-6 squadron had the same incident a month or two ago. They unfortunately really dicked it up, missed the wire, went off the runway, and had over $200,000.00 damage to their jet, ruined both engines—a total abortion. Both aircrew were unhurt fortunately. So what's my point? It really makes me look that much better.

It was so funny when everyone (Captain of the Base, etc.) walked up to Ron and shook his hand and told him what a super job he did and he looked at them and said, "Thanks, but she was flying." And then they shook my hand and got all flustered.

Kara wrote her Dad on 23 October "I'm so salty now. I've crashed. A Blue Angel got the whole thing on video—I'll bring it home at Christmas."

She signed the letter "Karash."

"My troops think I'm a hero," she wrote Pam on 2 November 1992. "You can imagine how I must hate to be idolized. I must have had 200 troops come tell me how glad they were that we were safe and how cool they think I am. It was so cute."

Then she described her meeting with the executive officer, Milton Shadowtree.

> The XO is back in town and he called me into his office for a debrief about the Karash. At least he was interested. He said "I saw the video—it looks like you did a good job." I think he said "good job" about three times. I think I'll just change my name to LT GOOD-JOB. 1-900-GOODJOB. He is such a snake. Brackett said to Harv— "Maybe this will bring her back up to zero." What a fucking shit. Billy Ray, the raving righteous one, is a complete stark raving lunatic. No explanation necessary.

Kara did get a Bravo Zulu, which is a navy version of "well done" in the navy safety magazine *Approach,* but the tribute that meant the most to her was that the maintenance chiefs in her division proposed that she be awarded an Air Medal. They prepared the whole awards package, the required form 1650 with citation and justification. Kara was honored and touched by that because it was not only a recognition of her aviation skills but also proof of the high regard in which she was held by the people many consider to be *the* most important group in naval aviation—the chief petty officers.

That package, however, was not endorsed by her commanding officer, "Billy Ray" Puckett, and Kara got no official recognition for what pilots call "a neat piece of flying."

Chapter 38 *The Firebird Ball*

"We had the Firebird Ball last night," Kara wrote Pamela on 7 November 1992.

> What a nightmare! I almost got Karen to set me up with a long-haired rocker with a nose ring—completely unpresentable—someone desperate for a free meal. I had my hair done up in a beehive bouffant instead. I just couldn't put anyone else through a squadron event, no matter how hungry.
>
> They had us dressed in a gulf rig, which consisted of our white CNT shirt with shoulder boards, miniature wings, and miniature medals, our black skirt, and a red cummerbund. I've never felt so ridiculous in a uniform. We had this thing at the Hyatt too—so I had to go out in public in this get up.

Kara had taken her physical readiness test ("yes, 300 points," she wrote) the morning of the party and had played softball all afternoon at the squadron picnic, so she was very tired when she got home—just in time to dress for the party.

> I got to the Hyatt and had three Heinekens and was completely lit. I was just slumped in my chair with an evil little grin and by the time they brought out the dessert I had to leave. I went out to sit in Ron's car and puked in the parking lot. Good form—fortunately there were no witnesses for that one.
>
> I hear that I was crawling around on all fours and lobbing rolls at the head table. Good girl—I'm sure I'm back into the negative numbers after last night. I also barely remember throwing banana pieces at Lester. What was my problem? I've never been that drunk on three beers before. Ron and Amy put me to bed by 2130. Amy had the duty so she took the watch. . . .
>
> Oh I actually got my FCF qual last week. Evidently the Skipper [Puckett] almost didn't sign it. But he did. He was concerned about sending me the wrong message.

Two days later, Kara updated Pam on the FCF qualification.

Yo Spam:

I was told today, "Not so fast on the FCF qual." Evidently the Skipper *didn't* sign it and he is going to talk to me "when he is (God-damn good and) ready." He went on leave for a week shortly after Chuck gave me that word. I hate being jerked around by these buffoons. I'm glad he didn't have his little talk with me today—I was ready to tell him to take his FCF and cram it up his ass. I'm outta here.

We had an AOM [All Officers Meeting] this morning and I must say I was in rare form. The Skipper made a comment to Nancy Nichols that when Captain Currie saw her at the Firebird Ball he remarked that he wanted to fly with her. So I piped up and said, "Yeah Nancy, the Hulkster has some good gouge [useful information] for you before you take the Captain up." The entire Ready Room exploded, and the Skipper just put his head down. The Skipper is so cludo he doesn't even realize that Nancy didn't attend the Ball.

Then the XO [Shadowtree] stood up with his flight jacket in hand. Someone, and I don't know who, sewed his sleeves up and put some huge (size 30) lavender women's panties in one pocket and a magical glow-in-the-dark condom in the other pocket. The Skipper promptly put Anita Petty in charge of a JAG investigation. I of course said, "Anita will surely get to the *bottom* of this . . . no bun intended."

We had training today introducing the LAN (local area network)—it's a cool computer network linking everyone together, but that's not the interesting part. The woman instructing the class looked and sounded just like Deborah Winger (Sissy) in *Urban Cowboy*. All I could think about was Bud saying, "I apologize from the bottom of my heart, Sissy, right back to the first time I hitchoo."

"Writing letters on my computer is like keeping a journal," Kara wrote Pam on 16 November in her running commentary on life in VAQ-33. "I'll need these letters," she had once written Marc, "so I can refer back to them when I write my memoirs, 'Breaking Heads as Thick as Coconuts.'"

Her letter to Pam continued:

I hope you aren't offended by the impersonal typed aspect. This way I won't repeat myself either.

Last Friday we had a boatex to woman key. It was Wedge and Moose's wetting down (Moose aka Laura Sherman). We had a great time—no wives, water football, and water skiing. I was pretty sore on Saturday from the full tackle football, thank you Jelly—my lower back was hatin' life.

I spoke to CDR Mariner tonight and she thinks the policy will change but it will take another 8–12 months. That's real encouraging. I'm getting more than a little sick of this. The raving righteous one [Puckett] still hasn't spoken to me about the FCF.

What else? I'm turning over with Amy in Maintenance. I didn't realize how much I did until I started passing it on to someone else. I can't wait to get out of this job now—I'm burned out. Harry told me today that I was the best division officer he had ever worked with—and he said he has told the CO/XO that at every opportunity. That was nice. I am a little concerned about this next Fitrep though. I have to break out in order to be competitive for a transition, or anything. I have a lot of support for my statement in the event of a poor fitrep. I'm already working on a statement—just in case. The CO/XO haven't made any phone calls for me—which is probably good, who knows what they would say.

A fitrep is the annual fitness report that is given to each officer in the squadron by the commanding officer. It's supposed to be a positive event, to let the officers know how they have been doing and where they rank among their peers. It's just like a report card in school except that the officer's career is on the line.

Her letter to Pam continued: "The XO called me in to talk about career options and instead of offering to help me he just agreed that I had no options and to keep him posted on what the Detailers tell me. Sure XO, I'll keep you posted. Mariner thinks I should get Skipper Foulk to help me through the back door since my chain of command is so useless. This shouldn't be so hard. Whaaaaa."

Kara was wonderful about writing her friends, old and new. Bound by their common goal to fly combat aircraft, she had become close to women pilots in other navy squadrons, and they shared their experiences. She wrote Brenda Scheufele about her CO, Commander Puckett, on 18 November: "My Skipper still hasn't talked to me about my FCF qual. He hasn't signed it. I flew the check flight two and a half weeks ago. I figure he needs to decide if he trusts me. If he does then let me get my quals without reservation. If he doesn't then Board me or trade me. I don't understand these non-confrontational wishy washy buffoons. It just isn't that hard."

Kara sent her mother a copy of one cartoon that pictured Indians with bows and arrows riding horses around a covered wagon. The sign over the entrance to the wagon said "CO's Office" and underneath there was a smaller instruction that said "Fitrep Debriefs Here." Beside the covered wagon, a friend is comforting a man who is lying on the ground with eight arrows protruding from various parts of his body. In the original cartoon, the arrows came from the Indians, but in the amended version everyone in the Ready Room understood that the arrows had been fired from Commander Puckett's office.

The wounded, arrow-pierced man is labeled "Kara," and she says, "Yeah, Ron, I hurt. But y'know, it's a *good* kind of hurt."

Kara finally had the long-anticipated conversation with Commander Puckett about her flight qualification and her performance in general. Their meeting didn't go at all as she expected it would. She described his revelations with amazement in a letter to Pamela dated 24 November 1992:

I had an interesting chat with Skipper Puckett yesterday. He finally decided to explain how he had NOT been sitting on my FCF qual (for three weeks), but that he wanted to make sure he had a chance to talk to me. He actually signed it three weeks ago.

In a nutshell—The best PAO he had ever seen (he never witnessed your performance as PAO, not that there is a competition there)—The best Division Officer he had ever seen (on par with Sue Still, spare me)—An obviously talented pilot in view of the video tape (Karash)—pushing for an award for me (that's funny because the Safety Officer was told not to write one)—wants to endorse my transition package—wants to make sure I have the best possible orders before he leaves—he never saw my last transition package—had no idea that the XO had signed my last endorsement—he is positive the XO had no idea that would be interpreted as a slam in DC (oh yeah I believe it).

My big problem was that I obviously was competing with the men because I wanted to prove that I (as a woman) could transition to a fleet seat. (Little does he realize that I compete with everyone not to prove anything, but as a way of life.)

I had suffered because I was so actively pursuing this goal of a transition. It was good, but he worried that I had the "Rosemary Syndrome" (no, I didn't smack him, but I felt like it)—doing the right things for the wrong reasons, being defensive, not admitting my mistakes.

He is convinced that I overstressed that jet (117) because Linda Heid was positive that I had, even though she never looked at the G meter. Well let us not take into account the time frame or the fact that four other pilots flew it after me or that the A sheets clearly show that I did not—or that [that] was 18 months ago. I didn't even say a word to defend that one—wouldn't want to appear defensive. (I should have said that I caused more fuel leaks than any man—didn't I?)

He said I've really improved though. Let's get back to the talented pilot part, the part about the positive endorsement. So I suppose it is good. He even quoted scripture to me, the message was that adversity built character. Yup, I'm a character, and he, unfortunately, is a caricature. So I'm going to whip out an updated transition package. It was actually a mostly positive counseling unless he is the best bold-faced liar I've ever met—which is entirely possible. He might even be better than Marc. Not that he's competing—I'm just comparing.

What's the difference between being constantly compared to others and competing with others? I suppose it's O.K. to be compared by others but when you make any comparisons yourself that's competing? Do I have this? It seems to me that one would do a lot better in the comparisons of others if they were competing too.

Chapter 39   *The Poem*

It's navy tradition that on 1 January a poem will be the first entry in the log of every command. The person assigned to be the squadron duty officer on 31 December is responsible. Since the watchbill comes out for the entire month, the lucky person knows in advance and can give it some thought. The rest of the officers always eagerly await it. As luck would have it, or possibly the intent of those who wanted to make sure the poem would be a memorable one, Kara was scheduled for the duty. She didn't disappoint them.

At the first AOM after 1 January 1993, Kara stood before all the officers in the squadron and introduced the poem: "I was tradition bound by rhyme and not reason to write this poem. The duty officer is going to read it aloud, and remember, if you can't laugh at yourself, just wait a stanza and laugh at someone else."

Lt. Perry Christiansen gave an inspired reading to a packed Ready Room. The junior officers loved it. The leadership was considerably less enthusiastic. You would have to know the people in the squadron in order to appreciate every verse, but some can be explained. The poem began as follows:

1 Jan 93 Logbook Poem
By Kara Hultgreen

To reflect on the year of ninety-two
If I were kind I would say, "It just blew!"
The EP-3J has made our life hell
A story not pretty, but one I must tell.

"Billy Ray" Puckett, the commanding officer, had taken the squadron's P-3Bs and, through single-minded determination, gotten all kinds of upgrades, new equipment, and prototype electronic gear installed. Then he lobbied heavily with Washington to get it declared a whole new airplane. Behind his back, the members of the squadron took to calling themselves "VX-33"; the VX designation for a squadron signifies that its primary mission is flight testing of aircraft and hardware. It was generally felt that "Billy Ray" was much more interested in his pet project, the P-3B, than in his responsibilities as skipper.

We wonder if Billy Ray has any clue
Morale of the men could stick to his shoe.

One stanza targeted a lieutenant commander, call sign "Jabba the Hut," who was not liked by anyone in the squadron. He addressed everyone by rank and last name. The story circulated that when he was a lieutenant (jg) in VQ-1, he had been regularly counseled on his lack of hygiene, one of his peers vowing that she would cross the street rather than give him first aid.

She zeroed in on Lester Cook for apparently never having heard the phrase "sexual harassment," and on a commander who was labeled the Excess O because he was promoted to commander but failed to screen for command.

"All the P-3 crew boast 40-knot brains," began one verse. (The dig was that the plane was slow and so was the crew.)

She gave praise where it was deserved also.

Now Harry and B. B., there's quite a pair
The advice they dispense, impartial and fair
Look out for your people, treat them with care
Be where you're supposed to be, when you're supposed to f'n
*   be there.*

Harry was Harry Ennis and B. B. was Tom King, a pilot whose favorite line for those who worked for him and those who flew with him was, "Be where you're supposed to be, when you're fuckin' supposed to be there!" The F word was his favorite expletive.

Harve in Safety with Wedge at his side
Safety standdowns so boring, we all nearly cried
Bring back old Boris, and standdowns of yore
Watching Jelly get smashed, we all cried—more, more!

"Harve" was Tom Walsh, the safety officer, and "Wedge" was Scott Wise, the NATOPS officer, both A-6 pilots and great guys. They supported Kara when she was trying to get her division lead and FCF qualifications. The reference to safety standdowns went back to when "Boris" (Pete Burris-Meyer) was safety officer. During a safety stand-down, he set up a demonstration on stage with the state police where various volunteers drank the same amount of liquor over a two-hour period. At the end, all were given breath tests to determine blood alcohol levels. The experiment backfired when one of the girls became hysterical at the barracks and threatened suicide. "Jelly" (Scott Hjelseth) was the only officer drinking.

Maniac and Moose, these O-4s are chicks
They fly in A-6s, but don't have the sticks
When compared to the men, the standard retort
Why on this earth would we sell ourselves short?

"Maniac" was Janet Marnane and "Moose" was Laura Sherman, both of whom were female naval flight officers.

Kara ended with:

We slave in a squadron bleak and bleary
Our futures not bright, my eyes are teary
With Clinton in office my vision through haze
A military "manned" with large women—and gays

Firebirds know we are only here to serve
But if you need a job—join the reserve!
Put that TAR package in, make it snappy
Bill and Hillary won't make you happy

I relieve the Duty this New Years Day
Oh, what's the point? We're Going Away!

The squadron was being decommissioned and people were bailing out or being forced out. Many tried the TAR route—training and administration of reserves—a program that gives officers a reserve commission and assigns them to reserve squadrons where they remain on active duty, doing the day-to-day work between reserve weekends. It is a popular community for pilots because they go to the logistics squadrons and fly C-9s, allowing them to get an ATP and type-rating, which are crucial for getting hired by the commercial airlines.

Kara told Pam, "Duty on New Years Eve was worth it just to write the New Years Poem."

⬛

Kara was moved to verse again a couple of months later after a cross-country flight she and Janet flew to Stamford, N.Y. The pitot heat switch was on, but the tube outside the fuselage that senses airspeed had gotten clogged, causing the airspeed indicator to go from 290 knots to zero. They managed to land safely and to have the mechanical problem fixed. However, before they could take off again, they got stuck in low ceilings and fog. Then, just as the weather cleared, they were picketed by right-to-life demonstrators.

A Poem

On a cross-country adventure and never merrier
In the goo at 290 it got a little scarier
Airspeed dropped to zero and we ain't no Harrier
There's one more seat cushion up my derriere

[A Harrier is capable of a zero forward airspeed because it can take off and land vertically.]

A malfunction of our naughty pitot heat
Caused this great tension in my seat
Lucky, we were, the AOA didn't fail
This card might never have seen the mail

[The AOA (angle of attack) gauge was working.]

Stuck next on the deck and the ceiling sank
On takeoff mins in this fog we could not bank
The weather was nasty, no need to pretend
This just might be the trip with no end
Takeoff from Stewart was further thwarted
Picketed by right to lifers after our takeoff was aborted
In the first trimester of runway, to abort is no sin!
Who are they to tell me, when does flight begin?

Chapter 40 ❧ *America Close-Up*

Kara had her mother writing letters again when the Bush-appointed Presidential Commission on the Role of Women in the Armed Forces recommended that a new law be passed to keep women out of air combat jobs. Though the conclusion was not unexpected in view of the makeup of the commission and although George Bush already had been defeated in the election, the female aviators were very upset. They had worked so hard, and now an appointed body stacked with Republican right-wing conservatives wanted to turn back the clock.

Sally Fountain, an aviator from VAQ-34 on the West Coast, wrote Kara on 11 November 1992, "The only thing I'll say is that everybody in D.C. realizes the commission has no credibility and no one really expects congress to act on the recommendations. I think the worst that will happen is that we'll be delayed a little longer, but it's conceivable the navy could still press."

On 15 November Sally wrote, "Talked to Commander Mariner tonight. She says she thinks everything will change in 6 months. And that even the Bush Administration is distancing itself from the Commission's report."

Rosemary Mariner had been leading the fight for women in naval aviation for a long time and was a mentor for Kara and her peers. Kara admired her greatly and looked to her for advice and counsel. On 23 November 1992, she wrote:

Dear Skipper Mariner:

Enclosed is the exciting Karash tape. If I can I'll copy my NBC three-second interview from last year onto the tape. It's a lot tougher than it looks to sound poised, intelligent, energetic, enthusiastic, focused, and natural on TV than I thought. If my sister Dagny (aka Dingy) can do it how hard can it be? I know what you're thinking— "Kara Hultgreen, just be yourself!" Well, as much as I like myself I think I'll stifle my personality a bit next time. My mother's only comment when she watched it was, " . . . (long pause) . . . weeellll . . . your skin looked good." I just couldn't ask for a better mother. I've also enclosed a copy of the letter Mom sent to Clinton.

The letter her mother wrote on 6 November 1992 to the newly elected president of the United States, Bill Clinton, was much like the letters she had written to members of the Senate Armed Services Committee in 1991, when she was supporting repeal of the combat exclusions laws.

"NBC wants to interview me again," Kara wrote Pam on 5 January 1993. "They are trying to arrange a flight with me and it is making Shadowtree and Brackett squirm. I get quite a bit of pleasure watching that." Naomi Spinrad, who had produced the NBC story on women in combat in May 1991, had remembered Kara, and nearly two years later, it was Kara she wanted to spotlight on the update.

On Wednesday, 13 January 1993, a television camera crew from *NBC Nightly News* came to Key West. The timing was critical because Clinton was about to be inaugurated, and it was expected that one of his first actions would be to direct that military policy be changed to allow women to fly combat aircraft.

It didn't happen exactly like that. The new socially aware president let himself be drawn into the emotionally loaded question of whether gays should be allowed to serve in uniform, and the women's cause was lost in the outcry. Fred Francis, busy covering the gay fray, didn't actually come to Key West to do the interview with Kara until three weeks after the first camera crew left. Kara said the interview "was delayed, rescheduled, canceled, delayed, rescheduled about six times."

She described the interview with Fred Francis in her journal: "He came to Key West and we sat by the pool at my complex. He was really nice. I was nervous. It would have been easy had they done it three weeks ago—I was used to having a camera two inches from my face. They sent down new camera people too."

The January crew had been cameraman Jim Nicholas; soundman Joe Valley; and producers Naomi Spinrad and Louis Clemens. They filmed for three days and got almost four hours of raw footage—Kara was the focus of most of it. She said that when Fred Francis interviewed her on 4 February, "Jim Nicholas' son, Chris, was the sound man and a camera guy I can't remember, and his daughter, Mimi. So there I was, surrounded by strangers, nervous as a long tail cat in a rocking chair factory, with the sun in my eyes—I'm sure I was squinting."

Sally Fountain, Linda Heid, Susan Dee, Nancy Nichols, and Janet Marnane were interviewed, but none of those interviews was used in the final piece; nor were the pictures of Kara and Janet walking down Duval Street at night in downtown Key West. Kara, Janet, and two men from a reserve unit, Chuck and Bucky, were taped playing golf, and although there was some great footage, it didn't make the cut. Kara had taken out her driver, the one her dad had given her for Christmas, and hit a huge drive straight down the fairway; then she kissed her "Big Bertha" on the clubhead, looked into the camera, and said, "Thanks, Dad." Another unaired segment showed Kara climbing out of her plane. She took off her helmet, shook out her hair, winked, and said, "Hi, Mom."

Amid rows of her navy squadron mates dressed in their whites, standing at attention during the change of command on 13 January, a striking profile of Kara looking straight ahead and serious was shone with her voiceover, "I say the pledge of allegiance and it means something to me. This country stands for freedom, equality, opportunity."

The next day, Kara was filmed getting into her flight suit, walking out to the plane, examining the plane, climbing into the cockpit, and sitting in the cockpit. Janet Marnane was flying with Kara, and in addition to her navigation duties, she agreed to take pictures with her HI-8 compact camera during the flight. "Shadownerd wouldn't let the [NBC] cameraman fly with me. He is such a worm. Janet did a super job though," were Kara's comments in her 1 February 1993 letter to Marc.

Kara wrote in her journal what she remembered saying to Fred Francis. "If I had thought of it, I would have taped the interview with my tape recorder. That would have been smart."

The first question he asked her was, "The gays in the military have gotten so much attention, do you think this will further delay a decision on the women's issue? Will the President not want to rock the boat by acting on another controversial issue?"

Kara responded:

I hope that doesn't happen. I also don't think this is a very controversial issue. Congress already represented the will of the American people and changed the law regarding women in combat aircraft. We have been studied for over twenty years. We are capable,
qualified, and willing. The Presidential Commission was disappointing because they spent a year on a fact-finding tour and
instead of basing their decision on the facts, they decided that
women shouldn't be POWs. The facts clearly indicated that women
are qualified, capable, have no negative effect on unit cohesiveness,
and should be given the same opportunities for advancement based
on performance.

She said she had her hair done for the interview "at Visible Difference,
and thankfully the humidity calmed it down. I told the chick I wanted
it to look conservative. Blow-dry it straight, take out the frizz, and use
a curling iron. I had three-mile hair by the time she was done. Yikes!"
Her recollection of the rest of the questions and answers was as follows:

> Q: This issue had a lot of momentum after the Gulf War. What hap-
> pened to that?
> A: A year of fact finding, stalling, and delaying is what happened
> to that.
> Q: What is your response to people saying that here is an attractive
> young woman and this is not who I want defending the coun-
> try and being placed in harm's way?
> A: I think it's about providing the best possible defense for our
> Constitution. That means placing the most qualified individual
> anywhere based solely on performance. The same type of indi-
> vidual is drawn to aviation [regardless of gender]. We are going
> to be aggressive, intelligent, athletic, and competitive. Not every
> woman or man is going to be successful as an aviator.

He asked her about Tailhook but they didn't use it in the segment, and
he asked her about landing her crippled airplane in Pensacola.

The interview aired the next week on the *NBC Nightly News*. Tom
Brokaw introduced the "America Close-Up" segment saying that there
had been "a lot of attention [given] lately to gays in the military, but

for many, the role of women in combat remains equally controversial. NBC News has now learned that the navy is ready to propose that all of its ships and planes be open to women, and that could force the combat issue."

It was interesting to see the result of hours of video taken and edited to make a story lasting only a few minutes. There was Kara in her flight suit on the runway at NAS Key West ready to climb into her EA-6A, her hands smoothing her hair, collecting wandering strands, "I swear, people always ask me that. What do you do with your hair?" She said it with a sideways glance at the camera, smiling and relaxed, an old hand at it now. Not only had they been filming her for three straight days, but also during the past couple of years, she had appeared on local television programs and given numerous newspaper and magazine interviews. She was used to it.

The next sequence showed Kara and Janet wriggling into their gravity suits. "Hardly high fashion," commented Fred Francis.

And back to the first shot of Kara beside her plane twisting her hair and tucking it under the collar of her flight suit. "I do this!" she said, hiding her hair with a flourish. "Now I'm ready to *don* the helmet." Her emphasis was on "don" and her expression was one of wry amusement.

Then Kara, dressed in shorts and a blue flowered shirt, was walking along the Key West Beach with Fred Francis. Next they showed the tape of Kara landing her crippled EA-6A at Pensacola that past October, her voice narrating what happened, "and the right main landing gear wouldn't come down."

Then the camera was again on Kara, the sun in her eyes, sitting by the swimming pool, and she was indeed squinting a little. Fred Francis asked her whether she was thinking that she had better not screw things up because she was a woman. "You don't necessarily want to be the chick that everyone talks about that screwed it up," she replied, then added, "but, you don't want to be the pilot that screwed it up, either."

The camera angle changed; Kara was saying, "It's about putting the most capable, qualified individual in any job based on their performance and abilities. The military doesn't hire killers. The military trains killers. And I'm just as willing and just as able to execute my training as any man."

Francis asked her how she would respond to those who focused on the consequences of being captured and raped.

"Raped? I can get raped walkin' across the street goin' to the grocery store and I don't see a presidential commission on how to prevent me from doing that.

"I'm willing to take the same risks that accompany all the opportunities. I'm willing to make those sacrifices."

The last pictures show Kara and Janet in their flight suits walking away from the plane; the focus is on Kara, holding her helmet under her arm, shaking out her hair and running her fingers through it like a comb.

Speaking for the soldiers in the culture war against women was Master Sgt. Sarah White, a member of the presidential commission that had found women just weren't qualified for any combat job. Master Sergeant White reminded Tom Brokaw of "unique specific differences between men and women. Men have the combination of strength and intelligence to do it."

Brokaw interrupted, commenting that not all that much strength was needed to fly an airplane. White responded that "Once you hit the ground, you instantly become a ground soldier and you have to escape and evade and you need every bit of your strength, and you can't depend upon your looks and your intelligence then."

Kara was perplexed at the sergeant's answer. She didn't know if her looks would help her or not if she were shot down, but she thought her intelligence would be a great asset. And she had been through survival training—stranded for several days without provisions in the cold and snow of Maine. She'd considered it a fine adventure.

After the interview aired, Kara wrote Pam: "I have had a lot of positive feedback from the NBC interview. My mother even liked it. Of course, when pressed for criticism she confessed that I really shouldn't have used the verb 'screwed'; it's not very classy, you know. Several reviews of the tape revealed that I need to work on my 'ing's'; that's right, it's flying not flyin' and going not goin'. Noted."

Monique also counseled that it would "probably be better if you don't use words like "chick" and "screwed." Kara had protested, "Mo, that's what my mother said. You're my best friend. You're supposed to tell me how wonderful I was. But instead, you sound like my mother."

Then Kara had laughed, "I just hate it when she's right."

When she was getting ready for the interview, Kara called Dagny to ask for advice. After all, Dagny was the television personality, the expert. She'd studied broadcast journalism at the University of Texas and had reported and anchored news broadcasts for the past seven years. Kara wanted to know what questions to anticipate, what to do to calm her nerves, how to deal with cameras, photographers; in other words, she wanted to know the tricks of the trade. Dagny thought about it for a minute, hmmmed, and said, "I think you should wear false eyelashes."

Kara loved to tell that story on her big sister— "typical Dagny," she said. Nevertheless, she took the advice, along with a few of Dagny's other makeup tips, and she looked beautiful on television.

Kara spent many hours preparing for that interview with Fred Francis. A lot was at stake and she wanted to do well. She found herself the spokesperson for all the women who were now her peers or who would follow her in naval aviation, and this was an opportunity to advance their cause on national television.

She began by making a list of possible questions and she started with the funniest, tritest queries she could remember ever having been asked. It was bizarre that the first question she came up with was the one that actually opened the NBC story.

1. What do you do with your hair?
2. Do you go med down when you suffer from PMS?
3. A friend of mine is in the navy, John Smith, do you know him?
4. Have you had to deal with a lot of chauvinism? [Her preferred answer to some of the questions could only be given in a select group of friends. She wrote them down for her own amusement.] Some of my best friends are chauvinists—and they know who they are. I always say, don't hate me because I'm a woman. Get to know me. I'd prefer you hated me because I'm so much smarter and more successful.
5. Can women kill?
6. Do you wear nonflammable lipstick?
7. Doesn't [flying a plane] take a lot of upper body strength? [The comparison of the upper body strength of men and women was

the fallback position for anyone determined to prove that women couldn't physically compete on an equal basis with men. But Kara did fifty regulation (male not female) push-ups every morning of her life, and many more than that on her Physical Readiness Tests. She figured everyone had to agree that anyone, male or female, who could do fifty push-ups had enough upper body strength to fly an airplane.]

8. Have you ever been scared?
9. Have you ever had to eject?
10. Have you ever crashed?
11. How do you go to the bathroom?
12. Why did you want to join the navy and fly?
13. Do you date men in the navy? Actually, I don't even encourage my boyfriends to join the navy. I tell them to finish high school and go to college.
14. Do you have a tattoo?
15. How do you feel about gays in the military?
16. Are you concerned about flying in the Bermuda Triangle? Only during the ³/₄ lunar phase.
17. How do you respond when someone says here is an attractive intelligent young woman and that is not who we want our warriors to be? If they aren't going to let the attractive intelligent young women defend the country, I don't think we should allow the attractive intelligent young men to do it either. Can you see the recruiter saying, "I'm sorry, not only are your test scores too high, but you are too good looking. The best thing that could happen to you now is an industrial accident. My suggestion is that you settle down and start reproducing more attractive intelligent Americans like yourself." Instead of, "be all that you can be," we could recruit with, "the ugly and ignorant only need apply. If your heart is set on being a navy pilot, lose a few teeth, scar up your perfect complexion, and shave your head, then come and sandbag the test scores."
18. Were you in Desert Storm?
19. How did you choose this career? Actually, it was really just a typo. I thought I was joining the USO and I ended up in the USN. I

thought I'd be singing for the troops and the next thing you know I'm tap dancing for the Skipper.
20. Were you at Tailhook?
21. Was your father in the navy?
22. What kind of little girl were you?
23. What's it like to land on a carrier?
24. How do they decide which aircraft someone flies? It's a mysterious process. I was under the assumption that it was based on performance and ability but now that I've been in the community a while I've determined that it is in fact based on looks. They send the best-looking pilots and NFOs to F-14s, the second best go to F/A-18s, and after that it's not pointy with afterburners so who cares.

Then the serious preparation started. She had learned that she had to think out her answers beforehand. When the question was put to you, the response had to be automatic or else you might say something you didn't mean, or worse, just stammer and look foolish because you were nervous. She had anticipated the questions asked in the actual interview and she had prepared for others:

> I joined the navy to serve my country, not for a career. The navy doesn't owe me, women, blacks, or any minority group a career path, but we should all be interested in providing the best possible defense for our Constitution. That means placing the most talented, dedicated, patriotic individuals in any position based on performance. Women have proven themselves capable in aircraft and have earned the right to fly in combat. We are willing to take the same risks and make the same sacrifices that accompany the opportunities.
>
> Why? Because I swore to uphold the Constitution of the United States of America. This country means something to me. It stands for freedom, and equality, and opportunity and these things are worth fighting for. They are worth killing for, dying for, and even being a POW for. It's even worth living on an aircraft carrier for six months at a time.
>
> I'd rather be a POW than be dead.
>
> My future in the service is entirely dependent upon the upcoming political policy decisions. I have a lot of confidence in President Clinton. I think he will look at the facts and make an educated

decision. If the policy had changed when the law did over a year ago, I could be on the USS *Kitty Hawk* right now. That is where I want to be.

If the policy does not change, I'll be out of a job as a navy jet pilot. That is an incredibly frustrating thought. I have almost one thousand hours in tactical jet aircraft. I've worked hard to get here and I have earned a fleet seat—based on performance.

Why should I be allowed to fly in combat? Why shouldn't I? It's about being an individual and realizing your potential as an individual, not being a man or woman or black or white. Being a woman is only one of my assets. Talent, intelligence, character, integrity, aggressiveness, spirit, and other qualities are going to play a bigger part in defining my abilities as a leader and a pilot.

You cannot convince me that women can be protected from the horrors of war. Or protect me from being raped. No one seems to care if I get raped on the way to my local grocery store; I'm just not allowed to get raped by the enemy. It doesn't make any sense. We are allowed to die in war. We are allowed to fly all the number one targets, like tankers. We are just not allowed to carry a gun and defend ourselves.

Tailhook: Yes I was there. My experience was much different than Paula's [Coughlin]. Her experience was not typical. The criminal actions of a very few people need to be dealt with, but fairly. The navy needs to move on.

Women on carriers: I absolutely agree with Secretary O'Keefe's comments to the Naval Academy Midshipmen. All naval ships and aircraft should be opened to women, and I also agree that women should be subject to the draft.

Stumbling blocks aren't in the fleet with Navy personnel; they have been with policies that are set by political appointees. It's doubly frustrating when the people making policy have often never served and have no concept of what affects combat readiness.

Why did I want to do this? The same reasons that attract men to aviation attract women. It is challenging, exciting, rewarding, and I love it.

The presidential commission: I agree with retired air force general Herres, the chairman of the commission, and the only fighter pilot on the commission. He argued for gender-neutral assignment to combat aircraft on a best-qualified basis.

Standards: You can bet the foot soldier calling for close air support cares that the best qualified aviator is going to get the job done and put the bombs on target. He or she won't care if that pilot is a man or woman when they do the job.

Black people do not serve because we "need" blacks. It's about having the best-qualified, best-trained individuals doing their job. Women don't have some right to do this, but it should be predicated solely on ability. We are held accountable to the same standards as the men to earn our wings. Allowing women to compete for jobs will only increase the quality and readiness of our forces.

POW issue: I am willing to take the same risk as anyone else. Freedom, democracy, equality for all people under the law, the Constitution, Mom, apple pie, ideals worth the risk and obligation.

Finish on an up note: Being a naval aviator is absolutely the greatest vocation in the world and I recommend it to any young man or woman.

Chapter 41 ✱ *I Have to Get Out of Here*

In little more than a month after that February 1993 interview Kara would complete her first navy tour. She was twenty-seven years old. The downsizing navy was causing career anxiety among men as well as women, but it was certain that very few women aviators would have any future in the navy if more positions were not opened to them, and that meant the combatant ships would have to be integrated. If they were not, Kara's choices would be either to fly A-6s in a reserve unit or get out of the navy. Her navy career would be over, along with her dream of becoming an astronaut.

Kara continued to send in her transition packages. She sought an endorsement from Capt. Kenneth Cech, commander, Light Attack Wing 1 (CLAW-1) and had an interview with him on 22 January 1993. She wrote her friend Marc, "The interview was slightly confrontational, but I think it went well."

> I also interviewed last Thursday with Admiral Bowman (F-18 pilot) [Rear Adm. Michael L. Bowman, chief of legislative affairs] for a job at the Office of Legislative Affairs at the Pentagon. I would be working directly for the Admiral as basically the Admin. Asst. He asked me, "So tell me Kara, why did you join the Navy?" and I replied, "Well, Admiral . . . sometimes I just don't think things through." He just about fell out of his chair laughing.
>
> I thought it was funny. I think that interview went well and I hope I get the job. I wouldn't be flying, but I would roll out of this chicken shit outfit in April and it would be a great place to be while I'm waiting for the combat policy to change.
>
> I keep thinking of that ancient Chinese curse— "May you live in interesting times." D.C. will be interesting this year.

Kara had considered requesting a transition to the marines to fly the Harrier, which really is a remarkable airplane. It is a Marine AV-8 jet aircraft designed specifically to support combat troops on the ground from close proximity. Using vectored thrust, the Harrier is capable of vertical take-offs and landings. The Harrier can be refueled and rearmed on the battlefield, and it doesn't need an airfield to take off and land.

One of her marine friends gave her what he said was a filched copy of the "Marine Aviation Qualifying Exam" so she could have a "heads up" if she decided to try to become a marine. The topics covered history, medicine, public speaking, biology, music, psychology, sociology, management science, and engineering.

The first question was on history: "Describe the history of the papacy from its origins to the present day, concentrating expecially [*sic*] but not exclusively, on its social, political, economic, religious, and philosophical impact on Europe, Asia, America, and Africa. Be brief, concise, and specific."

The assignment on biology was "Create life." On music: "Write a piano concerto. Orchestrate and perform it with flute and drum. You will find a piano under your seat."

To test engineering proficiency: "The disassembled parts of a high-powered rifle have been placed in a box on your desk. You will also find an instruction manual, printed in Swahili. In ten minutes, a hungry Bengal tiger will be admitted to the room. Take whatever action you feel appropriate. Be prepared to justify your decision."

And so on.

"As you can see I'm weak in the punctuation skills," Kara wrote Brenda Scheufele.

Maybe I'll make an excellent knuckle-dragging Marine. My mother says she really likes their "costumes" a lot better anyway. So I've got her support—which is nice. (What planet is she from you ask?—Texas—maybe Pam can explain. If so . . . explain it to me.)

The more I think about the idea—the more I like it. I'd fly Harriers in half a heartbeat and Hornets quicker than that. Think how proud my drill instructor would be—he thought I'd be President someday. He was a Marine, not a genius.

She wrote Suzanne Parker on 8 March 1993: "I had a very fun weekend—hung out with a couple of Harrier pilots. L.J. and Collin were a lot of fun. We snorkeled, sailed, watched *Seinfeld,* and ate sushi, but I didn't get any of the other S word—sleep. I am in lust with L.J. I kept thinking—this guy has such white teeth. . . . Hmm . . . I wonder what they taste like? I would have had to break *THE* major rule of engagement: *NEVER* date a Marine. Sex with a Marine is fine as long as it doesn't involve dating."

Kara was trying to go anywhere, just so long as it was out of VAQ-33. Ironically, however, even the option of holding over in the squadron for a while longer to try to wait out the policy decision was about to be taken away because the squadron was slated to be decommissioned in the fall. For Kara, each day of delay in changing the combat exclusion policy was critical.

She was unsettled and unhappy. Kirsten had sold her business in Austin and had moved to Los Angeles to be with Dagny, and Kara wanted to be closer to them. She wrote Pam on 3 January 1993 that she had "turned into a hermit in Key West. I hang out with Janet and Mike [Marnane] sometimes. Mike, an English major, is very well read and he has me reading all kinds of books and short stories. They broaden my horizons." Mike had been commanding officer of the squadron several years before Kara arrived.

Kara and her sisters spent Christmas 1993 at her dad's house in Appleton, Wisconsin. She told Pam: "Christmas was awesome. I was spoiled rotten—more than usual. Dad was in rare form and I am the proud owner of a new set of PING ZING golf clubs. Shot a 93 on 1 Jan [1993]—no pun intended. These clubs are amazing. I've been going to the driving range every day after work."

The squadron commanding officer, "Billy Ray" Puckett, was scheduled to turn over his command to Milton Shadowtree in less than two weeks. Kara had submitted a transition package that still hadn't left the command. "Calgon take me away," she moaned. "I didn't want to come back from leave." She was growing more and more anxious about how "Billy Ray" would deal with her request to transition to fly F/A-18s.

As it turned out, she was pleasantly surprised. She updated Pam two days later.

My transition package actually went out of the command yesterday. RRO (raving righteous one) actually wrote a very nice endorsement. Foulk is also going to endorse it and I'm sending it through CLAW [Captain Kenneth Cech in Cecil] and CNAL. ADM Less made a point of meeting me when he was at the squadron. He wanted to shake the hand of the pilot who landed that A-6 with a hung main. Having my gear not come down is turning out to be the best thing that could have happened to me.

Vice Adm. Anthony A. Less wrote Kara's mother on 28 October 1994 about his meeting with Kara. He was at that time president of the Association of Naval Aviation in Falls Church, Virginia.

I was the Commander Naval Air Forces Atlantic Fleet during a portion of Kara's tour at VAQ-33 in Key West. Approximately one month before Kara's very professional display of airmanship in handling the EA-6A main gear up landing in Pensacola, a young lieutenant encountered the same emergency, this time in an A6E at NAS Oceana Virginia, and considerable damage was done to the aircraft. When I heard how effectively Kara handled her emergency and how the aircraft damage was so minor that her EA-6A flew the following day, I made a note that on my next trip through Key West, I'd congratulate and thank this young female pilot. The opportunity presented itself and when I went to Kara's office I found her hard at work in her ground job, humble in accepting my praise and gratitude, and confident in her abilities. Needless to say, I was impressed and proud to have had her in our Atlantic Fleet Air Force.

Just wanted you to have the benefit of knowing your daughter was most respected and proved her unique capability to handle high performance jet aircraft. You can be justifiably proud of her accomplishments.

Kara spent a lot of time, as did other female aviators, doing everything she could do to bring about the demise of the combat exclusion policy as soon as possible. Kara and Brenda Scheufele drafted letters to the secretary of the navy, compared their drafts, and redrafted. They discussed what they should write and how they should write it. Kara didn't want to be "proselytizing or accusatory." She crossed out a paragraph, "about the attitude of people who would like nothing better than to see this fail."

Between the first and the final drafts, both the addressee and the message of Kara's letter to the secretary of the navy had changed. In early January 1993, before the NBC photographers came to Key West, Sean O'Keefe was navy secretary. By 4 February, when she actually did the interview with Fred Francis, Adm. Frank Kelso had been acting secretary of the navy for two weeks. And before Kara and Brenda had decided upon the final draft of the letter, Kelso recommended to the new secretary of defense, Les Aspin, a plan lifting the combat exclusion on navy ships.

All the navy women aviators were elated. Of course, they realized it wasn't a done deal; the final decision would be a political one. The fact that the navy formally had come out in support of its women aviators, however, was very satisfying. None of them cared whether the new navy position was a response to the bad publicity generated by the Tailhook scandal or whether the navy leadership finally realized it just wasn't fair to arbitrarily keep women out of certain positions. The important thing was that the women saw a glimmer of hope that things might actually change.

But after the women reviewed the plan, they were concerned about what Kara called its "quota-generating" and "standard-compromising" components. It stipulated that two women would be placed in each squadron in two airwings. A lot of schedules would have to be manipulated in order to guarantee two women in each squadron, including training and airwing deployments, not to mention squadron-manning requirements. Kara was very much opposed to quotas or any artificial rules just for women, and the letter she finally wrote to the acting secretary of the navy on 22 February 1993, was about that.

> Any quota system that places emphasis on numbers and timing rather than performance hampers operational readiness, jeopardizes safety, and creates an adversarial climate. Such discrimination on the basis of gender, both male and female, must be avoided. [She didn't think women needed the protection from men or the moral support from each other that a policy of having at least two women in each squadron assumed.]
> They [women] have already integrated successfully, both indi-

vidually and as a group, in the helicopter, VC, VT, VAQ, and VRC communities. Women will continue to integrate successfully on the basis of mutual respect for professional ability, regardless of numbers, in an individual unit. [Her position was that eliminating restrictions on women in the service should alleviate detailing problems, not create new ones.]

No professional aviator wants to be in a unit for any other reason than the basis of ability. Women are no exception. To work effectively, the detailing process must be able to disregard gender and continue to assign aviators to every community and airwing based upon *needs* of the Navy, performance, and desires.

Chapter 42 *DACOWITS Meeting*

On 17 April 1993, Kara flew to Washington, D.C., for the Defense Advisory Committee on Women in the Services (DACOWITS) spring meeting in Falls Church, Virginia, which was to begin the next day. DACOWITS was established in 1951 by George C. Marshall to assist and advise the secretary of defense on policies and matters relating to women in the military services. The committee had been recommending since 1975 that the combat exclusion laws be repealed.

The official navy recommendation that the combat exclusion on navy ships be lifted had been made two months earlier, and the female aviators wanted to do everything they could to keep the momentum going. Cdr. Rosemary Mariner had urged the young women to take advantage of the opportunity to talk to the DACOWITS members.

Lori Tanner from Pax River and Sally Fountain from VAQ-34, located at Point Magu Naval Air Weapons Station in California, came for the conference. Linda Heid arrived from VAQ-35 on Whidbey Island, Washington. She stayed with the Pucketts, who had moved to the beltway area after leaving Key West. "Billy Ray" had taken Linda under his wing when they were both in Key West.

Brenda Scheufele, Pam Lyons, and Sharon Cummins came from California and, along with Kara, stayed with Rosemary Mariner and her husband— "Mom and Dad Mariner's house," according to Kara. She labeled it "the DACOWITS spring slumber party and it was a blast. We all went to the cocktail party in our flight suits and schmoozed with the DACOWITS people."

Linda met Kara at the airport when she arrived Saturday, and they visited Naomi Spinrad and Naomi's small son, Luke. "Luke is adorable," said Kara. Naomi and Kara had become very good friends during the time they spent together in Key West while Naomi was producing the NBC stories in 1991 and 1993. That evening, Kara and Linda went to dinner at Chi Chi's with the Mariners.

Gen. Merrill A. McPeak, chief of staff of the air force, welcomed the assembly on Sunday. He was on the record as being against women in combat bombers and fighters, but his talk to the DACOW-ITS was about how much the air force had been doing for women. Kara and her friends were skeptical since the air force recently had decided that since women couldn't fly combat, it made no sense to train them to fly jets at all. After his speech, McPeak opened the floor to questions. Kara told Marc about it in a letter dated 25 April 1993.

> I immediately sprang to my feet and peppered him with several pointed inquiries. "General, I am LT Kara Hultgreen, an A-6 pilot from Key West, Florida. Why didn't the Air Force open all combat aircraft to women when the law was changed over a year and a half ago? Why, sir, do you think it is the wrong thing to do? Have you ever served in a squadron with female pilots, flown with or worked alongside women to come to this conclusion? I am currently in a squadron with men and women flying tactical jets and we don't have any unit cohesion problems."
>
> Lori Tanner got up next and said, "Unit cohesion is the only reason you have against women in combat squadrons? You currently have women in fully integrated tanker and transport squadrons; are you having any significant unit cohesion problems in those squadrons?"
>
> McPeak was stunned. There was a long pause and then he said, "None that I know of." He began to babble about how his argument was completely illogical but it was a cultural hang-up he had. He "felt" it was wrong for old men to send young women into combat.
>
> I was a hero to all the Air Force pilots that were too afraid to stand up. Apparently I was quoted in the *European Stars and Stripes* and made the Early Bird paper. It was a successful week all and all. Of course if the combat policy isn't changed soon, I'll be pretty much out of a job.

In her journal Kara wrote, "The Air Force women loved us. Lynn Martin, prior secretary of Labor, approached me afterward and said, 'Super job . . . I'm Lynn Martin and if you have any negative repercussions from this, you call me—I'm very powerful.'" Then Kara quoted Church Lady, one of her favorite *Saturday Night Live* characters, "Isn't that special?"

Capt. Rosemary Mariner said, "It was Kara taking on General McPeak that was the precipitating event responsible for changing the combat exclusion policy. Kara wouldn't back down and finally McPeak said what he really felt—that he had no real reasons why women shouldn't be flying; he was just prejudiced against it." On 28 April 1993 Les Aspin, the secretary of defense, announced: "The services shall permit women to compete for assignments in aircraft, including aircraft engaged in combat missions."

Chapter 43   *Wing Crunch*

"I just can't stand to be out of the negative numbers—zero is too high for me," Kara wrote in her journal after she got back to Key West from San Diego.

On the dark evening of 20 March 1993, she had crunched the left wing-tip of aircraft number 104, "trying to taxi from final checkers." "Luckily," she said, "it was only $25 damage to the fiberglass blister under the wing."

A detachment of her squadron was in southern California, getting ready to take off from Miramar. It was Kara's division lead check. The planes were lined up adjacent to each other on the taxiway and Kara had already gone through the first series of checks to make sure the moving parts of the plane were working and the engines were firing properly.

The plane captain signaled Kara that it was her turn to pull out of the line so that the "final checkers" could inspect the plane. Final checkers were plane captains and troubleshooters who went through their checklist before a plane took off to determine that there were no fuel or hydraulic leaks, that the wings were down-folded and locked, and that the flaps were down and ready for takeoff.

Kara taxied forward and pulled out of the line a little too far. The plane captain signaled her to make a hard right turn, then gave her an immediate brake signal. She turned to the right and came to a full stop so the final checker could complete his inspection of the aircraft.

Then the plane captain gave her a straight forward signal. She eased the throttle forward and released the brake, but after she started to pull forward he gave her an emergency stop signal. She felt the jerk and bounce of the brake lock. Neither she nor her navigator realized at the time that the wing of their plane had hit the wing of one of the other squadron planes parked in line on the other side of the runway. The pilot, Lt. Ellison, and the navigator, Lt. Ron Lotz, were standing on the wing near the fuselage, waiting to get into the cockpit.

The damage was easily repairable and under the $150 limit that would trigger an investigation and a ground mishap report, but the wingtips had impacted and they were "down," which meant they couldn't fly the mission that night. Kara's ECMO, Lt. William J. McDevitt III, who was also the assistant safety officer, was requested to write a memorandum about the incident to the VAQ-33 commanding officer.

The memo stated that when the plane captain appeared to give the straight forward signal, Lieutenant McDevitt attempted "to look across the cockpit and behind the pilot's seat to see the port wingtip. There were several ground crew standing at the wingtip to ensure clearance, several holding flashlights up, I assume to see the clearance better."

McDevitt thought the plane captain mistook the flashlights for the night "thumbs up" signal and that their wings were clear. "It was my feeling that all concerned acted properly, and that the impact was caused by what the Plane Captain perceived to be an 'all clear' signal when in fact it was not, only ground crew checking closer for wingtip clearance."

Kara had not forgotten the hard lesson she learned when she stood before the All Officers Meeting in 1991. She accepted responsibility and let others offer the excuses. On record in the safety report, she stated that as the pilot-in-command, she understood it was her ultimate responsibility to determine the wingtip clearance, and this crunch could have been prevented had they folded the wings before taxiing out of the line.

She had to depend on the ground crew to guide her because it was pitch black outside, and from the cockpit she had no way of judging the distance between the planes, but she wasn't going to be the one to say it.

But McDevitt's report was clear:

We hesitated folding the wings due to (1) not having folded the wings all week while accomplishing the same basic maneuver, (2) generally not folding the wings in this command, (3) having a tube on the outboard wing station. (Although this is not prohibited by NATOPS, in general, we do not fold the wings with stores on out-board wing stations.) (4) having already completed final checkers, we were hesitant to clean up, fold the wings, pull forward, respread, and reconfigure at night. The possibility existed that due to a break in concentration, we might not have dirtied up and ended up with a clean takeoff.

He meant that if they interrupted their normal checklist procedures by raising the flaps and folding the wings, and then lowering the wings and putting down the flaps, it would create so much confusion with other planes waiting their turn to take off on that dark night, something a lot worse could go wrong.

Chapter 44 *The Last Straw*

A twenty-five-dollar "fender bender" seemed a paltry catalyst considering the reaction it generated. Then again, it was a typical "last straw," a kind of nothing occurrence taken by itself that assumed great significance only because of what it meant to a particular person at a specific time. In this case, the person was Milton Shadowtree, who had become commanding officer of VAQ-33 on 13 January 1993—Kara's fourth CO in her nearly three years in the squadron.

In accordance with normal navy policy that, barring any unusual circumstances, the executive officer of a squadron always becomes the commanding officer, Shadowtree had succeeded "Billy Ray" Puckett. The electronic warfare support training community had fought to have the commanding officers of its squadrons come from the VAQ/VQ community and Shadowtree had screened through the normal aviation screening board. He was married to Cdr. Mary Shadowtree who was, like Pam, a general unrestricted line officer serving at that time in Washington, D.C. She was supposed to be coming to Key West for her next tour.

The navy had just gone on record that it was in favor of women being allowed to fly combat aircraft, and it was looking as if Kara might actually be successful in her quest to fly fighters. As her commanding officer, Shadowtree would have to endorse her transition, and he wasn't sure what to make of her.

Shadowtree had arrived in Key West to become "Billy Ray" Puckett's executive officer at the very end of 1991. But he heard the true account of how in the beginning of the year, Kara almost lost her airplane and her life—and he heard the Kara "fables" that were founded on jealousy and speculation. Gossip clung to Kara like steel shavings to a magnet.

If she was at the officers club in her flight suit, laughing and telling jokes, brash and beautiful, basking in the special light she lived in, a newcomer like Shadowtree or a visitor would ask, "Who is that?" And there would be someone to tell him how she had overstressed her airplane in May, landed on a "taxiway" in Norway, folded her wings with the flaps down in Spain, and blown her tire landing in Denver. "She's one of those females who wants to fly off carriers. She's a competent enough pilot, but she's overconfident and aggressive, always trying to prove something because she's a woman," they would explain.

As a "P-3 tube guy," Shadowtree was used to dealing with the "I'm a pilot, you're not, so don't tell me how to fly the airplane" swagger of male pilots, but he hadn't been subjected to that direct look-you-right-in-the-eye "attitude" from a woman pilot. He hadn't forgotten that Kara had caused him to be reprimanded by Captain Foulk for telling her she should get out of the navy and have babies.

However, she did make perfect scores on her physical readiness tests and nearly perfect scores on all her NATOPS exams. Her fitness reports from her ground jobs in maintenance and electronic warfare were outstanding; she never shirked any responsibility, and whatever extra job she was assigned she did promptly and expertly. Of course, he rationalized, these also were characteristics of what older aviators used to call "failing aviator syndrome," where a struggling pilot strives to make up on the ground for shortcomings in the air.

But what about her excellent performance in October when she had brought her plane in for a landing with only one main landing gear functioning? The video had been broadcast in all the navy Ready Rooms in the country and on the carriers as an example of a picture-perfect emergency landing. Kara clearly loved flying, and with the exception of a couple of lieutenant commanders from the days of the old O-4 Brute Squad, everyone who flew as her ECMO loved to fly with her. She had to be a competent pilot because navigators don't want to risk their lives flying with a pilot they don't trust.

On the other hand, she was continually creating a stir talking to the press and appearing on television. She submitted transition packages every quarter, which caused everyone a lot of trouble, and she was not only trying to get out of the squadron but also lobbying congressmen and senators to change the law. That was not something a military person had any business doing. To top it off, she was doing it in her flight suit, which though it had been romanticized in movies, was considered "work clothes" by the navy and wasn't supposed to be worn off the base.

In September 1992, when a detachment of the squadron was in California, Shadowtree decided he would do QA, or quality assurance, flights with Kara to check up on her and see how she was doing—get firsthand knowledge of her aviation skills.

Shadowtree had never crewed in the right seat of jets before coming to the squadron nine months earlier. Then he flew some in the back of the A-3, which is a jet but doesn't have ejection seats, and some in the right seat of the EA-6A, but he went on very few detachments and most of his flight time accrued in transit to various conferences and meetings. Kara at the time of the QA flights had more than 850 pilot hours.

Shadowtree hadn't had an easy time getting through his navigation training in the A-6. One instructor had found it necessary to write a script for him so he would know what to say on the radios and said he didn't even know how to call ground for taxi. His decision to QA Kara's flying caused more than a few snickers in the Ready Room.

Kara's opinion of Shadowtree's aviation qualifications was a one-line entry in her journal in January 1993, "The XO failed his closed book NATOPS test. What a joke!"

NATOPS is the sum of all knowledge relating to flight written down in manuals. It describes all the aircraft systems, how they work, emergency procedures, and other information to safely fly the aircraft. Naval aviators have to memorize it and every mission brief and officers' meeting is an occasion to review NATOPS procedures. Annual tests are required for every pilot and flight officer. The executive officer of the squadron should pass the annual NATOPS test.

One of the QA flights was a night flight. Janet Marnane, who was an experienced and capable naval flight officer, briefed Shadowtree extensively on operating out of NAS Miramar because radio communications out of San Diego are extremely busy at night and are a crucial aspect of flying there. The ECMO has to understand the system thoroughly in order to communicate with the different agencies that control the crowded southern California skies between San Diego and Los Angeles.

When Shadowtree flew with Kara that night, he stepped on other transmissions, was too verbose, and didn't listen. Kara didn't have a good flight either, but Shadowtree probably had no idea what her shortcomings were until he listened to the safety officer, "Wedge," debrief her after the flight.

Kara commented on her experiences flying with Shadowtree in her 4 October 1992 letter to Pam. "I just got back from Miramar—I love SOCAL. Unfortunately I spent the DET flying with the XO. He wanted to evaluate me for himself—like his years of experience in the tube of a P-3 qualify him." And she continued wryly, "Fortunately I was able to fly very safely and I only rolled inverted when it was absolutely necessary."

But whatever Shadowtree's qualifications were to evaluate her aviation skills, in March 1993 it looked as if he would have to decide whether or not to endorse Kara's request to transition to fly a combat aircraft. He had heard from the day he arrived at the squadron that Kara was overconfident and a bit of a daredevil. Maybe it was understandable that he would be scared to death of sending such a controversial woman to be one of the first women ever to fly in a fighter squadron.

With the twenty-five-dollar wing tip crunch fresh in his mind, the XO picked up the telephone and called his administrative boss, Capt. Kenneth Cech, commander, Strike Fighter Wing Atlantic, at the naval air station in Cecil to talk to him of his concerns about Kara.

Shadowtree told Janet Marnane that he and Captain Cech came to the mutual decision that a Human Factors Board was an appropriate response. Janet, along with the safety officer, the A-6 NATOPS officer, and the training officer, tried to convince Shadowtree that a board was not required.

A Human Factors Board (HFB) is a safety tool available to every aviation command to help reduce mishaps due to aircrew errors. Its purpose is to identify aircrew whose flying performance is being adversely affected by personal problems and recommend positive measures to help them get back on track before they cause a mishap. The board investigates whether there is something bothering the pilot. The intention is to find it and fix it.

The HFB is not like a Field Naval Aviator Evaluation Board (FNAEB), where the purpose is to review the competence of aviators and by the time they get there, they had better have some good facts on their side or they will find themselves grounded—FNAEBd. The FNAEB addresses the aeronautical judgment and flight discipline of aviators. It doesn't make recommendations for disciplinary action, but it does make recommendations for their continued service.

Navy publications stress that the Human Factors Board is not a reactive measure to be taken when the aircrew's performance is so unacceptable that he or she is one step away from being FNAEBd. Human Factors is to be used as a positive step to improve aviation safety.

A board is usually convened at the squadron of the person who is called to appear before it. Back in September 1992, "Billy Ray" Puckett, the commanding officer at that time, had issued instructions establishing a Human Factors Standing Board for his command. His instructions stated that the membership of the board "shall consist of the Commanding Officer, Executive Officer, Operations Officer, Safety Officer, Flight Surgeon, and such others as the Commanding Officer may direct."

But Kara's HFB was to be held at NAS Cecil rather than at the squadron, and no squadron member, not even Milton Shadowtree, the commanding officer, was to be a member of the board. That caused a lot of talk.

Shadowtree's version in his explanation later to the Ready Room was that having the board take place outside the squadron would give Kara the best possible chance for a fair hearing, since rumors had been flying for so long about her abilities. Janet said she didn't understand that reasoning since none of the A-6 crews scheduled to appear as witnesses thought Kara deserved the board.

In fact, the rumors had stopped flying in the A-6 community long before, when "Lightning" and "Weasel" had transferred out. The only people who still seemed misled were the P-3 community, which included the commanding officer, the executive officer, and Commander Brackett, a P-3 pilot who had come to the squadron, some suspected, to actually do "Billy Ray" Puckett's job. When "Billy Ray" was XO, he spent most of his time on the phone and had never even visited the enlisted barracks, something most XOs do on a daily basis. It appeared to squadron members that Captain Cech had taken the decision out of Shadowtree's hands. It didn't make sense that the commanding officer of a squadron would voluntarily give up a major responsibility of his command—which included not only the powers to convene and appoint the members of the board but even his right to sit on it. After all, that board would be deciding the fate of one of his officers.

Kara told the whole story to Marc Baron in a letter dated 25 April 1993, beginning with the wing-tip crunch:

> How's life with the Shadow and Briquette? Well, let me tell you the latest tale of Firebird buffoonery:
>
> On det in SOCAL I was under positive control of a plane captain and very cautiously taxiing at night, and I crunched the left wing tip. $25.00 worth of damage—my fault—sorry—bill me. The Shadow decided to call up the Commodore (Capt. Cech) in Cecil and give him the "Kara history." The Commodore had previously interviewed me and strongly endorsed my transition package; he was naturally quite concerned when my CO tells him about a departure, an overstress, an aileron roll below 1K, a taxiway landing in Norway, a dirty wing fold in Spain, a VIP scare with Capt Curry, and now a $25.00 wing tip crunch. . . . Let's not mention that most of these things are "rumored" to have happened before the Shadow came to 33. I think Milton wanted the Commodore to take his word for everything and just sabotage my chances for a Hornet transition.
>
> Things backfired on him when the Commodore decided to have a Human Factors Board up in Cecil.

Kara prepared carefully for the event. She got written statements from people who were no longer in the squadron including her prior boss in maintenance, Wayne Lockley, and a prior commanding officer, Capt. Bruce Nottke. She wanted to know what to expect and consulted with Cdr. Rosemary Mariner and Mike Marnane. As she did for her television interviews, she wrote down possible questions and answers. It wasn't difficult because she had documented in her journals all the events as each one happened.

The last thing she did was go shopping for the highest pair of brown heels she could find. They were going to have to look up to her.

Chapter 45 *The Human Factors Board*

The letter came in a bright yellow envelope addressed to LT KARA HULTGREEN at the squadron. The words "PREGNANCY TEST RESULTS" were printed in big letters across the top of the envelope and it was marked PERSONAL AND CONFIDENTIAL. It was postmarked Key West FL, 6 April 1993, and it looked authentic. Everyone from the mailman to the commanding officer expressed great interest in that envelope before Kara ever saw it; and there was a crowd around to watch her open it.

The joke wasn't up to Comedy Club standards, except for the spelling and punctuation, but everyone, including Kara, thought it was pretty funny. It relieved some of the tension she was feeling about having to face a Human Factors Board.

The letterhead, poorly typed, said, "KEY WEST FAMILIY SERVICES CENTER, 801 DUVAL ST, KEY WEST, FL 33040."

> Dear Miss Hultgreen,
>
> This letter is to inform you that your pregnancy results from 1 April 93 are complete. CONGRATUATIONS!!! YOUR PREGNANT. You must be thrilled! The thought of little Kara's running around must be heart warming.
>
> We understand the joy of this ocasion is deminished somewhat by the fact that you do not know who the father is. Well, we understand these things happen. We suggest that you contact your United States Department of Social Services for some free money from the Aid to Families with Dependent Children Program. In addition, we have enclosed some birth control information for future reference in case you decide to use some.
>
> We would also like to inform you of our other fine services available;
>
> 1. *ABORTIONS 'R' US CARE CLINIC:* should this news not be so happy.

2. *HAPPY LAND HOME FOR UNWED MOTHERS:* only if you decide to carry this baby to full term. (some restrictions apply)

3. *DISCOUNT BABY ADOPTION AGENCY:* (all expenses paid!!!!) Guarenteed to be delivered to a family that knows quality and is willing to pay for it.

For further information feel free to contact us at our new offices at 801 Duval St. or call us at BR-555.

WARMEST REGARDS,
DR. I FEELGOOD DR, ASC, QUI, OBGYN, AFU

On Thursday morning 20 April 1993 at 0615, Milton Shadowtree, six lieutenant commanders, and Kara piled into a P-3 in Key West and left for Naval Air Station Cecil. Kara summed up the delegation in her letter to Marc: "So last Thursday the merry band of morons from 33 jumped in a P-3 and flew to Cecil for my Board. B.B., Putt, Chuck, Janet, Bill McDevitt, T.J. (big fat new guy Safety Officer loser don't know why he went), Shadowslime and I all went to tell the sad story. [Amy Boyer, Kara's roommate, was already in Jacksonville on detachment.]"

"Walking up to CLAW 1, Skipper Shadownerd asked me how I was feeling," Kara recorded in her journal. She was recovering from a bad cold. "I said my voice is almost back to normal and I'm off the drugs, so I'm feeling better. He said, no, I mean emotionally how are you doing? I said, I'm fine, this is just another trial and tribulation that I'll live through and write about in my memoirs. He looked pale and pasty and nervous."

Cdr. Carroll L. White, a Hornet pilot who had been the commanding officer of an F/A-18 squadron, chaired the meeting. The other members of the board were Lt. Cdr. Karen L. Builder, a reserve C-9 pilot; Lt. Steve Parker, an instructor at VFA-106; and Lt. Cdr. Leonard R. Klein, the flight surgeon. Kara's description of the makeup of the board was concise: "A post command FA-18 skipper headed the board, a female LCDR made it politically correct, an instructor and the flight surgeon from the Hornet RAG were also board to death."

In addition to Kara, the following officers from VAQ-33 were interviewed: Cdr. Milton Shadowtree, Lt. Cdr. Tom King, Lt. Cdr. Tom

Jones, Lt. Cdr. David Dominicci, Lt. Cdr. Marvin Gardner, Lt. Cdr. Janet Marnane, Lt. William McDevitt, and Lt. Amy Boyer.

Statements from Lt. Cdr. Wayne Lockley, who was then stationed at Strategic Air Command in Omaha, Nebraska; AMCS(AW) Paul Jensen from VAQ-33; and Capt. B. A. Nottke who was with Navy Space Command were received and reviewed.

It was afternoon by the time Janet talked to the board. "The questions were fairly innocuous," she said, "and didn't deal with any real specifics but were more along the lines of what I thought of Kara as a pilot, officer, and person. I got the distinct impression as I talked that everything I said had already been heard by the board from others, and that their minds were already made up."

Lt. Cdr. Leonard R. Klein, the flight surgeon, interviewed Kara alone before the formal meeting. It was fortunate for her that he was a flight surgeon in an F/A-18 squadron and dealt every day with people whose attitudes were just like Kara's—straight ahead, go-for-it kind of people. Kara's account to Marc of their conference was as follows:

> I spoke to the flight surgeon first and he finished asking about all the "incidents" and then said, "Why in the hell are we doing this? These all seem really stupid. I don't know a pilot on this base that hasn't come into the break faster than 400 KIAS or rolled inverted on an airway. And $25.00 of damage is hardly worth discussing. Is your Skipper out to get you?"
>
> Now I had already decided to avoid the horses-ass vindictive SOB interpretation of my Skipper. I felt the innocent victim would yield more sympathy—even from hardened warriors. So I said, "Absolutely not! He is genuinely concerned. He's just not an aviator. He spent his entire career in the tube of a P-3 and doesn't have the background to sift through this. Unfortunately, I think he didn't really have all of the facts before he initiated this. I didn't know he was concerned about all of the rumors from the past—he never asked me about any of them."

The flight surgeon's evaluation report dated 23 April 1993 was sent to the senior member, Human Factors Board, Light Attack Wing One (Captain Cech). The report summarized the facts in paragraph one, and then concluded as follows:

2. LT Hultgreen reported to VAQ-33 after completing a CAT-V flight syllabus at the A-6 FRS. This syllabus entailed only 30 hours of actual flight time in the A-6. With only 170 total flight hours, she was flying home in poor weather, had a partial panel and nearly departed the aircraft while on final approach to NAS Cecil Field. She recovered without incident, but upon reporting this incident at a hostile squadron safety AOM, she was labeled as an unsafe aviator. Since that time, she has felt that she was under a microscope and everything she did was scrutinized.

Since that time, she has had multiple incidents while flying the EA-6A that do not appear to be anything more than "nugget" mistakes. These incidents include an alleged aircraft overstress, an inadvertent wing fold causing damage to the wing, landing on a taxiway used as an alternate strip in Norway, doing an aileron roll to descend while on an IFR airway, entering the break at NAS Oceana at 350–400 knots, and most recently, taxiing the starboard wing of her aircraft into another aircraft.

Taken as a whole, these incidents appear to be significant, but taken individually, LT Hultgreen appears to have acted appropriately in most of these incidents. She did not appear to be at fault for some of these events, yet it was passed from the outgoing CO to the incoming CO for three Changes of Commands that she was unsafe. When the current Commanding Officer observed the wing crunch occur, a[n] HFB was convened to see if a trend was developing.

3. LT Hultgreen began the Training Command in January 1988 and received her wings in August 1989. During her training, she received only two SODs [signal of difficulty], one during a T-2 safe for solo, and one during a T-4 tac turn hop. Both times she responded without difficulty. She completed the A-6 FRS without difficulty. LT Hultgreen's ultimate goal is to be an astronaut, but currently she desires to fly the F/A-18 and is active in campaigning for women in combat aircraft. She currently has an application pending for transfer to the F/A-18. She describes herself as an above average pilot and is very dedicated and motivated to continue flying.

4. LT Hultgreen is single and occasionally dates, though this is not a priority in her life at this time. She feels that her career is more important, and a family will come later. She has multiple friends in the squadron to confide in, but she has a strict policy not to date any-

one from her squadron. She currently denies any financial burdens, legal proceedings, extended family problems, or sexual problems.

Kara's description to Marc of that part of the interview is more vivid than the written report: "Then he started asking all the personal questions, 'Do you have a boyfriend? No? Is that a problem? Do you wish you had a boyfriend?' And I said, 'Are you flirting with me? Hey look, I live in Key West and I've met a lot of cute funny nice guys, but unfortunately they already have boyfriends.'"

The flight surgeon's report continued:

Her parents have been divorced since she was very young, but she still keeps in touch with both of them, and they are very supportive of her career choice. She does not smoke and drinks alcohol on occasion. She is very active in "Women in the Military" issues but denies being outcast from her squadron for her position. She also denies sexual harassment from her squadron mates and does not feel that she is prejudiced against or for her gender. She denies any medical illness at this time, but she is awaiting a return to flight status after being grounded for a short time for a mild cold.

She appears appropriate and cooperative and displays no evidence of psychological disease. She describes herself as aggressive and competitive and strives to be the best. She states that she learns from all her mistakes and has even included items into her pre-flight brief that she felt caused her near mishap. She remains extremely motivated to fly, and especially would like to fly single seat aircraft.

5. In conclusion, LT Hultgreen appears to be the typical aggressive, competitive, and confident Naval Aviator. Her only problem appears to be that she has been a nugget under the microscope. While her mistakes have caused some damage, she appropriately has learned from them and has incorporated these changes into her habit pattern. Since VAQ-33 has changed command officers three times since her arrival, she has been unable to shed the "dangerous aviator" label, and thus had been scrutinized by each CO.

Appropriately this HFB was called to explore her trends and stresses. She appears to be a solid aviator and would most likely make an excellent single seat pilot. No other human factors are involved at this time. LT Hultgreen is currently physically qualified and aeronautically adaptable for duty involving actual control of the aircraft as a Service Group I aviator.

Janet and Kara talked about what had happened at the board when they got back to Key West. Janet said Kara "got the impression from the flight surgeon that after their talk, he was equally as stumped as the rest of us as to why she was there."

Kara summed up the Human Factors Board meeting in her letter to Marc:

> Well to make a long "boarding" story short—the board had no problems with me, my attitude, my flying, anything. The head of the board said I would do fine in any fleet squadron including any one in Cecil. He said this event would not hurt me and it will help me if anything. My debrief lasted about 3 minutes.
>
> The Shadow's debrief lasted over an hour with the Commodore. I would have loved to be in on that one. He tracked down Ben Jergens for a statement about me. Good old Ben. I can't wait to read that one. Last December he had tried to get Linda Heid to document in writing that I had overstressed the jet two years ago. [Linda thought Kara had overstressed the jet, but she couldn't be absolutely sure of it, so she refused Commander Shadowtree's request.]
>
> It was gratifying to see real pilots listen to these stories and roll their eyes in disbelief. I was so proud of myself too.

Although no minutes or written reports were required, in this case, since it was the commodore who requested the HFB, a report was prepared by Cdr. Carroll L. White and sent to commander, Light Attack Wing 1, with a copy to VAQ-33 and Kara.

In the first three paragraphs, the report listed the members of the board, personnel interviewed, and statements received. The findings were set out in paragraphs four and five:

> 4. The HFB was precipitated by a minor ground wing tip crunch that was the latest in a series of actual and alleged incidents in which LT Hultgreen was involved. She is a 1310 with 1000 flight hours who has been flying EA-6As for VAQ-33 for three years. She is active with women in the Navy issues and has applied for transition to Hornets. The board found no life "stressor" or medical conditions that would adversely affect her performance.
>
> Her involvement and alleged involvement in several air incidents was examined for adverse trends in performance and judgment. Several incidents were totally unsubstantiated and several other inci-

dents involved a perception of poor judgment that was unsubstantiated. LT Hultgreen has made mistakes, which she fully acknowledges, but the board found no pattern of performance that is unsafe.

She is an aggressive and ambitious officer whose development parallels that of the typical junior aviator. LT Hultgreen is respected by both pilots and aircrew with whom she has flown and is considered by her peers to be a thoroughly professional pilot and flight lead.

5. LT Hultgreen was highly motivated to return to flight status. She exhibited no physiological, psychological, social, or professional traits that could preclude her ability to safely operate tactical jets.

Chapter 46 *The Fortune Teller*

"This is sort of like being able to vote. This is historic. . . . I feel super, I'm ecstatic, I'm thrilled," Kara told the *Navy Times.*[1] She said she felt like a pioneering suffragist in early twentieth-century America. Secretary of Defense Les Aspin had announced on 28 April 1993 that all combat aviation squadrons in the navy would be open to women. "As opposed to last week," Kara continued, "when they said my best option was to get out of the navy."

"I'm really proud of the navy," she exclaimed. "It was the navy that said, 'We have a plan, we'll implement it, we'll have people on carriers within a year.' The navy was ready to move two years ago, well before Tailhook. The only thing holding us back was this law." Kara was referring to the exclusion laws prohibiting women from flying combat aircraft. Though the laws were repealed in October 1991, it took another year and a half for the services to formally change their policies. Dick Cheney, secretary of defense under George Bush, had decreed that the services could take no action until the presidential commission made its recommendations.

Kara summed it up: it was either open squadrons to female aviators or face "a huge setback for women in the Navy."

She sent the *Navy Times* article to her mother, explaining,

> We affectionately refer to this rag as the *Navy Enquirer,* but I am featured in the article. I can't decide if I'm glad they didn't have a photo of me on file or not. I almost wish the publicity would go away now that the policy has changed. On the cover are Brenda Scheufele, T. J. Shults, and Pam Lyons.
>
> I still don't know what is in store, but I've been talking myself into F-14s. There is no way they will let me go F/A-18s on the West Coast, and it would be so nice to live in San Diego. The F-14s may move to Lemoore CA in two years though. Lemoore is where the F/A-18s are now and north of Fresno I think.

The Tomcat community would definitely be the toughest community to crack into (no pun intended). There has never been a female Tomcat driver. If anyone is going to do it—I really think I'm best suited to be the first. I've spent the last three years training in an abusive environment and I will have the advantage of having made mistakes here that I won't have to repeat there.

Keep your fingers crossed!!

Just days after she wrote that letter, Kara was assigned to Miramar Naval Air Station in San Diego, California. She would train to fly the F-14A Tomcat of *Top Gun* fame, the epitome of "something pointy with an afterburner." It was the navy's premier fighter with sophisticated weapons systems allowing it to track up to twenty-four targets and attack six at a time. Though appreciative of the mystique surrounding the F-14, it took her a while to understand the significance of her orders. For naval aviation, a female flying the F-14A variable wing supersonic fighter with its fierce weapons was a huge event.

For Kara, it was something of a letdown. Her dream of flying a combat aircraft had come true, but she had always thought it would be the F/A-18 Hornet, the newest navy aircraft, with a single seat and state-of-the-art electronics. Never, until the last few days, had she considered flying the F-14.

It was an old airplane and worse, a two-seater, and she would be flying the A model of the F-14 rather than the D model with its improved systems and General Electric F-110 engines. The A model was powered by Pratt and Whitney TF-30 engines, infamous for being underpowered and stall-prone, "an airline engine on a fighter," making the F-14A a dangerous airplane to fly. More than 120 F-14s had crashed before Kara got her orders. It was not disputed that all the TF-30 engines must be replaced, but $2.5 billion dollars was needed to do it, and apparently the government had better places to spend the money. In the meantime, the pilots were required to "fly the engines" rather than the plane.

Kara told her mother about her assignment with pride, but she didn't have the same excitement in her voice as she had when she told her that all the combat aviation squadrons in the navy were now open to women. It was a muted reaction considering all the effort she had expended to achieve her goal.

Kara had things to do in order to check out of her squadron, including attending the official Hail and Farewell. Milton Shadowtree introduced her to the gathering, wished her well in her new assignment, and then congratulated her for having her name cleared by the Human Factors Board. It was entirely inappropriate for him to bring that up at a party, and Kara was very embarrassed. The new people just checking into the squadron were completely confused, and it just invited speculation and questions all over again.

Kara rolled her eyes, but she got up and said, "Thank you for your kind words, Skipper." Then she said she was excited about flying F-14s, and she sat down. She had learned that in VAQ-33, nothing made any sense, and she left the party as soon as her part was over.

Janet and Mike Marnane gave a wonderful party for her before she left Key West. The highlight was a song played by Tom Walsh on his guitar and sung by Tom's wife, "George," and Janet Marnane. The words, written by Tom and Janet, were set to the tune "Eighteen Wheels and a Dozen Roses." Kara inspired the choice when she explained to a television reporter in Miami that the difference between flying an F-18 and an EA-6A was like the difference between driving a Ferrari and a truck with "eighteen wheels and a bad alignment." It made a great song title.

Eighteen Wheels and a Bad Alignment

Kara got her gold wings
Thought they'd mean everything
Then she spent her years runnin' round the world with Thirty Three
Well, Kara's seen some real strife
Now she's off to live the good life
Gonna fly her fighters and finally be free

Of eighteen wheels and a bad alignment
One more night and then she's through
With three long years in a bad assignment
Now she'll spend the rest of her life in a jet she can love

These years have been a real test
Tryin' to stay away from Key West
Knowin' there was somewhere else she'd really rather be

But Kara's gotta leave now
Gonna go away to sea now
With the Blacklions on the Lincoln *and then she'll be free*

Of eighteen wheels and a bad alignment
One more night and then she's through
Three long years in a bad assignment
Now she'll spend the rest of her life in a jet she can love

Yes, she'll spend the rest of her life in a jet she can love.

Kara wanted to make sure she had a tape recording of the song, so Tom came over later to Janet and Mike's house with his guitar and he, Janet, and Kara sang it for posterity. Mike was the audience. Kara forgot to turn her tape recorder off and it picked up their conversation after they finished singing the song.

"Look at my car," Kara giggled, pointing to the Mazda RX7 she was going to drive across the country from Key West to San Diego. "It's *so* small." But it didn't really matter to her that she could hardly get her gear in it. It more than satisfied the "jet pilots must drive fast sports cars" requirement, going from zero to sixty miles per hour in 4.9 seconds. "Five very fun seconds, I might add," she had written Brenda Scheufele in November 1992 when she got the car.

The tape continued, recording the conversation between Kara and Janet about their visit to Rachel the fortune teller.

"You remember everything bad that happens to you," Rachel told Janet.

Kara laughed. "She said the same thing to me." And somberly imitating Rachel, Kara intoned, "I don't hold grudges, but I don't forget either."

Janet said Rachel advised her, "For the rest of this year your relationship will be good."

"For the rest of the year?" they laughed, "Oh, great," Kara said. "You will have a good relationship for almost a year." Janet's husband, Mike, halfway listening, chuckled.

"Did she see you moving?" asked Kara.

"She said that in the next year I would be offered opportunities that I had been denied previously—that I really deserved," responded Janet. "But she said I may have a lot of enemies that I might not know who they are, so 'It's best to keep all your plans to yourself.'"

"Actually," said Kara, "that's pretty funny, because Rachel was saying similar things to me about not trusting anybody or anybody else's advice, because there were all kinds of people who were trying to give me advice and a lot of them were trying to give me bad advice on purpose."

"Well, that's pretty close," agreed Janet, Mike, and Tom, laughing.

"Do you see a light-headed man doing that?" Kara had asked Rachel. That drew more laughter; she was referring to Shadowtree.

"Yes, I see a lot of men doing that," the fortune teller had replied.

Janet said, "She told me I need to look for a fat guy with gray and black hair."

"Maybe my dad's coming to visit," guessed Kara, "planning to give you some advice."

"I wasn't in there nearly as long as you were," Janet said.

"Did you ask many questions?" Kara wanted to know. "Because I asked her a lot of questions trying to pin her down. I pressed her because I thought she was pretty vague so I asked her for specifics. She told me, 'You're leaving but I see you coming back. You'll be back here. Please come see me. I want to see you again.' She was like crying at one point. . . . I thought that was either the best act I've ever seen or . . ." Kara paused.

"Why was she crying?" asked Janet. "She was just all over you when you came out."

"The first thing she said when I came in, and it just cracked me up because I was thinking of the TV thing, was 'You have beautiful skin.'" In her "Church Lady" pursed-lips voice, Kara said, "Thank you," and told Janet, "I had just put on this tanning stuff to make it look better for my television appearance next week."

"She said that I had been famous in my previous life," added Kara.

"You had a previous life?" Janet inquired.

"Yes, she was talking about my past life, and how I had been denied achieving certain things that I needed to achieve in my last life, and that I was very determined to achieve them in this life, and that I shouldn't let anyone stop me. Then she said that people were supposed to know my name."

In a low, vibrating "fortune teller" voice, Kara mimicked, "You are not a stranger. People are supposed to know your name," and chuckled in the particular way she had, and Janet and Mike laughed with her.

"So, how many kids will I have?" Kara asked Rachel. "Am I going to have any kids?"

"You're supposed to have four, but there are only two," said Rachel.

"What does that mean?" asked Kara.

"Well," explained Rachel, "that either means you are going to miscarry two or two aren't going to live very long."

"That's nice," was the doleful reaction. And the tape ended.

Chapter 47 ✾ *Miramar*

Three women were to be trained as F-14A Tomcat aviators with assignment to a fleet squadron as their destination. Kara and Carey Dunai (later Lohrenz) were pilots and Christina Green was a naval flight officer who had flown in the backseat of the F/A-18D in one of the West Coast electronic warfare support training squadrons, VAQ-34. The F/A-18 was designed to be a single seat aircraft but some are two-seaters, used by the navy primarily for training. The VAQ squadrons also had a few two-seaters; a switch controlling the jamming systems was installed in back for the NFO. Kara and Christina checked into VF-124, the Gunfighters, at about the same time in June 1993. Carey had not yet arrived, so Kara and Christina went together to meet the skipper of VF-124.

Cdr. Tom "Sobs" Sobieck had the challenging assignment of supervising the training of the first three female F-14 aviators. He didn't underestimate the capabilities of women; he had two teenage daughters. The younger one had played first base for a boys' baseball team when she was eleven years old, and the team had won the Mira Mesa League. But still, he wasn't sure women in combat was such a great idea, and he knew that many, if not all, of his instructors had that same fighter jock mentality. On the other hand, his orders were to train these women aviators in the F-14 and, assuming they were trainable, that's what he was going to do.

As commander of the largest fighter squadron in the navy and with about thirty-six hundred hours in the F-14, he had to be smart and competent. In addition, "Sobs" was good-natured and a genuinely nice person; he tried to put Kara and Christina at ease. After awhile, he walked them over to introduce them to his boss, Rear Adm. "Wick" Parcells, who was then the fighter airborne early warning wing commander. The admiral was cordial but very direct. "Why do you two want to do this?" he asked the women.

Kara and Christina weren't intimidated. They told him they had worked hard for this opportunity and they intended to be the best F-14 aviators it was possible to be. "I've been trying to do this for as long as I can remember," Kara said. "I want to do it and I can do it." Kara and Christina left no doubt that they meant to complete the program and fly Tomcats in the fleet.

A young lieutenant, Neil "Waylon" Jennings, saw Kara check into the Replacement Air Group, or RAG, where pilots go for warm-up and refresher training. An instructor with an aggressor squadron, the VF-126 Bandits, he was there to fly a training mission as an adversary against some of the instructors and F-14 students. "Waylon" knew he would soon have to train females to fly combat aircraft and he was not enthusiastic about the prospect. He saw Kara wandering the halls in her khakis. "She had a solid reputation and was thought of as an above-average pilot and not a female who used her gender to get by," he said, "but still, I wondered how well she would fit into this previously male-only profession."

The air force was already showcasing its new female fighter pilots, and the navy didn't like being left behind. The carrier USS *Abraham Lincoln,* scheduled to deploy in the spring of 1995, was to be altered to accommodate females. The F-14A squadron assigned to the *Lincoln* was VF-213, and that was the destination squadron for Kara, Carey, and Christina. Commander Sobieck made the decision to push the women to the head of the line for the next class because the airwing wanted the nuggets to join their squadron as soon as possible so they would have some time to settle in before going on cruise. That meant other junior officers were bumped back, and some of them had been waiting for as much as a year to begin their F-14 training. They were not happy.

Kara anticipated resentment from the junior officers who were affected by Sobieck's decision, but her view of it was that women had been waiting forever to fly combat airplanes, and she had been waiting for three years. She didn't feel guilty about starting before some of her peers, but she knew it would cause jealousy and resentment, and she very much regretted that. She had been around long enough to know how much trouble those emotions could cause. However, there was nothing she could do about it. She was determined to keep as low a profile as possible and earn the respect of those very talented but not quite "liberated" individuals.

It turned out that training for Kara's entire class was postponed because Christina Green had to be sent to VT-86 to learn to run intercepts. It wasn't her fault she hadn't had the normal intercept training that most NFOs receive. Like Kara and all other female naval aviators, she had been serving in a shore-based, noncombat support assignment. Just as Kara hadn't had weapons or carrier-landing training in the A-6 because she was prohibited by law from joining the fleet, Christina originally hadn't been allowed the opportunity to learn the full NFO syllabus.

The skipper gave his welcome aboard kick-off to the class as it was about to start F-14A ground school. "You'll learn to fly and fight the F-14," Sobieck told them. "You'll be taught the basics of the fighter mission and become good wingmen. You will be safe on and around the ship both day and night, or you won't go to the fleet. Your instructors will do whatever they can to assist you in developing your skills, but the final answer rests in your performance and motivation."

Sobieck had given that talk many times before and he was on familiar ground. There was another subject, however, which he had to address, and with this topic he was less comfortable. He called the three female aviators in his squadron into his office to give them the standard "no fishing off the company dock" lecture—meaning they weren't to date any of their instructors.

As "Sobs" told it, he was embarrassed, not quite sure how to phrase it, and as he was searching for the right words, Kara chimed in, "I understand, Skipper, you mean, don't fuck the help, right?" With that not so delicate summation, Kara put her CO at ease and he had his first glimmer of hope that things might work out.

"That was a tremendous relief to me," Sobieck said. "That was exactly what I was trying to say." Then Kara asked if that meant the aggressor squadron VF-126 Bandit pilots were off-limits too. He thought about it for a minute and then said he couldn't think of a reason why they would be. "I thought that by the time they were fighting the bogeys, they'd be so damn busy with the airplane and tactics, a relationship would be the furthest thing from their minds."

It was by design that the navy placed the women in the same training squadron and then assigned them to the same fighter squadron and the same carrier. Renovating a carrier to accommodate women with separate sleeping and bathroom arrangements was a major project, and for some time the *Lincoln* would be the only one on the West Coast ready to welcome females. Kara wondered if it weren't also by design that the first three women assigned to F-14s were so statuesque. At five feet, ten inches, Kara felt petite beside Carey and Christina, who were each at least six feet tall.

Also, it seemed reasonable that breaking the gender barrier would be easier in a group. That was the theory. But in practice, it didn't work well for these particular women. They were very different from one another.

Kara was the most senior of the three, although Christina had served for a year or so in an electronic warfare support training squadron before this assignment. Christina, however, hadn't been an active protagonist in the fight to have the combat exclusion laws repealed, and because she wasn't a pilot, she didn't automatically spark male ego defense mechanisms. Most men could somehow tolerate a woman in the cockpit, so long as she wasn't actually flying the plane. The pressures Christina might have experienced were very different from Kara's.

Kara had learned some hard lessons during her three-year tour in Key West, and she was toned down and determined to fit in. "It just wasn't worth it to be a maverick," she told her sister Kirsten. Kara was well aware that all eyes at Miramar were on the women, and that as the first females in a fighter squadron they had to make a statement; they had to be perfect and they couldn't just leave that up to chance. They had to try harder, work harder, and be better than most of the men.

Carey was fresh out of the training command and, unlike Kara, hadn't had to fight Congress and the U.S. Navy for that F-14 jet slot. Her feeling was that she had made the grades and she was entitled to it. She had been in the right place at the right time. This was her first assignment; how could she know what she was facing? Kara had been full of enthusiasm after flight school too, but school is school, and Kara had learned things are different in the real world. Carey had no idea what she was up against. The microscope was only beginning to focus on her.

Before they started formal training, Kara was studying and spending time in the simulators, learning the systems of the plane. She wanted Carey to do the same because she knew she and Carey were a team, whether they had planned it that way or not. Carey reacted to Kara like a rebellious teenager to a doddering parent, and like a teenager, she didn't bother to try to hide her disdain.

Maybe for the first time, Kara began to have some pangs of regret for the way she had reacted to some of the lieutenant commanders when she first arrived at Key West. Carey treated Kara like Kara had treated Ben Jergens, as if she were all caught up in her seniority, taking herself too seriously, and out to get her. Not that Kara compared herself to Ben, but she had the uneasy feeling that was the way Carey saw her. Somewhere along the way, Kara had grown up from a young, enthusiastic, gung-ho jet pilot to also become a dedicated professional naval officer. She was the most senior in rank of her classmates and therefore the class leader, and she felt responsible for them.

Kara was taking everything seriously. She knew all too well how serious it was, but Carey couldn't understand what the big fuss was about. If she wanted to go visit her fiancé over the weekend she didn't see why she should have to be back early for FOD walkdown. If Kara insisted, Carey practically sneered at her.

Another thing that caused a rift between the three women was Kara's request that they not be required to give interviews to the media. Commander Sobieck was getting calls from some very senior public affairs officers requesting that the women talk to the press. The navy was anxious to promote the fact that women were being trained in fighters.

Kara had lived through that scenario in Key West when the higher-ups in the navy had encouraged her to give interviews. Not until later did she realize that as she attracted more attention from the media, she also attracted resentment and criticism from her peers, and from some of the senior officers in her squadron. The men who were doing the same thing she was doing hadn't appreciated it that the focus was on her; after all, there just isn't much difference between the boys and the girls once you climb in a cockpit. The women who weren't being spotlighted weren't happy about it either.

Besides sidetracking animosity, Kara had another motive for not talking to the press when she got to Miramar. She said it was enough learning to fly the plane; she didn't need the added pressure of preparing for and giving interviews. She knew from experience that a good interview didn't just happen and had worked hard to make them interesting.

"I'll do the interviews, of course, if I am ordered to," she told Commander Sobieck, "but if it's left up to me, I'll wait until I've finished training." He was relieved because he knew that any attention focused on the women would rankle those junior officers who weren't pleased to have females there in the first place.

Although "Sobs" "thought Kara's stand was great," the navy hierarchy wasn't pleased. Now that it had changed its policy, it wanted to show off its new female fighter-pilots-to-be and enjoy the good publicity, but there was no one up the chain of command willing to order Kara to pose for pictures and deliver clever sound bites.

Kara tried to explain to Carey why she took this position, but Carey couldn't relate to it. She wouldn't have minded talking to the press and posing for pictures. She was young and attractive and set to enjoy the attention that being one of the first women to fly the F-14 was bringing to her. Kara could understand how Carey felt because she had thought it was fun when the press first discovered her.

Kara realized there was no way Carey could understand without having had the experience herself. All Carey understood was that if Kara refused to give interviews, she couldn't either without looking as though she was out for glory. It got around that Kara was the one who wanted to stay in the background, so Carey didn't even get credit with the senior officers for being modest. She didn't seem happy about any of it.

Chapter 48   *The Gunfighters*

"I thanked God for Kara rescuing me from my stammering problem," "Sobs" said when he told the "no fishing from the company dock" story to "Waylon" Jennings in March 1994. "Waylon's" squadron, the Bandits, and Kara's squadron, the Gunfighters, were on a combined detachment in Pensacola, Florida. The Gunfighters were flying tactics during the day against the Bandits and bouncing for the boat at night.

"Waylon" said later, "I can report that I know of no romantic liaisons on that detachment, although I do remember one particular night at Seville Quarter where Kara was dancing with several of my squadron mates. It looked like she was having a great time hanging out with our group."

In the first phase of her training, Kara finished number two out of her class of five—in spite of blowing both tires on her instrument familiarization flight. She was at slow speed with one thousand feet left on the runway at Fallon, Nevada, and used improper braking technique. It wasn't unusual for a new pilot to blow some tires learning to land at a high altitude, but her pride was hurt and she acquired a new call sign, "Boom Boom."

She had another bad day on the weapons detachment to Fallon. She missed hitting the altitudes and airspeeds that were required by the sortie and had allowed the "switchology" to get the best of her. Her difficulties in hitting the numbers caused her to finish last in her class of five in conventional weapons. Kara put her mind to mastering the proper techniques and three days later she reflew the hop, receiving an above-average grade of 3.05. (3.00 was average.) Her class-standing in basic weapons was three out of five.

In tactics she did very well. Commander Sobieck praised her, saying, "She was a superb airplane driver, always searching for more knowledge about the proper way to employ the Tomcat. JOs loved to fly with her. She was a 'kick butt' kind of woman and a surprisingly good fighter pilot for her experience level."

Kara finished two out of five in tactics, one out of five in advanced fleet air superiority, and one out of five in air refueling.

Kara's mother arrived in San Diego on 31 March 1994, to watch her practice her field carrier landings—FCLP in navy jargon. Night landings were different from the day landings her mother had seen when Kara was practicing field carrier landings in 1989 in Beeville.

The runway was lighted to duplicate the landing area on the carrier. The landing area is about seven hundred feet long and wide enough to provide about six feet on each side of the wings of the F-14. The wingspan of the F-14 is a little over sixty-four feet—the plane is a twin-engine, two-seat, variable-sweep wing, supersonic fighter. The variable-sweep wing, which is automatically positioned by a computer, is its most prominent aerodynamic feature.

Sally rode in a navy van with the landing signal officer (LSO) and his assistant to a little glass house that sat next to the runway. Visitors are allowed, but that night she was the only one. The young officers were polite but they were all business. Kara had walked to her plane with the other pilots and navigators, who are called radar intercept officers, or RIOs, in the F-14.

Six planes were circling in the pattern and they had each done about three touch and gos before the LSOs pointed Kara's airplane out to her mother. After that, she learned to listen to the calls over the radio and knew when Kara was beginning her approach. She also began to understand when the LSO was pleased and when he wasn't, and it was obvious he wasn't editing his comments about Kara because her mother was there.

At 150 mph, each plane in sequence attempts to touch down at the spot where the tailhook would catch the third of four wires on the carrier deck. After it got dark, the pilots had no reference points and had to rely totally on instruments and what they call the "meatball."

Five vertical lights are on the side of the landing area. The top three vertical lights are amber and the bottom two lights are red. The "meatball" is the third amber light; it is in the center of a horizontal row of green lights. As the plane comes in, the pilot will see one of the top two amber lights if he or she is too high or one of the bottom red lights if too low. The objective is to see the amber light aligned with the row of green lights. This will keep the plane on the proper glide slope.

During an actual carrier landing, being too low is very bad because you can fly into the end of the carrier. Being high isn't great either since you can't land—but at least you get another chance. The LSO gives a grade for each landing. If your accumulated grades aren't good enough at the field, you don't get to try landing on the carrier.

Kara had some difficulty during practice at the field. It took her a while to figure out that her experience in the A-6 did her more harm than good. Her habits, ingrained by three years of flying the A-6 with its quick response engines, were a handicap. The Tomcat's fan engines took longer than the A-6 engines to respond, and the throttle movements were magnified when she didn't stay right on top of the deviations from glide slope. She was rough with the power while she was trying to retrain her motor skills.

Easter lunch ran late and Kara had to hustle to get her mom to the airport in time to catch her flight, driving with a special combination of skill and speed honed in RX-7s and F-14s. Kara rolled down the window and leaned out to kiss her mother goodbye, but a policeman with a no-nonsense look on his face signaled her to move on. So instead they waved at each other and Sally ran for her plane. It was the last time they ever saw each other.

Kara's field carrier landing practice grades were less than satisfactory. She was nine out of nine, but her trend was improving toward the end of the FCLP period. The LSOs told the skipper they would be willing to take her to the boat for a look-see because they knew they could trust her when they told her to do something. But her grades were only a little better at the boat, and she didn't qualify.

After a long night in the cockpit, "having had the hell scared out of her," she and Carey, who also had not qualified, were called to the skipper's office. Commander Sobieck said, "It was obvious to me that they had just experienced their first real failures. They didn't know for sure if they could master landing twenty-five tons of fire-breathing airplane on a ship steaming through the pitch blackness of the night. I told them they each would get a Human Factors Board to make sure there was nothing physically, psychologically, or mentally wrong with them, and then we'd try it again as long as my LSOs said they could work with them."

Kara was disappointed not to have qualified the first time she tried. She said it wasn't easy to land on the carrier at night and being catapulted into total blackness was about as scary as it gets, but she didn't feel it was something that was impossible for her.

Three out of the five in her class failed to qualify. Four other pilots who went to the boat with her class qualified, but they were all doing it for the second time. Kara's class had been hurt because weather and scheduling difficulties had shut them out of training at San Clemente. There, a runway begins at the edge of a huge cliff beside the ocean, and it is as close an approximation of landing on a carrier as you can get. "In fact, it's scarier than the boat" is the general consensus. Practice at San Clemente is invaluable for preparing for the real thing. The Human Factors Board took that into consideration and recommended to Commander Sobieck that everyone be allowed to try again.

After she got over her initial dismay, Kara handled this setback the way she did most things she couldn't do anything about—with humor. "I decided on a unique tactic when I went before the Human Factors Board," she wrote on the inside of her Mother's Day card. "I didn't want to admit to trying hard to be so below average, so I blamed my performance on too many all-night drinking binges and roaring around. They said, 'That's the fighter spirit.'"

Because the F-14 is by far the hardest plane to maneuver aboard the ship, the carrier-qualification failure rate is much higher than for other aircraft. Statistics illustrate the disparity between the disqualification rate for F-14 pilots and pilots of other aircraft and put Kara's failure to qualify on her first attempt in perspective. For the eighteen-month time frame comprising calendar year 1994 through 26 June 1995, 255 category 1 naval aviators attempted to carrier qualify in the Pacific Fleet. Thirty-six didn't qualify, a failure rate of 14.12 percent. The failure rate for the F-14 pilots was 33.33 percent, more than twice as high. The breakdown by aircraft type is as follows:

Aircraft type	No. to Attempt	No. to Disqualify	Percent to Disqualify
A-6	28	3	10.71
EA-6B	37	4	10.81
F-14	30	10	33.33
F/A-18	83	14	16.87
S-3	50	4	8.00
E-2/C-2	27	1	3.70

Barring extreme circumstances, the pilots were all given a second chance to qualify.

Around the end of April, "Waylon" checked into VF-124 for refresher Tomcat training and carrier qualification in the F-14A. He was scheduled to go to the USS *Constellation* at the same time as Kara, who was making her second attempt. They got to know each other pretty well while they were hanging around the Ready Room waiting their turn to fly. "Her demeanor was perfectly suited to being a fighter pilot," he said. "She was good-natured, had a great sense of humor, and was competitive to a fault. If you told a joke, she told one better, if you had a story, she would try to top it. In short, she fit in fantastically. It was solely because of her that I changed my mind on whether or not women would be able to do this job. She made a believer out of me."

Around 22 June 1994, Kara told her mother she was doing great with her field carrier landing practice and didn't anticipate any problems when she tried again to qualify at the boat. On 24 July 1994, on the USS *Constellation,* Kara qualified to fly the F-14A on and off an aircraft carrier. Her performance summaries from the final Replacement Air Group carrier qualification were as follows:

Event	GPA	Boarding Rate	Class Standing	Summary
FCLP	3.24	—	3 of 7	Above Average
Day CQ	3.22	89%	1 of 7	Above Average
Night CQ	2.82	71%	6 of 7	Below Average
Overall	3.05	81%	3 of 7	Above Average

Overall, she rated third out of a class of seven. She placed first in her class in daytime landings at the carrier, but her class rank was pulled down by her night-landing performance.

Chapter 49 *The Press*

"I made it to the fleet!" Kara wrote in her journal on 26 August 1994. "Qualled at the July boat in the RAG and then joined VF-213, the world famous fighting Blacklions, at FFARP [Fleet Fighter Air Combat Maneuvers Readiness Program] in El Sweato."

In accordance with policy, the navy also assigned her a ground job. It was the one she liked the least, public affairs officer. As the navy's first female F-14 pilot, she was "encouraged" by Washington powers to give interviews, thereby filling the dual capacities of producer and star.

She and Carey were interviewed on local television in San Diego. In a 10 August 1994 television interview with Susan Farrell on KNSD News in San Diego, Kara described her first carrier landing: "You see this boat at about ten thousand feet and you think it's a fishing boat or something and you say 'No possible way!' And then you fly by at about eight hundred feet and you think, hey, that's huge, I can land on that—and I barely remember my first four traps, because all I could think of was how can I work the rest of my life to buy this drug? It's just an adrenaline rush!"

The *Compass,* an authorized navy newspaper in San Diego, ran a front-page story on Friday, 29 July 1994, headlined "Women Pilots Soar Off Carrier." Kara, whose twenty-first landing of the five-day training exercise on the USS *Constellation* made her the first fully qualified female F-14 Tomcat pilot, was quoted as saying: "It's the most intense carrier landing training that you'll get in your career. This is definitely the most challenging thing I've ever done. Landing a Tomcat is sort of like dancing with an elephant. . . . You can kind of nudge it over to the right and ease it over to the left, but when it decides it's going to sit down, there's not a thing you can do about it."

Kara told the reporter she had requested assignments to fleet squadrons on numerous occasions. First she was blocked by the combat exclusion laws, then by policies of the services, and most recently because, due to budget cuts, the jet squadrons women were permitted to fly in were being broken up. "About a year and a half ago they were telling me that I didn't have a future in the Navy and that I might as well get out . . . because there were no female jet slots open."

Kara also said that being a female aviator hadn't been a factor—good or bad—in her F-14 training, and she was glad about that. "Being female hasn't been an issue in our training at all. We've pretty much gone through like any guy. We certainly weren't accorded any attention for [being female]. I've been flying jets for six years and I never thought this was a real question of whether women were capable of doing this; it was just a policy issue. It has more to do with politics than anything else."

What she said to the press, about how being female hadn't been an issue, wasn't entirely true. There were a few F-14 instructors who didn't go out of their way to help her. For example, one instructor wouldn't comment or offer instruction during the training flight but would wait for the debrief to bring up mistakes for the first time. The purpose of the training flight is to teach, not to catalogue mistakes. The instructor is there to help the new pilot, to offer the lessons of experience when they are needed, not after the flight is over.

But the battle was won now and Kara wasn't going to sabotage the peace. She said she foresaw the spotlight on female aviators dimming as more were integrated into fleet squadrons. "It'll probably not even be an issue in a few years."

The *Compass* later ran a two-part series on Kara and Carey joining a fleet fighter squadron. The caption of the first part was "The Jet Doesn't Know the Difference."

Kara described her mother as "a perfect role model. She's very independent and smart." She said her mother taught her she could do anything, that her gender was not a limiting factor. Because of that influence, she felt her dreams held no boundary.

"As a little kid, I always thought I would be an astronaut. And there are two ways to do that. You can either be a Navy jet test pilot, or you can go to school and get your Ph.D. in something and ride along."

The article explained that Kara experienced a "culture shock" when she moved with her mother to San Antonio, Texas, from Canada.

I was playing basketball and somebody told me girls don't play basketball. I said, "What do you mean? I played all the time in
Canada." It was different because all of the girls in Texas were
cheerleaders or on the drill team. They were allowed to play golf or
tennis. It was a completely different attitude. But I played basketball and tennis and anything else I wanted to do. I just never noticed
being treated any differently when I was in Canada. This whole girl-
guy issue was never an issue.

She talked about getting selected for jet training after primary flight
training in Corpus Christi.

At that time there was a limit. They could only select five female
jet pilots a year because there was a limited number of female jet
slots available. There was a quota because they only had four or five
jet squadrons that had women in them. The whole time I was going
through primary they told me there was no way I could get jets
because they already had given out all five slots that fiscal year. And
I just said, "It's my destiny. You cannot make me believe that,
because it's my destiny."

She described her training in the T-2 and the A-4 Skyhawk. "Even
though we couldn't go to combat squadrons at the time, we still got
the exact same training as the guys. We dropped bombs, we shot rockets, we did air-to-air gunnery, we did carrier quals, we did dogfight-
ing, everything. It was very frustrating at the time to have done well
and have very limited options just because I was female. So I got the
best thing I could get as a female jet pilot and went with A-6s."

She said she felt unchallenged in the electronic warfare support
training squadron in Key West where she flew the EA-6A, and she
tried everything she could to get fighters.

About three months prior to changing the policy the detailers were
recommending that I get out because they said I didn't have a
future in the Navy and they had no place to send me. All of the
squadrons with female jet pilots were being decommissioned
because of the budget cuts. I was just waiting for the policy to
change, and wondered if it would. Everyone was telling me that it
would never change. I was just thrilled when they actually did
change the policy.

Kara ended the interview with, "I've flown F-14s for a year. It's been great so far. For me it was just what I wanted to do all along, and the three years before that was just sort of a sidetrack."

In the second part of the two-part story published by the *Compass* on 9 September 1994, Kara described how she felt after her qualifying carrier landing on the USS *Constellation*. "That was the best feeling in the world. After your last trap, they say '103 . . . you're qual'd.' And then I thought. 'I hope I don't crash into anything and ruin this.' I didn't want to screw up the parking. It's sort of like being in the Olympics and winning the gold medal. It is the final exam in most people's eyes."

She said she felt her personal achievement was more important to her than what it did for the advancement of women in the military:

> I think obviously the change in policy has affected the status of women in the military. The fact that I've done this is not really to me a reflection of all women. It's just a sort of "great, I did this." I never thought that I had something special to prove for women, because women have been flying tactical jets [in noncombat squadrons] in the Navy since 1972. It's just always been a personal goal. I think that the status of women in the military has obviously changed in the last year. It's been a tremendous change. I never believed women couldn't [fly combat aircraft]. There are a lot of guys who couldn't do this, and there are a lot of women who couldn't do this. I think given the right attitude and motivation and talent, just about anybody can do this. It always surprises me when people ask me, "Why do you want to do this?" And I think, God, who doesn't want to do this? This is the greatest job in the entire world. These are the best looking jets on the planet. I mean, don't you think an F-14 is just gorgeous? I feel fortunate to come to work, and I don't take it for granted.

Marina Pisano, who had written two earlier articles for the *San Antonio Express-News,* wrote another article about Kara that was published on 13 October 1994. She quoted Kara describing night traps: "Tell you what, it is the scariest thing. There's so much adrenaline pumping. In the daytime, flying one of these planes is the sport of kings. At night, it's a blue-collar job. . . . It's so hard you think, 'I must be crazy. What am I doing up here?'"[1]

Kara talked about disqualifying on her first try at carrier night traps in April: "It's not uncommon to 'disqual' first time. Three out of five of my classmates disqualed. It was sort of the first time I ever struggled with anything, but I also thought, 'Hey, this is doable.' I realized what I needed to fix, and it made going out the second time easy."

Kara told Marina that navy officials had asked her to be available for media interviews when her duties permitted. Kara said the only time she had a problem with the press was when a reporter suggested that women fighter pilots received special treatment. She disagreed: "We were treated the same. We were under a microscope just like any junior pilot."

Georg Thurmann, an enlisted man in Squadron 124, said, "As far as all the reports go regarding her training, if anything, the navy made it tougher for her since she was the first female F-14 pilot. The male pilots have a very large ego problem!"

Around the first of October, *National Geographic* expressed interest in doing a TV documentary on Kara. In the November issue of *McCall's* magazine, Kara was one of several young women featured in an article called "Women Who Will Brighten Your Future." Julia Roberts was on the cover. Kara said she didn't interview for the story nor did she furnish the picture, which she believed was taken right after her carrier qualification.

There was the inevitable grumbling from some of the male aviators about the attention Kara and Carey were getting, but the person who was really affected by it was Christina. The press only wanted to talk to the female pilots, and Christina felt that her accomplishment as the first woman RIO in the F-14 was being ignored. Because Kara was the public affairs officer for the squadron and it was her job to deal with the media, Christina blamed her for not bringing any attention to her or the maintenance women.

Chapter 50 *The Blacklions*

Soon after Kara joined VF-213, Kirsten went to San Diego to visit her. She was amazed at how slim her sister was. A friend of Dagny's once described Kara as "sturdy," and Kara had been insulted. It was true that Dagny and Kirsten were slimmer, but Dagny had a much smaller frame than Kara had, and Kirsten's business was exercise.

However, after Kara moved to Solana Beach, she ran on the beach every day, and went surf boarding or worked out at the gym when she wasn't flying, and that extra 10 pounds she thought she would never lose just melted away. She weighed around 140 pounds and Kirsten thought she looked terrific.

Kara had to work at the squadron's nacho booth at the air show the weekend Kirsten was there, a duty that always fell to the squadron nuggets, which in a fleet squadron meant non-cruise-experienced pilots. Worse, she was the booth captain—an honor bestowed upon her by the commanding officer of the squadron, Cdr. Mike Galpin, because he said, "I trusted her to take care of the money." Kirsten wanted to be with Kara so she worked with her in the booth that Saturday for a full eight-hour shift. It was a thankless job in the hot August San Diego sun.

In her capacity as the Blacklions public affairs officer Kara wrote an article in her typical fashion. Doug Sayers, her public affairs civilian boss, kept the copy she gave him. "It's been on my wall since she sent it over—still good for a few chuckles," said Doug.

Lions Work Air Show in Support of MWR
By Lieutenant Kara Hultgreen

MIRAMAR—Fighter Squadron 213 provided cheap labor for the concession vendors at Miramar's 1994 air show in an effort to raise money for the station's Morale, Welfare, and Recreations Department.

Volunteers from the squadron beginning with the commanding officer on down served nachos, pretzels, sodas, and beer in six different booths during the weekend. The food and drinks were severely overpriced, but the Blacklions were flat rate labor.

Next year, smart people will bring coolers from home and refuse to pay $3.75 for a soda.

The nachos dripping with fat and cholesterol were described by many as "terrible at best" yet had the longest lines all day. Medical experts may someday link nacho sales to sun poisoning. The hard-earned money will go to the squadron's Moral Welfare and Recreation fund and will help pay for squadron "all hands" functions.

Kara wanted Kirsten to see the F-14A demonstration. When it was about to begin, she shut down the booth and pulled Kirsten out into the sunshine. She didn't have to ask her twice. Kirsten would have welcomed any excuse to get out of that steamy nacho booth, but besides that she was excited about seeing the F-14s perform.

"I'm dying to see your plane," Kirsten said. She described the scene:

So we went out there, and I'm watching this jet and Kara is standing beside me, and I'm thinking, "Wow! That is unbelievable." This feeling of awe just hit me. I'm so impressed. I'm so amazed. That plane is just so beautiful and then I look at Kara when the whole thing is over and I go, "Kara, you are so cool." And Kara was still looking after the F-14s in the distance, with this blissful glow about her. "Yeah," she said. "Isn't it great?"

Kirsten continued, "I'm taken aback. I had this feeling of pride for her. It was unbelievable. I just wanted to say, 'That's my sister and she's just so great!'"

Right after the air show, the squadron deployed to spend a week at sea. Kara wrote in her journal on 26 August 1994: "Now I'm on the USS *Lincoln* for TSTA III (not sure what that stands for). Flew aboard yesterday got my 2/2/2 (2 day traps, 2 day touch and gos, and 2 night traps). I haven't been debriefed yet but it went OK—the last pass I was lined up way right at the start but fixed it." Kara did very well during those exercises. She ranked first among the new pilots in her squadron. On six carrier landings her GPA was 3.17 and her boarding rate was 100 percent, ranking her in the upper half of all air wing pilots. Because the grades for F-14 aircraft landings are lower as a group, for an F-14 pilot to be ranked in the upper half of all the pilots is quite an accomplishment, and especially so for a nugget F-14 pilot.

"Waylon" Jennings, who had also successfully carrier qualified on the USS *Constellation* and checked into VF-213, described Kara's performance on that first detachment at sea:

> A carrier pilot's true reputation rests mostly on how well they land their aircraft aboard the ship. On Kara's first at-sea period, she emerged as the best nugget pilot in our squadron. She was a pleasure to fly with and was one of those unique individuals with an insatiable appetite for knowledge. I was quite happy when she was assigned as my wingman and I was looking forward to taking an active role in her training and development as a fighter pilot. Because of her talent, and my former adversary experience, I knew she was the girl I could train to beat all the boys at 1 V 1 ACM (one pilot and aircraft dog fighting against another—the ultimate sport). I was also convinced that she would be the first female Tomcat skipper.

Kara figured out what TSTA III stood for because as PAO she had to write an article about it:

Blacklions Complete Refresher Training at Sea
By Lt. Kara Hultgreen

The VF-213 Blacklions recently returned from a week aboard the USS *Abraham Lincoln* participating in TSTA III (Tailored Ships Training Assessment). TSTA used to be called REFTRA, which stood for refresher training, but that too clearly explained our purpose and wasn't nearly important sounding enough hence the name change. The carrier itself was always referred to as "The Abe," but now with the advent of women on board, we affectionately refer to her as "The Babe." I won't tell you what they are calling "The Ike" now.

We packed up the entire squadron for a short week at sea designed to train damage control and flight deck crews. Every day a General Quarters was announced at least once to interrupt sleeping, eating and any plans for exercise. The aircrew was relegated to sitting in the Ready Room with flash hoods and gloves (fire-fighting gear) while the maintenance personnel, also engulfed in fire-fighting equipment, were fighting mock fires. Of course the drills were not allowed to interfere with the aggressive air plan. The Blacklion maintainers proudly provided quality jets while our plastic jet Hornet brethren were breaking down and missing sorties.

The Airwing spent the first three days performing carrier qualifications and the final four days flying cyclic ops. The cyclic operations included bombing sorties, mixed section tactic training, and a long-range strike to Fallon, Nevada. The airwing and the ship worked together for a successful week in preparation for our upcoming deployment.

Her journal descriptions of the TSTA III training were more personal.

So far this has been fun. All of my night traps have been pinkies though. Tanked off a 135 yesterday—not too bad. Two of my join-ups on Sprout were a little hot, otherwise an uneventful day. I missed my own strike planning meeting on Saturday morning and that wasn't good. I helped the Skipper on his Strike planning team—meaning I printed on the slides. I'm not scheduled for the Long Range Strike though.

Irritations on the boat are all the stupid blackshoe drills. General Quarters, MOP levels, Man overboard etc. You can't eat sleep or workout during these things.

My PAO calendar will be full the week we get back. *Navy Times*, *McCall's* magazine, *Hopscotch*, *National Geographic*, and Channel 9/51.

I was pretty excited about the little things like my first clearing turn [after the catapult shot] on the 26th, my first EMCON [electronic emission control] recovery on the 27th—I actually screwed that up a bit. [The use of some electronic equipment is restricted within a certain range of the ship so the ship's location is concealed as long as possible.] The cut lights for power didn't really register and they thought I should have responded with more power, hence my first no grade one wire. I followed it up with an OK though. I bombed smoke for the first time—it was hard to see and a Hornet was chasing us around the pattern so instead of 20 deg dive from 8k we were 35 deg. Computer target didn't work well—I didn't have time to designate by the time I found the switch on the left. Computer pilot mode gave decent hits though.

The SDO on the ship is a red ass to be sure. I had it [she was squadron duty officer] for the fly off on the 31st. I woke up at 0330 after two hours of sleep and didn't want to sleep past the 0430 brief time so I got up. I wonder what type of breakfast food I could keep in my stateroom. I get hungry in the morning and when they call GQ it really ticks me off because then I can't get breakfast.

Linda [Heid] is two doors down the hall and Pam [Lyons] and Brenda [Scheufele] share a room as well. It's exciting to be here. It wasn't long ago that we were all in D.C. trying to make this happen. Linda likes her squadron, but Pam and Brenda are not thrilled with theirs. I'm really lucky to have Flex [Cdr. Mike Galpin] and Killer [Cdr. Fred Kilian] for CO and XO—they are awesome.

As Kara was climbing out of the cockpit, one of the plane captains aboard the *Lincoln* approached her. Catching her eye, he started to say something, but as she turned toward him, her commanding officer called out to her. The enlisted man stopped and receded into the background. As soon as Commander Galpin left, Kara looked around for the plane captain and when she spotted him, she walked over.

"Did you want to talk to me?" she asked.

"Uh, well, Ma'am," he said haltingly, "I just wanted to ask you how it felt to land that thing on the ship, you know, being a woman an' everything."

He later told Scott Watkins, senior editor of *Woman Pilot Magazine,* he wanted to kick himself for asking such a question, since all the navy programming emphasized he wasn't supposed to notice that "she" was anything but a naval aviator. But Kara just said, "It feels wonderful! I'm so lucky to have the opportunity to do this. Is there anything else you wanted to know?"

"No, Ma'am," he replied. "Thanks for taking the time to talk to me."

"Anytime," Kara said.

He said to Watkins that when she had taken off her helmet and shaken her hair free, he had been shocked at how beautiful she was, but the fact that she would remember him and seek him out was what really impressed him.

✖

The relationship between Kara and Carey and Christina continued to be cool, and Kara decided to confront both of them, hoping to come to some solution. They were going to have to spend a lot of time together in close quarters during the next three years and she wanted them to get along. Their discussion was frank, so frank that Kara was amazed at the intensity of their resentment toward her, and it wasn't only about media attention. Kara told Kirsten about it in a letter dated 18 September 1994.

> I had a chat with Carey and Christina last Friday and hashed out why Christina was giving me stink eye and the silent treatment for the last two months. They both were concerned about my *drastic* weight loss (a whole 10 lbs. in the last year). They think I look sickly and I used to have nice legs but now they are skinny and look bad.
>
> They both think I'm bulimic and shared that with the flight Doc. Anyway, I have apparently hurt Christina's feelings and told her she was fat or said things like weight was psychological and a matter of exercise and discipline.

In her journal on that same day she recorded: "Carey kept saying that 'we just have two different personalities and this just can't be resolved.' (I'm sure she would like that.) I said I think we have a communication problem because obviously I've said or done things that have hurt Christina's feelings and nothing has been said and then these things have festered for months and months."

"Well," she continued in her journal, "I'm glad we talked about it. I know I feel a lot better knowing what the problem is." But she didn't know what to do about it.

The week on the *Lincoln* was to prepare the squadron for three weeks of airwing strike warfare training with Carrier Airwing Eleven that began in Fallon, Nevada, 18 September 1994. Kara wrote an article on 16 October 1994 titled "Blacklions Invade Fallon Nevada."

"The Blacklions returned from an 'absolutely brilliant' detachment in Fallon, Nevada, according to the commanding officer CDR Mike 'Flex' Galpin. Flying an unprecedented 18 sorties per day the Lions completed 196 of 200 scheduled sorties with 10 jets on the flight line over the three week period."

For three weeks they planned and flew coordinated strikes on simulated targets in the Fallon, Nevada, ranges. Each strike was conducted as though launched from the aircraft carrier. The enemy had a complex integrated air defense including simulated surface-to-air missiles and airborne F-5s and F-18s. The Tomcats were the primary air-to-air fighters, but they also dropped bombs.

Kara described how the F-14 could interrogate the identification friend or foe (IFF) equipment to determine whether the aircraft was signaling that it was friendly so that "blue on blue" kills (like the air force F-15s killing U.S. Army helicopters for example) could be prevented. "The Blacklions prided themselves with zero blue on blue during the three weeks (unfortunately one F-14 was lost to a 'friendly' Hornet)."

Kara described the detachment in her journal entry on 25 September 1994.

Fallon Airwing Det has been pretty fun. Sharing a room with Christina—I'm glad we had our talk Friday the 16th or it would be uncomfortable. . . . The room is O.K. Two twin beds, a toaster, and coffee machine. The shower is wild. There is no volume control; it's like a fire hose. Luckily we can control the temperature, but the water is soft and you never feel totally clean. The flying was great the first week. The days were pretty long 18–20-hour days during the ITP (Integrated Training Phase). Strike planning is a pain in the ass but the flying is a blast. I flew every day last week. A high point was a 1V1 with a Hornet and I got two Fox 1s off. Apparently he (K-9) was hang dog and taking a lot of shit at the club.

I landed pretty skosh on fuel a couple of times. I thought I was going to flame out on deck prior to the chocks—100 pounds in the right feed and 200 pounds in the left feed at shutdown—apparently we had a "small" leak from the left main fuel pump. I dropped a[n] LGTR on Saturday for a bull's-eye then we raged at low level in the Clan Alpine mountain range and did low pops into B-17. What a blast.

I went to Reno with Pam, Brenda, and Joan Demarzio last night (Sat). We bought tickets for B. B. King, Little Feet, and Dr. John, but it got cold and rained and the lightning was impressive and I retreated with Joan into the Hilton casino. I lost 20 bucks playing craps. Joan is up 150. We couldn't find a room in Reno or within 50 miles and ended up sleeping (I use the term loosely) in the mini-van. It was cold and uncomfortable. I'm tired. Luckily tomorrow I'm free until 1630—I'm sleeping in.

Chapter 51   *Flipper*

"Kara was a great asset to the Ready Room," "Waylon" said. "Although she wasn't in the squadron long enough to become well known, she was well liked and [well] thought of among her squadron mates. There wasn't anything she didn't excel at. Whether in her ground job as PAO, or in the air flying her jet, she gave it her all. Given the chance, she would have easily emerged from her peer group as one of the leaders."

"Waylon" was known in the community as an exceptional air combat maneuvering pilot and a solid carrier aviator, a "good stick." Kara loved flying on his wing. When he was an adversary instructor pilot in VF-126, he had the ability to communicate his talents and skills to his students, who all wanted to become as proficient as he was. He could take the less-experienced pilots out and teach them the meaning of respect in the air. Even among the special breed called "fighter pilot," he was outstanding. He had what Tom Wolfe was speaking of in his book *The Right Stuff,* and he had taught Kara a lot. She couldn't wait to learn more.

In Fallon, "Kara's reputation was sustained," "Waylon" said. "That was also where she earned her call sign 'Flipper.'" (Previously, she was known as "Revlon" due to the fake eyelashes and makeup she would occasionally don in anticipation of one of her many interviews with the media.)

"Waylon" continued:

As the story goes, a group of several Lions were coming back from a late night in town and arrived at the BOQ in a squadron van. Rambunctious as they were, one of the guys jumped on Kara's back to wrestle her around a bit. Thwarting him, she immediately flipped him off her back, sending him flying to the ground. Hence "Flipper" as a call sign. Over time, her nickname was affectionately referred to in the dolphin vernacular rather than the karate move from whence it originated.

As a side story to the "Flipper" incident, the guy who jumped Kara that night landed on his head and required several stitches before he was able to retire for the evening. The next morning, someone acquired some chalk and drew a body outline on the sidewalk where he landed. There was a bloodstain in the appropriate spot where his head was drawn, and the whole thing was quite hilarious to look at. We chuckled about it every day as we walked by the spot on our way to and from the squadron. Kara was a little embarrassed, but I think she liked the attention. The guy with the stitches wore them as a badge of shame for the rest of the det. He should not have underestimated her.

Kara's version was in her journal entry dated 1 October 1994:

Fun week last week. Cancelled for weather on Wednesday night and went to the Bird Farm with Smash and Hob (Head of Bone) Dino, Dog, Chuey, Craw, Snort, Haggis, etc.

Wrestling, Dog's face meets pavement. 1 million stitches by Doc Miller. New call sign Flipper. Chalk outline of Dog in parking lot. Bubba (Beat up by bitch again). Cartoon for entire airwing brief *Far Side* two bears (labeled Revlon and Ralph [Carey's call sign]) over dead hunter (labeled Dog). Caption— "Maybe these guys will finally take us seriously."

The new call sign is because the story is that I flipped Dog and threw him face first into the ground—kicked his ass. Of course this bears little resemblance to the truth but we never let the truth get in the way of a good story. So I'm famous in the airwing.

Kara had told her mother that what really happened was she saw Dog coming at her and just stepped aside, and he hit the pavement. Kirsten told the story of how a high school friend of theirs had visited Kara in San Diego and then had gone on to see Kirsten in Los Angeles. Kirsten said he talked and talked about Kara. He said that he asked her how she got her call sign "Flipper," and she had said, "Well, I'll tell you, but what do you want, the truth or the legend?"

On 1 October 1994, still in Fallon, Kara sent her mother a postcard from Lake Tahoe. "Flying has been great! Went to Lake Tahoe

today. Rented mountain bikes—no broken bones! Beautiful scenery."
But writing in her journal that night, she was pensive.

I'm wondering if this is what I want to do for the rest of my life. I
don't really like dealing with people. I look at Skipper Galpin and
he is an awesome leader. I don't think I could be as good. Lately I've
thought about being a hermit. Living in a log cabin with very little
exposure to the outside world. I would almost say I'm depressed but
I'm not. I'm actually happy. I love flying this jet. I love the squadron.
I feel very lucky. Key West was so hard. I'm glad to be here.

Chapter 52 ❋ *The Last Day*

Kara lived just a block from the ocean in Solana Beach, a few miles north of San Diego. She shared a rented house with a friend who didn't have a traveling job and could look after things while Kara was on cruise for six months or deployed somewhere else on the planet.

She loved to be outdoors. The southern California weather was wonderful all the time, but in October it was perfect—sunny, crisp, gentle during the day and cool at night. Kara's new passion was surfing and she focused intensely on learning the skill, tackling it with all her heart and soul, as she did with everything she undertook.

Her life was full and happy. When she wasn't flying or surfing, she was playing beach baseball or tennis or golf or working out in the gym or walking by the ocean or eating out with friends at one of the wonderful restaurants in the area. Or she was packing. She had been a fleet aviator for just under three months and had been away on detachments about half the time.

"Here are some pics. I'm going to the boat next week until 9 Nov. Should be fun." In that letter, which she wrote to her father on Sunday, 23 October 1994, two days before she was to leave, Kara enclosed recent pictures showing her with her F-14A in the background.

"I'm also in November issue of *McCall's* magazine. See ya, Love Kara. P.S. I haven't made Christmas reservations yet. I'm waiting for LV. approval. Prob dates 23–28 Dec."

She had spent part of the weekend gathering things she would need for the coming at-sea period, and after work on Monday she took her gear to her room on the USS *Lincoln,* which was docked at North Island Naval Air Station, just across the bay from San Diego. She brought the old down comforter she wouldn't let her parents throw away, the one they had bought when they lived in Germany the winter after they were first married. It was scruffy, the down lumpy, clumped, and bunched, but Kara loved to wind herself around it when she slept. She had several yards of a heavy dark forest green cloth that she had bought to shield her bunk from her roommate's lights, and by the next cruise she intended to have it sewn into a proper curtain.

She brought flight suits, khakis, and workout clothes. She knew they would all smell oily after a short time. You would think that with nuclear power there wouldn't be that pervasive fuel odor, but not so. There was still that "good ol' ship smell."

Kara felt a sense of anticipation as she boarded the gigantic vessel with her bags in tow. There is a lot of activity on a ship as it is being readied for voyage. The aviators bunked in the same general area of the ship and she ran into friends and squadron mates who were also preparing for the sixteen-day detachment. The new fleet aviators were excited and they showed it. The old hands at the drill were excited too—after all, this was what they lived for—but they affected rather bored expressions.

Kara, always organized, found a sense of peace and stability as she arranged her small space. When she was satisfied that everything was in place, she went home to eat dinner and get to bed by 11:00 P.M. Tomorrow would be a big day.

She woke up early the next morning, too wound up to sleep late. She stretched and savored the promise of the day. She had worked hard for this adventure and she meant to enjoy every minute of it. The morning seemed to move in slow motion as she ate breakfast, reviewed the checklist of items she needed to have on board, and tried to decide whether or not to wear her khakis to the base or just put her flight suit on at home.

Wearing flight suits through the gate was frowned on—shouldn't be prancing around in work clothes no matter how glamorous the image—but it was really inconvenient to have to dress up, then change as soon as she got to work. So she blew off the flight suit rule. "Everybody does it," she rationalized as she pulled up the long zipper.

She was determined to once again have the best landing grades of all the new pilots in her squadron this cruise. Or why not the best grades in her entire squadron? She just had to be a little smoother with the power. Her performance on the six carrier landings since she qualified had placed her in the top half of all the pilots in the air wing, which was amazing for a new carrier pilot, and an F-14 pilot at that. And she had been recognized as the top nugget pilot in the squadron since 28 August. It was so satisfying, especially since she hadn't carrier qualified her first time around.

She was feeling the beginning stirrings of a familiar adrenaline surge.

Kara arrived at the squadron at 11:45 A.M. for "Wink" Winkowski's brief of the overall carrier qualification mission. "Wink's" experience as a carrier aviator made him a good teacher. She listened and learned about how ships try to kill you every day. She knew it paid to take aboard what he had to say.

He went over the administrative procedures required to take planes to the ship's operating area. He reviewed not only daily carrier operations but also emergency procedures, which take on increased significance to pilots flying to or from the deck of a ship that is moving though the water and is only sixty-four to sixty-six feet above that water.

After "Wink" finished his characteristically thorough briefing, "Waylon," who was the flight leader for Kara's element, briefed their hop in more detail. Then Kara and her RIO, Matthew "Klem" Klemish, went through the specifics of the hop together in even greater detail. They had to get their minds right for the mission, which was setting twenty-five tons of jet fighter down on a ship.

Kara had flown with "Klem" eight out of her last nine flights and they had fun together. Kara trusted him, and more importantly, he trusted her. "Klem" had been on one previous cruise, so he was no longer a nugget like Kara, but still he was comparatively inexperienced. He had only 697.7 total flight hours as compared to Kara's 1,241.9. However, 477.1 of his hours were in the F-14A, whereas Kara had only 217.9 hours in the F-14A. He had made more than three times as many carrier landings in the F-14A as Kara had—150 to her 48. He was one of the brightest young RIOs, not only in the squadron, but in the navy. "Flex," the squadron skipper, had a lot of faith in both "Klem" and Kara. He had assigned former RAG instructors to fly with nuggets he believed needed more help than Kara, and she took some pride in this.

Kara and "Klem" put on their flight gear and were ready to "step" for the airplane, an air force term that means "walk." The plane captain met them with a big smile on a face that was red from the afternoon southern California sun. Kara went one way and "Klem" went the other, and they looked for things that might be wrong with their jet, Lion 103. "Klem" found some fasteners that needed to be tightened, but other than that everything was in acceptable condition and they "mounted up" Lion 103.

Commander Sobieck had told them, "When you fly fighters, you don't get in the jet. You put it on and it becomes part of you. You know how it feels, how it responds, and what it will do for you if treated properly. It should be respected, not feared. Your envelope should be as big as the airplane's, but that will only come with practice and experience. Stay out in front of it and never turn your back on it, or it may bite you."

Kara taxied to the warm-up area near the takeoff end of runway 24 where they waited until "Waylon," in Lion 116, ran through the fuel pits to top off his jet. When he rolled up to the hold short, Kara gave him a "thumbs up," signaling they were ready. "Waylon's" RIO, Lieutenant Higgins, called for takeoff.

The Tower gave "Waylon" and Kara permission to position and hold. The winds were 280 at 9 knots. Kara took the starboard side, counting on the wind to take the jet wash from "Waylon's" jet off to the left side of the runway so she wouldn't have to deal with it while she was getting her plane into the air.

Tower's radio blared, "Lion 116 and flight, two four right, change to departure, wind 280 at six, cleared for takeoff." "Waylon's" right hand appeared above the canopy and he flashed two fingers in the air and wiggled his wrist. He was signaling Kara to run up the engines. He would be doing the same and if neither of them had problems with their jets, they would be rolling down the runway in a few seconds.

Kara ran the throttles up to mil (something less than afterburner) with her feet squarely against the brakes. The engines were spooling up, and as she moved the stick to the right, "Klem" watched for the appropriate movement of the horizontal tail and spoiler deflections. The RPM, TIT, fuel flow, and other instruments looked good. Kara asked "Klem," "You ready?" then she gave "Waylon" another thumbs up.

Lion 116 rolled down the left side of runway 24 right and "Waylon" selected afterburner. "Klem" and Kara counted to five, Kara pushed the throttles into afterburner, and Lion 103 lurched forward, first slowly, then faster and faster. The acceleration was a drug that made her feel ten feet tall. "Klem" said, "You're off the peg. There's 80 knots."

"Roger, nose wheel steering is disengaged," Kara answered. One hundred, 120, "Rotating," she said, and they were flying.

"Waylon" was at eleven o'clock and about one-half mile away, and he was cleaning up his machine. His gear was up and he was beginning a turn to the north. Kara accelerated through two hundred knots and then her airplane was clean. She turned to join up with "Waylon" so they would look good leaving Miramar. The two F-14s flew close parade formation until they crossed the coastline, then "Waylon" pushed out with another hand signal that told them to go into loose cruise.

Departure Control wasn't very busy that afternoon. They acknowledged Lion 116 and flight (meaning Kara's plane, Lion 103) leveling at two thousand feet and told them to head two two zero degrees and expect higher in four miles. It was a beautiful day to be on the beach. There was major league surf along the coast to the south, but then this was better than surfing. The cloud cover didn't start until they got a few miles out to sea.

"Lion 116 climb and maintain 14 thousand," San Diego Departure directed, and "Higgy" responded, "Roger leaving two for 14 thousand." One minute later they were cleared to switch to Beaver Control, the fleet area control and surveillance facility. Beaver was usually a big hassle because their radios were so bad they could never hear the aircrews.

"It's a little scary that these guys are the search and rescue coordinators," Kara said to "Klem." "You have to wonder if their equipment is going to work if you ever need them."

It wasn't long before they were transferred to the strike control frequency for the USS *Lincoln* and checked in with the ship. The ship's controller switched them to the Marshall frequency, which is holding in navy jargon, and provided an expected approach time. This gave them some idea of how much fuel they would be carrying when landing.

Things were going smoothly that day, because their push time was just twenty minutes away.

"This is so great!" Kara exulted. "Going out to the *Lincoln* for two weeks of flying every day."

"I can tell you haven't had a tour at sea yet," "Klem" laughed. "You'll be ready to come home after two weeks on the ship."

Then Kara went into her Monty Python routine about the difference in the wing velocity between the African swallow and the European swallow, interspersed generously with *Princess Bride* quotations. "Klem" laughed and they launched into one-up joke competition.

At about eight minutes to push, "Klem" recommended they dump a thousand pounds of fuel so they wouldn't have to wave off because they were too heavy. It seemed like an outstanding plan to Kara, so they squirted out a thousand pounds. The fuel would evaporate before it got to the surface of the water.

The ship was working Case Two, which meant Kara would fly on "Waylon's" wing through the clouds with him on instruments until he saw the ship, then they would be switched to the air boss in the tower for his control.

They "pushed" on time and were all done with the ship's penetration checklist including de-arming the spoilers and dropping the hook. Kara dumped more fuel until they were five hundred pounds above maximum trap weight. They would use that much flying the normal approach once they got to the VFR pattern.

"Waylon" leveled at twelve hundred feet, and at ten miles from the ship, "Higgy" reported to Marshall that we have a "see you," navy talk for "we see the ship."

Marshall switched them to tower, and "Higgy" checked in at the three-mile initial. The ship's wake was underneath them and the water was light blue and aqua, compared to the dark cold blue of the undisturbed ocean. The wake was white at the stern of the *Lincoln* as the mammoth vessel plowed through a relatively calm sea.

They were level at eight hundred feet doing about 375 knots. "Waylon" kissed Kara off about one mile past the bow of the ship and banked sharply to the left. They began their count. In theory, if "Waylon" pulled reasonable G in his break and maintained at least 150 knots until he reached the bow again on downwind, she could count to seventeen seconds, then break. If she pulled respectable G, she should arrive in the groove at an interval that would allow the flight deck to clear "Waylon's" aircraft out of the landing area, and reset the arresting gear so she could land without having to be waved off for a foul deck.

She knew the air boss didn't give a damn about theory. He wanted the planes there on time, not early, not late, but on time. The longer the captain has to stay into the wind, the more vulnerable the ship is to submarines, so the pilot's duty as a professional tailhook aviator is to be there.

She counted the seconds "fifteen, sixteen, seventeen." "Klem's" mask must have been a little loose, because she could hear air rushing on the ICS. They were pulling about three Gs at eight hundred feet and rolling out on a downwind heading of 125 degrees.

"Klem" said they were a little wide and recommended a cut to get them to the proper abeam distance. The LSOs only grade the groove portion of the approach to the ship (that portion from about three-quarters of a mile until touchdown), but they know when the pilot is wide or close abeam. They also know that the numbers they give the crew to use for "gouge" (helpful information) are of no use unless they get to a proper abeam distance. The LSOs coach them to work to get where they are supposed to be.

Kara made the correction and descended to pattern altitude of six hundred feet.

"In the groove, wave it off. Foul deck," was the call from the ship and "Waylon" had to go around again.

"He'll be hatin' that," Kara said.

Kara was one mile abeam, a little close for the pattern. "Klem" suggested they "extend a potato or two off the abeam" and she agreed that was just a grand idea. (To "extend a potato or two" is like Lawrence Welk's counting, just before the band starts to play, "andavon . . . andatwo." Aviators count potatoes.) They were on speed (the correct indicated airspeed for the aircraft's weight and configuration) and about thirty feet low at the 180-degree position. Kara's last recorded words to "Klem" were "140 degrees, 450 feet, 5 knots fast." What she was thinking and feeling can only be imagined.

✠

We're going to be a little wrapped up here, so I'll carry a few more knots, she calculates.

We're descending at 100 to 200 feet per minute and turning to final. I'm looking for 450 feet or so at the 90-degree to go position and a descent rate of 300 to 400 feet per minute to get back on the numbers. Don't peek at the boat yet. Wait just a little longer, until I get nearer the 45-degree to go position. We're crossing the wake now. We should be picking up a little high ball. There it is.

"Klem" comes up on the radio. "One zero three Tomcat ball Hultgreen."

The controlling landing signal officer, "Paddles," responds, "Roger ball."

But something isn't right. *What in the hell is wrong with this airplane?* Kara thinks to herself, her heart beginning to beat faster. *It's like there's no power coming from the left engine. We're settling like you can't believe.*

"Kara, you're ten knots slow. Get some power on this jet," "Klem" prompts.

"POWER! POWER!" commands the landing signal officer on the ship.

I don't know what's wrong with this machine, she thinks, all her senses heightened. *The power is coming up. Oh my God, the damn yaw rate is getting out of control and the nose keeps wanting to come up as I add power. If I step on the rudder I can almost control . . . No, I can't.*

"WAVE OFF," the backup landing signal officer (BLSO) instructs, his voice calm but insistent. He activates the wave off lights.

I usually like to hear those guys helping me, but right now I don't think they know what my problem is because I don't even know what's wrong with this thing. How much airspeed do I have? The ship is in the way. The goddamn ship is in the way. The water is getting so close.

"WAVE OFF! WAVE OFF!" "Paddles" directs. His voice is intense and very firm, cutting out the "level your wings and climb" call of the BLSO.

Damn it, I'm trying, Paddles. Why can't I level the wings? There's not enough rudder and stick here.

"WAVE OFF!" the BLSO calls as Kara's plane crosses the extended landing area centerline from right to left. His tone is urgent now.

I'm trying. I'M TRYING!

"POWER!

"RAISE YOUR GEAR!" The BLSO's voice is terse and tension filled.

The stick is just useless. I've got to get some airspeed.

"RAISE YOUR GEAR!"

"POWER!" The plane begins to roll to the left.

The stick seems to be doing more harm than good. We're getting so close to the ship and the water. I can't see the ship because of the angle of bank. If I can just get enough airspeed to raise the nose. The damn thing keeps rolling to the left, and even the rudder won't stop it anymore.

"EJECT! EJECT!"

She was conscious of a sudden explosion and a rush of cold air as the canopy was jettisoned from the plane. All the dust and dirt from the cockpit blew into the air, rushing past her windscreen. Lion 103 was starting to increase its roll rate to the left when "Klem's" seat rocketed from behind her.

She'd been so determined to save the aircraft, she hadn't considered ejecting. But "Klem" had made the decision, even before the command from the LSO, and she felt a sense of relief. *God, I hope he's going to be all right,* she thought. It seemed to take forever for her turn to come.

They'd have a lot to talk about when they got on board the ship.

Epilogue: Sally's Story

"It's Navy Lieutenant Gamber and Chaplain 'Somebody'"

It was not yet 5:00 A.M., still black outside, on the morning of Wednesday, 26 October 1994, when the doorbell rang. Such an unexpected sound, jarring in the silent darkness, crisp tingling tones, just two notes, one high, one low, echoing.

My clock radio was set to turn on later to Texas Public Radio, volume low, monotone voices soothing, crooning the daily news, nothing jangling—another ordered day in a fine life. I couldn't quite assimilate the clear, sharp two-note melody of the bells played out of context, but I was instantly awake, immediately out of bed, and at the top of the staircase calling down somewhat irritably to ask who was there.

And then came the response that I never anticipated but understood at once, the words dreaded by every person who has a loved one in the military, "Navy Lieutenant Gamber and Chaplain 'Somebody.'"

I knew at that crushing moment what I would learn at the bottom of the stairs.

"I don't want to answer the door, do I?" I said, not expecting or receiving a response from the uniform-clad beings awaiting me on my front porch.

I turned around, walked back into my room, and pushed the switch outside my closet so that when I opened its door the light shone, verifying that what I was experiencing was real. It took me a long time to decide what to put on to answer the door. Nothing seemed right for such an occasion.

A young female officer in dress blues, about Kara's age, and a tall man came into my house. I led them from the small entry hall, out of habit warning them not to trip on the step down into the living room, and invited them to sit down on the couch.

269

"Is she dead?" I asked them.

"Yes, Ma'am," said Lt. Amy Gamber, and then she said some formal words she had rehearsed, something like, "I regret to inform you that your daughter Kara Hultgreen has been involved in an airplane mishap and is lost at sea and presumed dead."

Amy told me the accident had happened at approximately 1500 hours, while Kara was attempting to land on the carrier. I knew that 1500 hours was 3:00 P.M., but I couldn't comprehend that my daughter had been dead since yesterday afternoon and so I thought it must have happened at 3:00 in the morning, just a couple of hours before. Then I tried to figure out whether it was California or Texas time. It was hard to think.

I had called Kara at 6:35 P.M. San Antonio time the evening before, thinking that she was going to the *Lincoln* on Wednesday, not Tuesday. Kara's housemate had answered the phone and we had laughed and talked for a time. Later, I realized that when I made that call, Kara had been dead for one hour and thirty-four minutes.

I asked if Kara had hit the ramp on the carrier and Amy said no, but that was about all she knew. Amy and the chaplain sat there a minute or two; they asked me if I wanted them to call someone to be with me. I said no, that I wanted to call Dagny and Kirsten in Los Angeles, and that I wanted to do it myself.

After I made those calls, I went upstairs and dressed carefully for the day.

Kirsten, Dagny, and Dagny's husband, Michael Dubelko, arrived in San Antonio that afternoon.

"What will we do?" I asked Dagny and Kirsten as they were unpacking. "How will we live our lives without Kara?"

"We were just talking about that," said Dagny.

"Yes," said Kirsten. "We feel so sorry for you, Mom. Your nicest daughter died."

In a way that was true. Kara was very protective of me. Kirsten was a good soul, but she could be blunt and insensitive. She had mastered saying "Mother!" in the tone used by generations of female children to intimidate their mothers.

Dagny occasionally refused to mince words either. When I suggested that I might have to take over the lease on Kara's tiny racy sports car, Dagny said, "Mother, you would look *ridiculous* driving that car!" I turned to my bachelor brother. "Never have any children, Jimmy," I said, about half serious. "They die and ruin your life—and they live and ruin your life."

It was so hard for all of us.

The Memorial Ceremony at the San Antonio Country Club

"Her time with the fleet was much too short, but her memory will long remain with her fellow aviators," Admiral Yakeley said with a catch in his voice, his grief obvious. He had known Kara and had come to San Antonio from San Diego to lead the program of military and family speakers at the memorial ceremony. "Kara knew the risk of flying high-performance aircraft off the carrier, day and night," he continued, "but it was a risk she accepted freely and with enthusiasm."

It was 5:00 P.M. on Saturday, 29 October 1994, four days after Kara's death. The day was bright, mild, crisp, and beautiful, the kind of fall day that makes San Antonio natives forget the hot, humid summer and remember why we love living here. I hadn't known at first where to have the ceremony. I thought it would be handy to be religious. Religion provides not only a remedy to the finality of death but also a physical place to honor it, and a familiar ceremony. It probably looked strange, the announcement in the newspaper that the memorial ceremony would be held on the terrace of the San Antonio Country Club. It surely was the first time ever such a service was held there. But it was a perfect place.

The chairs were placed so the mourners looked through the twisted, gnarled branches of the old live oak trees at the rolling green fairways of the golf course. There was just enough space between the branches to see the four F-14s from reserve fighter squadron 201 out of NAS Dallas when they flew over. The fourth plane, which broke away in the "missing man" formation, was framed in green leaves. It was heart stopping.

And Kara had loved it there. She had worked one summer as a counselor for the children's camp in the mornings, and in the afternoons she would play golf. Some of the people in the gathering that Saturday were men who had walked a few holes on the course with the leggy eighteen-year-old Kara and marveled at how far she could hit that golf ball.

The Fifth Army Band from Fort Sam Houston Army Base, which you could see in the distance, played "Anchors Aweigh" and other military marches. "Nothing sad," I told them. Then the colors were paraded and posted as the National Anthem was played. Kara's Uncle Jimmy thanked the many naval officers who had served with Kara in San Diego and in Key West and who had come to San Antonio to say goodbye to her.

Kara's best friend, Monique, was the first to speak. Her voice, always soft, was trembly, but she had great presence. "I know most people remember Kara as the first woman navy fighter pilot, but I remember when it was all just a dream. She would call and say, 'Hey Mo, want to go to a movie?' and I would grit my teeth and say, 'Kara, please don't make me see *Top Gun* again!'"

She talked of Kara's courage, "her courage to have a dream, and the courage to fulfill it; and as much as I will always miss my friend, I know she lived her dream." Monique ended saying, "Through her exceptional and extraordinary life, she has given me the privilege of living my life able to say, 'My best friend, Kara Hultgreen, is a hero.'"

Dagny rose to talk about her sister and she meant to tell the story Kara relished telling, about how Kara had called her, the television professional, to ask advice about how to do a good interview, and her contribution was, "Wear false eyelashes." The story was so funny the way Kara told it—even to Dagny because Kara made such gentle fun of her, but Dagny didn't pull it off. She said something like, "Kara wanted to know tricks of the trade to have a successful television interview and I told her that looks were very important."

No one in the audience noticed that the punch line had no punch, however, because Dagny started crying in the middle of the story and the ravaged face of the beautiful young woman expressing her love for her sister told a more poignant tale.

Kara's dad told how Kara had brought her jet to an air show near his home in Appleton, Wisconsin, and though he had hoped to take her to lunch, Kara wouldn't leave her plane because there were children lined up to talk to her. Lots of the pilots left their planes unattended, but not Kara. She stood there for hours explaining to her eager young audience what it was like to be a navy pilot and encouraging them to follow their dreams. Then he said he had come that day to say goodbye to his daughter, and he became so emotional he could say nothing more.

I was dry-eyed as I thanked everyone for sharing the day with us. "If there can be any good resulting from the loss of this beautiful human being, maybe it is that it reminds us that there are men and women who believe that we are so blessed to live in this wonderful country that they are willing to die to preserve it."

Kirsten did what she often did. She put the essence of the day into words. She told about going to the air show at Miramar with Kara and watching with awe as the F-14s flew overhead. "It was the first time I realized fully what an amazing thing Kara was doing with her life, and I told Kara how proud of her I was," Kirsten said. "Kara had been so happy that I finally understood how she felt about flying."

Then Kirsten told about the friend who asked Kara how she got her last call sign, "Flipper."

"Well, I'll be glad to tell you," Kara had said, "but what version do you want, the truth or the legend?"

"With Kara," Kirsten ended, "the legend was the truth."

Aftermath

When the news of Kara's death began circulating, the media requested interviews and pictures of Kara. It was Kirsten's immediate reaction that set the tone of how we would deal with the media.

"Of course we'll talk to the press," Kirsten said. "We want everyone to know how special Kara was."

We wanted the world to know more than just the fact that the first woman combat F-14A pilot had died. We wanted to share that a wonderful human being had been lost, that she loved to fly, that she had a great sense of humor and a gentle and caring nature. We thought it was important that Kara's spirit, her honor and patriotism, be recognized and remembered.

We gave interviews to everyone who asked. We talked to radio and television network news and their affiliates in San Antonio and San Diego, the Associated Press, Reuters, *Nightline,* and *Prime Time Texas.* We talked to newspaper reporters from the *San Antonio Express-News,* the *Houston Post* and *Houston Chronicle,* the *Dallas Morning News,* the *Chicago Tribune,* the *London Sunday Times,* the *New York Times* and the *Washington Post.*

The navy sent a public affairs officer from NAS Corpus Christi, Cdr. Nettie Johnston, to help with the press and with arrangements for the memorial service. She and Amy Gamber, the casualty assistance officer, were abiding presences in my living room. The phone rang constantly with friends expressing condolences, with media representatives asking for interviews, and with navy personnel helping us arrange the memorial service and the disposition of Kara's personal effects.

And then I received some calls that were dissonant, incompatible with the flow of activity that was carrying me along, not allowing me time to fracture. Only a day or so after Kara's death became public, Duke Cunningham, an ace navy fighter pilot during the Vietnam War, now a congressman from California, phoned to say that someone purporting to be a navy pilot had sent an anonymous fax concerning Kara to radio talk show hosts in San Diego.

The six or so single-spaced pages of the fax were filled with incorrect information. For example, the anonymous author charged that Hultgreen "never even got aboard [the flight deck] on the first attempt to night qualify," which was not true. And the low carrier landing scores attributed to Kara were not hers. But whether the allegations were true or not didn't seem to matter to those who aired the message.

The congressman said the fax made much of the fact that Kara didn't qualify her first time at the boat, but he said that didn't mean she wouldn't develop into a fine aviator. "I'll match my record with anyone's," he said, "and I didn't qualify my first time at the boat."

Roger Hedgecock, a San Diego talk show host, repeated the anonymous allegations without any known attempt to verify the facts and added his uninformed opinion that if the navy had not lowered its standards so that women could fly combat planes, Kara Hultgreen would be alive today.

Many of his listeners believed women had no business in the armed services, much less flying navy warplanes, and they responded. Some called in to say their navy careers had ended so that room could be made for less qualified women and minorities. A few claimed personal knowledge that navy standards had been lowered to accommodate women. "Kara wasn't qualified to fly the F-14," said the callers that Hedgecock encouraged. "The navy had pushed her through because it needed to get women in the pipeline to fly combat jets in the wake of the Tailhook scandal."

Kara's death became a rallying call for people who opposed the new expanded role of women in the navy. To my mind, one of the most outrageous and insensitive comments was made by Dick Cheney, former secretary of defense under George Bush, who was in San Antonio to campaign for Henry Bonilla's race for congress. Our family was incensed as they saw his offhand comment to television reporters that of course he was sorry about Kara's death but he never thought women belonged in the cockpits of combat aircraft anyway.

John Dalton, the secretary of the navy, Adm. "Mike" Boorda, the chief of naval operations, and Rear Admiral Yakeley called to reassure me that the "facts" stated in the six pages of accusations were not true and the navy would stand up for Kara. But even though the allegations against Kara were no more than unsubstantiated gossip, the national press picked up the story and repeated them on network television and in big city newspapers.

To put an end to gossip and speculation, I released Kara's carrier qualification grades. I had found the documents while going through Kara's papers, and I asked the navy if there was any reason I shouldn't publish them. I was told it wasn't navy policy to release training grades but those documents belonged to Kara. It was my decision. I released them on 21 November 1994, the morning of Kara's funeral at Arlington.

Kara had rated third out of a class of seven. In daytime landings, she had placed first in her class. Her night-landing grades had dragged down her class standing.

For a time the talk ceased.

The Jagman

Whenever someone is killed on active duty or an accident causes more than $1 million in property damages, the navy conducts an official investigation to determine the facts surrounding the accident. Investigators decide whether the deceased died in the line of duty and whether the accident was due to misconduct by the deceased. They produce a report specified by the *Manual of the Judge Advocate General* and usually called the JAG report.

In an aviation accident, the navy also conducts a safety investigation. Its purpose is to prevent the same mishap from occurring again. Results of the safety investigation are presented in a *Mishap Investigation Report,* or MIR.

The JAG is based on consideration of the facts. Just as in a court of law, hearsay, innuendo, and conjecture are not allowed. Witnesses testify under oath and are subject to disciplinary action if they are suspected of violating the Uniform Code of Military Justice. The JAG is the official report of the accident and a copy, which in Kara's case was more than three inches thick, is available to anyone who requests it.

The JAG report on Kara's accident was eagerly awaited. Because of the public interest in what caused the mishap, and because a JAG is hard to wade through if one is not used to reading navy reports, the navy decided to hold a press conference to explain the conclusions of the report and to answer questions. It was scheduled for Tuesday, 28 February 1995. As a courtesy, the commanding officer of Kara's squadron, Cdr. Michael J. Galpin, came from San Diego to San Antonio on Sunday, two days before the press conference, to give me a copy of the report and help me understand it.

"This mishap was precipitated by a malfunction of the left engine during an extremely critical phase of the flight," said Rear Adm. Jay B. Yakeley, who served as the investigation's spokesperson at the press conference.[1] An article in the *San Antonio Express-News* quoted excerpts from a telephone interview with Rear Admiral Yakeley: "Fighter pilots are trained to fly the F-14 with one engine. But Yakeley added that Hultgreen 'may not have known. There's a possibility she had no warning at all' of the stall as she went into the carrier landing approach at 600 feet altitude." The JAG states, "There are no caution or advisory lites [*sic*] that indicated an MCB valve malfunction."[2]

Kara's approach to the *Abraham Lincoln* wasn't flawless—she was overshooting a little—and she was taking actions to correct her deviation, using her left rudder and moving the throttles, but there was no reason to believe she wouldn't successfully board the carrier. "Neither the side slip [caused by using more than normal left rudder] nor the throttle movements were out of the basic design parameters of the flight envelope," according to Vice Adm. Robert J. Spane, commander of the U. S. Pacific Fleet Naval Air Force, in an article published in the *San Diego Union-Tribune* (see appendix A).[3]

Kara's actions may have been within the normal parameters the engine is designed to handle, but unknown to her, she wasn't operating under normal parameters. The left engine of her plane had a closed MCB valve. "The mid-compression bleed valve system was stuck in the bleeds closed position prior to impact" and that "reduced the stall margin" and added to the engine's "tendency to stall," the JAG concluded.[4] The rebuilt TF-30 engines in the plane Kara was flying have a history of stalling when the air in front of the engine is disturbed, Admiral Spane told me, and were known to be inefficient and stall-prone even when new and operating under the best conditions. The mechanical deficiency and the age of the engine had reduced the stall margin of the engine substantially, and Kara's attempts to correct her line-up reduced it further.

Kara may have faced other obstacles that will never be known. "Like many accidents, this one was due to a combination of factors; take away any one of them, and it would just have been a wave off, not a fatal accident," wrote Peter Garrison in the June 1995 issue of *Flying* magazine.[5] But whatever random combination of circumstances caused the engine of Lion 103 to stall, the problem occurred at the worst possible time during the flight. The fact that the engine stalled when Kara was in the landing pattern somewhere below 450 feet while trying to slow the airplane to an on-speed condition made this a very special mishap.

Kara's first hurdle would have been to figure out what the problem was.[6] Lieutenant Klemish said he heard a "single and barely audible 'pop' coming from somewhere behind him." The "pop" noise is notable because it could be an indication of a compressor stall resulting in reduced thrust and a break in speed. According to the JAG, "The 'pop' seemed insignificant, even in hindsight, and [LT Klemish] did not ask LT Hultgreen if she heard it, nor did he mention it to her."[7] Kara was farther away from the source of the sound and concentrating hard. No one knows whether or not she heard it, but the actions she took to try to fly the plane away were proper for a dual engine wave off, not a single engine wave off.

Both cockpit throttles were up in full afterburner range as they were supposed to be, but when she added power, only the right engine responded. That caused the airplane to yaw to the left and the nose to pitch up, thus increasing the angle of attack. That meant the wing was no longer producing the lift it should because of the angle at which the wind stream was hitting it. In addition, the F-14 fuselage is very long and large, which caused an additional problem. As the nose came up, it blocked the air from flowing over the vertical tails. Whatever directional control Kara had was reduced as the nose came up and the angle of attack increased.

Even if she had been aware of the engine stall and attempted to execute single engine emergency procedures, the odds against success were great. The procedures anticipate that the pilot will have some time to prepare and set up for a straight-in approach and to control the angle of attack and airspeed, and Kara had neither altitude nor time to prepare to salvage the situation. The warning found in the F-14A pocket checklist reads: "Extreme caution must be exercised when performing turns into a dead engine. Decaying airspeed or increasing angle of attack can rapidly result in a situation where there is not enough rudder authority to return the aircraft to level flight and insufficient altitude to effect a recovery."

Kara was trying to land, turning into her left engine, and it stalled in the midst of her turn. If she tried to correct by turning right, she would be pointing the aircraft back toward the carrier and she was very close to it. Admiral Spane told me in a telephone conversation on 14 February 1995 that he "thought that she was trying to miss the ship, but we will never know because there were no precise readings."

To keep her angle of attack below twenty units and avoid a mishap, she would have had to point the nose down. "With water rush occurring as the aircraft is descending [through] 200–250 feet, an extensive amount of flight time and experience would be required to accomplish this procedure properly," wrote Rear Admiral Yakeley in his letter forwarding the JAG report.[8]

The JAG report, even with Admiral Yakeley's explanations at the press conference, was difficult for reporters to understand and write about so that the public could digest it, and his statement that the engine malfunction precipitated the mishap satisfied their deadlines. It would have been impossible to summarize the complexity of the accident in a headline.

The MIR

About a month after the 28 February 1995 press conference, the report of the second investigation, the Mishap Investigation Report, or MIR, was nearing completion. The sole focus of this investigation is safety, and its purpose is to prevent the same mishap from recurring.

An Aircraft Mishap Board (AMB) made up of aviators with experience in operations, maintenance, and medicine, produces the MIR, which is meant to be used as a training tool for aircrews, to help them learn from the mistakes of other aviators. From testimony and material evidence gathered, the AMB tries to re-create the series of events leading up to and during the mishap. Then it analyzes the findings in an attempt to assign causal factors. It also identifies possible mechanical deficiencies so they can be rectified in like aircraft.

It can and does speculate on different theories as to what might have happened and neither an administrative forum nor a military court martial holds the witnesses accountable for their statements. The MIR is written by naval aviators for naval aviators and not for the general population. Members of the AMB may reach a conclusion based on their experiences and opinions. The conclusions in the MIR may differ from those in the JAG because the JAG conclusions must be based on hard evidence.

Because the MIR includes opinion (whether or not substantiated by fact), educated guesses, possible causes, and ideas, it definitely is not meant for publication. In fact, releasing it to unauthorized people is a felony. That did not deter someone within the navy from leaking it.

The person who leaked the report claimed that the MIR contradicted the official JAG report—that the MIR attributed the accident to pilot error.

The format of the MIR is unique. A statement is made and the members of the AMB must either accept or reject it. They don't need to prove that the action or circumstance described in the statement caused or was partly to blame for the accident; they need only a reasonable belief based on their analysis of the evidence and their experience that it was a causal factor. A causal factor "accepted" can and many times does result in action being taken to correct it. The format succeeds, in that it leads to formulating recommendations for changes to existing systems, materials, or procedures. After all, the reason for producing a Mishap Investigation Report is to prevent such an accident from occurring again.

The statement was made in the MIR that the pilot "failed to execute proper single engine wave off procedures" and it was "accepted" as a causal factor of the mishap. The accusation of pilot error rose from that statement. However, the MIR continued that the RIO "did not see any illuminated engine stall warning lights" and the AMB believed that "the left engine stall warning light was not illuminated." The inference is if she didn't know she had only one engine, she wouldn't have had reason to execute a single engine wave off.

But the MIR format doesn't allow for extenuating circumstances. It isn't relevant that the pilot's actions may be justified. If the board can reasonably substantiate the statement, it is accepted. Conversely, if a statement can logically be ruled out based on the knowledge and experience of the board members, it is rejected. For example, if a statement were made that "it was impossible for the pilot to have saved the aircraft" it would be rejected if the board believed there was one chance in a hundred or a thousand that the pilot could have saved the aircraft by doing something differently.

The navy learned much from Kara's mishap. Training for this particular failure during an approach to the carrier had been limited at best. In the future, pilots would be trained to respond to an engine compressor stall in the landing pattern. In addition, the old engines would be inspected more frequently.

A single-engine-landing configuration was added to the annual out-of-control trainer syllabus. The F-14A NATOPS manual now includes "single engine failure landing configuration" procedures emphasizing the importance of controlling the angle of attack during wave off. Single engine failure—wave off in the landing pattern was added to the familiarization carrier qualification phase of simulator training. Increased emphasis was placed on the proper execution of single engine wave off procedures during field carrier landing practice.

The MIR recommended one-time fleetwide inspection of the F-14A TF-30 engine midcompression bleed system and a review of previous recommendations for a newly designed directional control linear bleed valve assembly. Also advocated was more frequent use of the high-power trim box, which tests available thrust, stall margins, and the proper operation of the midcompression bypass system.

The recommendations for change to established policy and procedures reflected the navy's acceptance of its portion of blame for the accident.

Gregory L. Vistica, a reporter who revisited the Tailhook scandal every time the navy had a change-of-command ceremony, called me on a Saturday afternoon and read out loud portions of the MIR, claiming that this information contradicted the JAG report. For someone like Vistica, who was not accustomed to reading an MIR and did not understand its purpose, the starkness of "accepted" or "rejected" applied to each statement was misleading.

Vistica asked me if the navy had lied to me.

I said no, that I was not privy to the MIR (later, I got it on the Internet like everybody else), but the navy had explained all the things he was talking about, and that if he took the trouble to read the JAG report he would find the same information there.

It didn't really matter, however, what I had to say because Vistica was well into writing a book to be called *Fall from Glory: The Men Who Sank the U.S. Navy,* and my explanation of the seeming inconsistencies didn't suit the theory upon which his entire book was based—that "the Navy was covering up, that it had again lied to the public."[9] True to his premise and his upcoming publicity tour, Vistica's blurb in *Newsweek*'s 27 March 1995 issue questioned whether the navy had told the whole truth in the report it put out to the public.

The leaking of the MIR was enough to provide additional ammunition to those determined to sabotage the navy and any officer who supported equal opportunity for women. The navy had been accused of lying when it defended Kara's flight training record, and now "they" said, it was evident the navy had lied again in the Jagman report.

In an effort to provide all the information available and so there could be no charge that information was being withheld, the navy had released the videotape of the accident at the 28 February 1995 press conference. That was unprecedented, but it was a sure bet that the innuendoes and rumor would not be quieted so long as one piece of evidence remained unpublished. Our family agreed. The price of watching Kara's plane career into the Pacific Ocean played over and over on television was high, but we believed the truth best served Kara's memory.

Neither the navy nor our family appreciated that some would try to use the video to claim the pilot was incompetent. Those whose agenda was to keep women from combat roles rejected the navy's explanation that there was something wrong with the plane and claimed the accident proved the pilot wasn't qualified to fly the plane.

Commander Sobieck, who had watched the women aviators grow and learn their trade from the beginning, told me, "Sadly much of the speculation in the news was by people who couldn't carry those three women's helmets out to the jet for them. In fact, the total tonnage of what some of these people don't know about carrier aviation and flying the Tomcat, and specifically this mishap, could have sunk the *Nimitz*."

In his 13 April 1995 article in the *San Diego Union-Tribune,* Vice Admiral Spane stated that the Jagman and MIR reports were not inconsistent—just written for different reasons, and he explained in clear and simple sentences just what the two reports took hundreds of pages to say. The full text of the article is included in appendix A, but Admiral Spane's conclusions were

It was improbable that the aircraft could have been recovered. The pilot had to accurately analyze the emergency and apply precisely the correct control inputs in less time than it takes the telephone to ring twice. I believe Lt. Hultgreen did her best to recover the aircraft; the fact that she was not successful in no way diminished her stature as a fully qualified F-14 pilot. Her late ejection could have been due to her attempt to "save the airplane at all costs."[10]

This article inspired a fervent attack on Admiral Spane and the integrity of naval leadership in general by a man named Gerald Atkinson, another author of a book in progress, this one entitled *From Trust to Terror: Radical Feminism Is Destroying the U.S. Navy.* His commentary was published in the *San Diego Union-Tribune* on 7 July 1995.

Admiral Spane had written, "Another F-14A squadron commanding officer tried to replicate this situation in a simulator; eight of his [nine] pilots 'crashed' the simulator." Atkinson took him to task for failing to respond to accusations that the simulator test was rigged.

Robert Caldwell, editor of the Insight Section of the *San Diego Union-Tribune,* said that "sources" (anonymity apparently being the order of the day) told him that the tested pilots were reportedly ordered *not* to execute the F-14 manual's so-called boldface instructions for flying through an emergency situation comparable to Kara's.[11] The boldface instructions are mandatory procedures in a given emergency.

Cdr. James A. Winnefeld Jr. was the commander who conducted the training exercise for the members of his F-14 squadron, VF-211. He answered Caldwell's charges in a letter written on 10 April 1995 to Herb Klein, the editor of the *San Diego Union-Tribune.*

He explained that he conducted the training informally over the course of an afternoon or two, that the pilots were told in advance they would experience a left engine failure at some point in the approach and were instructed to perform all normal emergency procedures (with no restrictions whatsoever) to save the aircraft. As reported, eight of the nine pilots crashed on their first attempt, with all nine learning how to handle the situation on subsequent attempts. He wrote: "Ultimately, the exercise taught us a valuable lesson about a rare and very difficult flight regime. It also taught us that Lt. Hultgreen's accident should not be a gender issue. She was in a predicament that would have been terribly difficult for even an experienced pilot."

As Commander Sobieck explained it to me, "During training, pilots are taught to deal with an engine stall emergency in proximity to the ship, but the simulation is normally set up off the other end of the carrier. The pilot and RIO are accelerating off the catapult and they are staring at their engine instruments, not scanning outside the airplane preparing to board the carrier. In other words, instead of trying to slow the airplane down to land, they are trying to accelerate and climb. It is a very different situation."

Scott Watkins, senior editor of *Woman Pilot* magazine, was on assignment on the *Abraham Lincoln* just four days after Kara's accident and interviewed people on the ship. He wrote: "What is known is that although the F-14 had stopped flying, Kara kept fighting—had she not, the accident could have been worse. Aviators interviewed by this writer after the crash stated emphatically that even though flight control was all but lost, to just let go of the controls and give up would have accelerated the crash time significantly. Witnesses aboard the carrier consider her a hero."

The article continues: "'Who knows how many lives she saved? As far as I'm concerned, she sacrificed herself to save the ship,' says flight director Brian Kipp."

Airman Stephen Snow, an aircraft handler on the flight deck, echoed those sentiments. "It was coming in funny, with one wing more forward than the other, like a prop plane does when it's coming in. I remember thinking, 'It's too slow, and it's too low.' Then I saw the backseater [Klemish] eject just as the jet rolled away from the ship.

"The pilot was ejected into the water, head-first. But she saved a lot of people first. A ramp-crash could have started one helluva fire. Who knows what could have happened? That lady had some guts."[12]

Adm. Stanley. R. Arthur wrote a letter to the editor of the *Washington Times* after he became incensed by an article, appearing in the 18 May 1995 issue of the paper, by Paul Craig Roberts called "Washout on the Navy's Bridge." Admiral Arthur was a much-decorated aviator who had flown more than five hundred missions during the Vietnam War, commanded the U.S. naval forces in the Persian Gulf War, and had just retired as vice chief of naval operations. He said Roberts's article was "so error filled that I must break with my standard practice of ignoring such tripe." He continued:

> Roberts, an economist by training, armed with a pile of photocopied training records that neither he, nor the activists who are peddling

them, understand, has accused the Navy's civilian leadership of causing the death of a woman aviator. Nonsense.

As a naval aviator for 37 years, I can assure you there is no quota policy when it comes to earning the Navy's "Wings of Gold." Those charged with training young men and women to fly know that the student naval aviator they train today could be their wingman tomorrow. No one involved in this training would push through a pilot who was unsafe or unqualified.

A reading of Lt. Kara Hultgreen's records by those who understand naval aviation training would reveal that she was a fully qualified pilot who earned her wings through merit. The fact she did not achieve perfection in her training syllabus comes as no surprise to the many of us who also had some "downs" in our training days.

Roberts compounds his errors by repeating a canard. He says male pilots trying to replicate Lt. Hultgreen's crash were ordered not to follow procedures for avoiding a crash. This is simply not true . . . something he could have learned from the lips of the squadron commander who conducted the tests, if he had bothered to ask. . . .

Those who follow these issues know I have received some political heat for standing behind decisions to keep unqualified pilots out of the cockpit. Those decisions were made solely on the basis of the pilot's skills and not his or her gender.

Lt. Hultgreen was qualified to fly F-14s. Her tragic death is a reminder that naval aviation is a dangerous business. Her death should not be used by unqualified pundits to score political debating points.[13]

Admiral Arthur had had a direct hand in bringing women into naval aviation and then into combat planes. But then, asked to review the training records of a female helicopter pilot trainee named Rebecca Hansen, he confirmed the decision to wash her out of naval aviation. It put him at odds with a U.S. senator and, ironically, cost him his nomination to take over the Pacific command.

The consensus is that the nastiness arising after Kara's death came from the naval aviators, retired and active, who thought women shouldn't be allowed to fly the hot airplanes, and it isn't hard to find quotes from those who support that opinion. Probably the best example of true vitriol came from a man named Rolla Rich, who identified himself as publisher and editor of *Sports Leader.* He qualified as an expert on flying since he had, in his words, "stood with, eaten with, talked with, lived with Aces, astronauts, Blue Angels and other super pilots."[14]

On 22 November 1994, Rich wrote to Capt. Mark Grissom, the commander of all fighter operations in the Pacific Fleet, who had been quoted in the 20 November 1994 issue of the *San Diego Union-Tribune* as saying, "It infuriates me that someone is out there out-and-out lying or insinuating and passing off rumor and innuendo" about Kara's qualifications to fly the F-14.[15]

Quotes from Rich's letter to Captain Grissom include: "Frankly, I don't think Hultgreen is worth the ink on the paper. She wasn't much of a pilot, never was an aviator, and not much of a person. . . . She's buried, but she's no heroine, just another feminist. If you knew the Bible, you'd know why what she was doing was wrong."

And finally, the most relentless attacks on Kara came from Elaine Donnelly, who identifies herself as president of the Center for Military Readiness (CMR), an organization she established. The name of the organization is subtle, since its purpose is to oppose the idea of women in combat. It's as if keeping women clear of battle is the defining criterion for military readiness. Support for the organization comes from the retired naval aviator community and such guardians of "right-thinking" citizens as Phyllis Schafly, who led the fight against the Equal Rights Amendment and who is on the board of directors of CMR.

Support for CMR also came from a junior officer in the navy, Lt. Patrick J. "Pipper" Burns, an instructor in VF-124 who contended that Kara and Carey had been accorded special treatment in training to fly the F-14 and that the navy had misrepresented the cause of Kara's mishap. After requesting and being granted immunity from criminal prosecution, he admitted that he rifled through squadron files and, in violation of the federal Privacy Act, provided copies of Kara's and Carey's training records to Donnelly.[16]

The Center for Military Readiness published a special report dated 25 April 1995 titled "Double Standards in Naval Aviation." The table of contents page noted that "documents presented in this compendium of information have been selected to demonstrate a pattern of flexible or double standards in naval aviation." Excerpts from Kara's and

Carey's F-14 training records "selected" by CMR were included. A condensed version of the CMR report published in June 1995 claimed that "vehement protestations" by the navy that the women were technically "qualified" were meaningless as well as misleading, because "the *definition* of that word has been radically changed by practices that forgive low scores and major errors in training so that certain people will not fail."[17]

Lieutenant Burns's lawyer, Robert Rae, portrayed him as a hero who felt he had no place else to turn, but Navy Secretary John Dalton rejected that argument and recommended that Burns's name be removed from the 1998 promotion list for lieutenant commander. The *Washington Times* reported that Mr. Dalton sent Lieutenant Burns a letter of censure that stated in part as follows:

> I find that you intentionally violated the Privacy Act by releasing the personal training records of a fellow officer to an individual outside the federal government who lacked authority to receive such records.
>
> I expect all officers in the navy to exhibit our core values of honor, courage and commitment. . . . Your actions were not honorable, in that you violated federal law by releasing records of a shipmate knowing that such information would be used to humiliate the officer involved.[18]

The commander of the F-14 training squadron, Tom Sobieck, told me he was outraged by the CMR accusations and by the fact that one of his trusted officers would violate a federal law. He was also terribly disappointed that Lieutenant Burns didn't approach him when the training was being conducted because documentation was available at that time to prove that Kara and Carey had met all required standards.

Squadron policy required that any extra-time sortie or refly of an unsatisfactory sortie was to be completed on an instrumented range known as the Tactical Air Combat Training system (TACTS). The system records every second of flight while the airplane is on the range and is available for playback and debrief. It gives the crew a precise readout of heading, altitude, airspeed, angle of attack, and G readings, plus the relationship of that airplane to every other airplane on the range. It is a tool for teaching fighter pilots, and it also removes any subjective evaluation about performance on a particular sortie. Carey had reflown a tactics hop on that range and there was no question but that she had met the standards. "Had I known I was going to be accused of lowering standards for the women, I would have saved the recording," he said.

Commander Sobieck had instituted the policy as a training tool. In addition, the TACTS tape recordings could be used as documentation in the event a student wound up before a Field Naval Aviation Evaluation Board (FNAEB) to review his or her performance. "If I were trying to slide the women through, I certainly wouldn't have established a policy that would provide irrefutable proof of acceptable or unacceptable performance," he told me.

The same is true for carrier qualifications. Every landing is recorded on a camera system known as the PLAT. There is no way to fake performance while landing on a ship. Commander Sobieck said he told his landing signal officers to evaluate all the students carefully and make the call. If the LSOs decided that any of the students were not ready for the fleet, the recorded documentation would be in place and the FNAEB process would begin. "Though both Kara and Carey required two attempts to qualify on the ship with the F-14A, the documentation was available at that time to prove they had met the required standard," Commander Sobieck said.

Stories behind Stories

Sometimes the stories behind the stories offer the real explanations as to why things happen the way they do.

For example, the fact that John Dalton, secretary of the navy, attended Kara's funeral at Arlington caused a negative reaction among some male aviators. The 16 September 1996 *New Yorker* magazine quoted a former chief of naval aviation, Thomas Moorer, as saying, "As C.N.O., I must have attended five hundred funerals at Arlington, and I never saw a Secretary of the Navy at one of them."[19] The implication was that John Dalton was serving political correctness.

But why wouldn't the death in the line of duty of the first woman to fly the F-14 Tomcat merit attendance at her funeral by the secretary of the navy? She was a pioneer, and as such, would have a significant place in naval history. In addition, Kara was a hometown girl. The secretary had lived in San Antonio, and he and I had many friends in common. He was a good friend of my cousin Carleton Spears and of Mike Beldon, my friend since high school, and of my next-door neighbor Drew Cauthorn. They talked to him. He knew all about Kara.

The commanding officer of Kara's squadron, Cdr. Mike Galpin, brought a copy of the JAG report to me in San Antonio the Sunday before the navy press conference scheduled for 28 February 1995. He told me to read the letters forwarding the report along the chain of command first because they would state the essence of the report.

I began reading the endorsement letters and when I came to the letter he had written, I read one of his sentences several times. "This one," I said, "is what the headlines will be."

Commander Galpin looked over my shoulder as I read out loud. "In this mishap, whether the engine stall was brought on by (1) an overly-aggressive pilot using rudder to remedy a dynamic overshoot, (2) a failed or closed MCB valve, and/or (3) unknown additional causal factors, will never be definitively determined."[20]

"An overly-aggressive pilot using rudder to remedy a dynamic overshoot," I repeated, looking over at him. His face was flushed as he heard his words read by a nonpilot, a person who interpreted them without the benefit of any naval aviation background.

"But being aggressive is not a criticism," he said. "It was one of Kara's best qualifications for flying the F-14."

"I understand," I said, "but it sounds negative, and it's catchy—an 'overly-aggressive pilot' is much more quotable than your next description of her as 'a meticulous professional.'"

Telling the truth isn't as simple as it sounds, and eyewitness accounts are notoriously inaccurate. Describing an event is difficult, but explaining how and why it occurred is a monumental task.

Mike Galpin left that Sunday afternoon and I promised not to show the report to anyone or talk about it until after the navy held its press conference on Tuesday morning. I was very surprised on Monday night when CNN broadcast a short story that the navy report attributed Kara's accident to engine failure. Commander Galpin had been careful to explain to me about the interaction of the stuck air bleed valve, rapid throttle movements associated with a carrier approach, and the left side-slip. I was perplexed at the succinct conclusion announced by CNN and amazed that the navy had released such information before the press conference.

I considered calling Admiral Spane to ask what had happened, but it was late and his number was at my office. More important, I was anxiously expecting to hear at any moment that my first grandchild had been born. I was very worried because Dagny had toxemia and had been in labor at a Los Angeles hospital since that morning.

Never before, but for a year after Kara died, I had to take pills in order to sleep. Without them, I would lie in bed, my body numb as in deep sleep and my mind skimming along. Or I would become quickly unconscious, only to be jarred suddenly awake; that would happen over and over all night.

The night before the navy press conference, I took a ten-milligram Ambien at ten o'clock and went to bed. The phone woke me from a deep sleep an hour later. It was Pat Flynn, a reporter from the *San Diego Union-Tribune*. He had seen the CNN broadcast and an Associated Press release from the *Chicago Tribune* and he was panicked. His editor wanted to know why he didn't have the story since the *Chicago Tribune* and CNN did.

Flynn said the navy report was out and began asking me questions. I was caught off guard and I tried to answer. But his questions required complex explanations, and when I became more awake I asked him why he was discussing this technical report with me. I told him to call Admiral Spane or Admiral Yakeley, then I promptly fell back to sleep.

Kirsten woke me up again a couple of hours later to tell me that Dagny had delivered a healthy, beautiful eight-and-a-half-pound girl named Skylar. She didn't talk long. She said the baby was fine, but they were worried about Dagny, whose blood pressure was dropping. Even after that, I went back to sleep. Those miraculous pills that were helping me survive the death of my youngest daughter, saved me from dealing with the knowledge that my oldest daughter was now in danger.

At 5:30 A.M., a reporter from ABC called to ask about the navy report and the phone never stopped ringing after that.

Kirsten told me later that morning that Dagny had been in serious trouble, but she was all right now. After receiving that good news, I called Admiral Spane to see how the press conference had gone. He was extremely cool and I couldn't understand why until he told me that I had been quoted all over the front page of the *San Diego Union-Tribune*. He assumed that I was the one responsible for leaking the navy report.

It turned out that Michael Kilian, a staff writer for the *Chicago Tribune,* had released the story to the Associated Press. He hadn't had a copy of the Jagman report, but a "source" had informed him of its conclusions. This was not the first story leaked by someone in the navy.

The fact that the first news stories about the conclusions of the report were written on the basis of comments by "sources with knowledge of the report" in the case of the *Chicago Tribune* and Kara Hultgreen's mother in the case of the *San Diego Union-Tribune,* without either of the reporters having a copy of the report itself or the benefit of hearing the explanations at the news conference, probably was the foundation for the confusion to follow.

The headline in the *Chicago Tribune* was "Engine Cited in Fatal F-14 Crash." In the *San Diego Union-Tribune,* Pat Flynn quoted me as saying, "Basically, their report just says what they've been saying all along. It was engine failure." And, "It was determined without a doubt the engine stalled. They know part of the reason why, maybe not all of it. What they do know is that she didn't know [her engine was out]." After I read that article, I was shocked that I had said so much to Pat Flynn. In fact, I was so groggy when he called I am amazed I made any sense at all.

That story in San Diego, full of quotes by me, had to have affected the way the news conference went, and maybe it distorted the slant of those reporting on it. The subtleties and complexities of the navy explanations just didn't have the bite of "it was engine failure."

I was miserable that I had betrayed Admiral Spane's trust. I told him that I knew when I decided right after Kara died to talk to the press that I would make a mistake somewhere along the way, but I was truly sorry that it had to be with the San Diego press right before the navy news conference.

The worst thing about the whole episode was that those who were determined to use Kara's death to advance their own agendas had been inadvertently helped by her mother.

One Crowded Hour

"Waylon" Jennings wrote me a long letter as the anniversary of Kara's death neared. He had just returned from a six-month WESTPAC deployment to the Persian Gulf. The squadron had lost two more Tomcats during the cruise, and he was flying one of them. He and his RIO survived, crashing into the Philippine Sea on 20 September 1995. Lt. Cdr. John Stacy Bates had crashed the first plane the previous April, and he would lose another Tomcat and his life on 29 January 1996. His RIO, Lt. Graham Alden Higgins, also died; "Higgy" was "Waylon's" RIO the day Kara flew on their wing out to the *Lincoln*.

In the next month, two other F-14s from different squadrons would crash, bringing the five-year total of F-14 crashes to thirty-two.

"Waylon" wrote in his letter:

> We were very low, going very fast, and something caused the jet to explode before we knew anything was wrong. I've been through time-expansion experiences before, and based on what I know of them, they occur often in near-death experiences. As our aircraft came apart and we were tumbling through the sky towards the water, I knew I wasn't going to survive, and in the three seconds that passed between the explosion and initiation of ejection, by my RIO, time seemed to stand still. My reactions were still at normal speed, but my thoughts and pondering lasted for what seemed several minutes. My first thoughts went to my wife and what it was going to be like for her to be without me. I then thought of my two children and was a little sad by the fact that they were going to grow up without their father. I wondered how they would get along and whether or not their mother would be strong enough to be both parents for them. After that, I thought, "This must be what it was like for Kara in her last few seconds." I wasn't scared at all, and it was a very calm and reflective experience.

"Waylon" had been Kara's friend. Also, he had served on the Air Mishap Board that produced the MIR of her accident.

> After [Kara's] mishap I was one of the ones assigned the unenviable task of sorting out the events of that day. The media was intolerable and unjustified in their treatment of Kara. We will never know exactly what happened, but I am certain of one thing, Kara was as

qualified as any pilot at Miramar to be in the fleet, flying Tomcats aboard and off of a ship. There were pilots our squadron was concerned with at that time, but Kara wasn't one of them. I personally reviewed her records with a fine-tooth comb, and I also interviewed numerous witnesses, associates, and former instructors. It all added up to the same thing—there were no skeletons in Kara's closet.

These days, anytime her name is brought up in a negative light, I am quick to point out what I know and how the facts have been distorted by irresponsible members of the press. Every time some reporter or someone writing an editorial drags Kara's name through the mud, it just incenses me. I can't imagine what it must be like for you, except that I'm certain you know the truth and are able to ignore all else. Rest assured, the only thing Kara lacked in the Tomcat was experience. With more of that, I believe she would have been one of the great pilots in our community.

Kara wasn't perfect, but I wish I had a hundred friends just like her. Although I only knew her a short time, I was enriched by her friendship, her enthusiasm, her zest for life and for flying. Her excitement was contagious, and everyone who experienced her was affected positively.

Bernard Weintraub, a syndicated columnist, described Kara as "a young woman who, in her struggle to become a pilot, didn't so much want to transform the boys' club as to soar joyously into the thick of it."

And that is the essence of what Kara was doing. All she asked for was the right to try—the opportunity to compete for the job of flying a fighter jet airplane. Her struggle to find her place in naval aviation is an inspiration to everyone who has a dream that means anything, but her real legacy is that of a life well lived in every way.

In my own struggle to cope with the enormous loss of my extraordinary daughter, the words of Mordaunt comfort me: "One crowded hour of glorious life is worth an age without a name."

Appendix A ✣ *Anatomy of a Plane Crash*

"Anatomy of a Plane Crash: Evaluating, Explaining the Results of Two Different Navy Investigations" by Vice Adm. Robert J. Spane, commander of the U.S. Pacific Fleet Naval Air Force, was published on 13 April 1995 in the *San Diego Union-Tribune*.

Over the past several weeks there has been some confusion over the cause of last fall's F-14 accident involving Lt. Kara Hultgreen. This confusion is due to perceived discrepancies between the results of the Navy's Judge Advocate General (JAG) manual investigation and the results of the Mishap Investigation Report (MIR).

There also has been a concern voiced about the integrity of naval officials.

I would like to comment on these issues.

First, let me explain the difference between the JAG investigation and the MIR. The JAG discusses facts and bases opinions on these facts. Just as in a court of law, hearsay, innuendo and conjecture are not allowed.

On the other hand, the MIR, a privileged document, probes all areas. There are "no rules" concerning what can and cannot be included in the MIR. Facts, opinion (whether or not substantiated by fact), guesses, possible causes, ideas, etc. . . . all are allowed. This is to ensure that any possible factor can be brought forward and discussed without fear of retaliation and without the formal rules of evidence and fact.

My 32 years of experience in evaluating reports of this type (and my analysis after reading all 500 pages of these two particular documents) tells me that in Lt. Hultgreen's accident there are really two issues: What caused the engine to malfunction, and, once the malfunction occurred, could the aircraft have been recovered?

We will never know for certain all of the factors involved in each event, but let's start with the facts that we do know:

- The left engine experienced a compressor stall.
- A compressor stall is an interruption of the air flow which causes the engine to stop producing thrust. Sometimes the engine malfunction is momentary, and sometimes the engine must be shut down and be restarted in order to return the engine to normal operating conditions. Once the stall clears, the engine is usually capable of normal operations.
- One of an engine's safe operating parameters is measured in "compressor stall margin." This is a measure of the engine's design resistance to compressor stall.
- Engineering analysis established that the left engine in the aircraft had a failed mid-compression bypass valve. This failure reduced compressor stall margin in the landing configuration by approximately 26 percent.
- Compressor stall margin is also reduced as an engine ages. The left engine was an old engine with the commensurate reduction in stall margin. The exact amount of the reduction is unknown.
- Lt. Hultgreen used more than normal left rudder during her approach to the ship. This causes unbalanced flight called "side slip," which reduced compressor stall margin. Computer simulation of this accident based on video indicated the aircraft had up to 10 degrees left side slip. Engineering information indicated the F-14A engine is designed to operate in this configuration with up to at least 18 degrees of side slip.
- Lt. Hultgreen was moving the throttles during this approach. This also reduced compressor stall margin. All aircraft engines are engineered with an automated fuel control that meters the fuel to keep the engines operating within parameters. The fuel controls for both engines were operating normally.

The "bottom line" question is: Would this engine have malfunctioned if the mid-compression bypass valve had not jammed, reducing compressor stall margin by approximately 26 percent?

My opinion is no. Neither the side slip nor the throttle movements were out of the basic design parameters of the flight envelope.

As a counterpoint, if this conclusion is false, in the 20-plus years this aircraft has been operating, there would have been at least one approach with side slip and throttle movements at least as great as Lt. Hultgreen's, and another accident would have occurred, or at least we would have had a very frightened flight crew; we have been unable to find a similar incident.

My conclusion is that if the engine had 100 percent of its compressor stall margin, this accident would not have occurred. It occurred due to a combination of circumstances, but a failed engine component unknown to the pilot that reduces the operating envelope by approximately 26 percent must be a significant issue.

Once the stall occurred, the facts are:

- Lt. Hultgreen had four to six seconds to respond.
- The correct response would have been—full throttle, right rudder and lower the nose of the aircraft. The last two actions would have placed the aircraft in apparent danger of hitting the ship.
- Lt. Hultgreen had 217 flight hours in the F-14A.
- Another F-14A squadron commanding officer tried to replicate this situation in a simulator; eight of his [nine] pilots "crashed" the simulator.

My conclusions are: It was improbable that the aircraft could have been recovered. The pilot had to accurately analyze the emergency and apply precisely the correct control inputs in less time than it takes the telephone to ring twice. I believe Lt. Hultgreen did her best to recover the aircraft; the fact that she was not successful in no way diminished her stature as a fully qualified F-14 pilot. Her late ejection could have been due to her attempts to "save the airplane at all costs."

Since both the JAG and the MIR reports are now "in the public domain," anyone who reads both documents will find generally the same set of facts. The JAG defines what we know and the logical conclusions and opinions based on those facts. That was the information presented at the recent news conference.

The MIR, on the other hand, contains facts, conjecture, as yet unproven theories and opinions, some of which are not rigidly based on fact. This is appropriate for an MIR but should not be used as the definitive cause of the accident nor to malign the pilot.

Finally, recent articles by *Union-Tribune* Insight Editor Robert Caldwell (March 26 and April 9) question the integrity of naval aviation leadership. The integrity issue in this tragic accident is not naval aviation leadership, but rather the unauthorized "leak" of privileged information to advance a personal agenda.

During my career, the Naval Aviation Safety Program has reduced the naval aviation accident record by a factor of 10; the confidential MIR process has been a crucial contributor to this achievement. It should rightly continue to be a privileged document by which we inside naval aviation seek to reduce our accident rate even further.

Appendix B �֎ *Some Letters I Received after Kara's Death*

I always knew Kara was destined for greatness. . . . She captivated strangers not only with her outer beauty, but with her inner drive, motivation and charisma. When she'd tell a simple story people would be on the edge of their seats waiting and hanging on her every word.

A casual game of tennis was the match of a lifetime. If she had a bad serve she'd scream as loud as she could and the next serve would be the world's most perfect shot.

I only remember laughing when I was around Kara. Her funny little voices, her amazing memory for entire movies and songs! And, of course, her beautiful smile.

There will never be anyone else like her, and the world will be a far lesser place without her.

Letter postmarked 29 October 1994 from Krista Levitan, a college friend of Kara's

֎

I want to express my deepest sympathy on the tragic death of your daughter. . . . I've always respected her talent as an aviator. Never doubt for a moment that she was above average both in and out of the cockpit. Any rumors to the contrary are (as you probably suspect) the makings of men who never wanted women flying jets in the first place.

I certainly respect you and your family for the way you handled stabs at Kara's reputation in the media during a time of unimaginable grieving. The rest of us women aviators have Kara in part to thank for the changing of the combat exclusion laws. I for one am

grateful and very saddened that she wasn't able to enjoy her lifelong dream longer.

Letter dated 12 December 1994 from Lt. Sue Still (now lieutenant commander), who was one of the female naval aviators flying the EA-6A in Key West with Kara. Sue piloted two missions of the U.S. space shuttle *Columbia,* the first of which launched on 4 April 1997 from the Kennedy Space Center, Florida. Sue took Kara's miniature gold naval aviator wings with her in memory of Kara.

❋

When I first met Kara, I was the coach of the best high school tennis program in the state of Texas. Kara was 16 or 17, new to San Antonio, and new to that high school.

Kara wanted to be on that tennis team. She did not have the tennis training or the tennis experience of the other girls in that program. I did not think that she was good enough to make the team. It comes as no surprise, however, to those who knew Kara, that she did make that team.

Kara was such an outstanding athlete. She had such an incredibly infectious positive attitude.

Thanks Kara.

You dared to dream.

You had the courage, discipline, energy, and enthusiasm to make the dream come true.

You inspired us then.

You will *inspire us—forever.*

Letter dated 28 October 1994 from Larry B. Oxford, Kara's high school tennis coach

❋

I knew Kara in Key West where I did my last tour in the Navy (1990–94). I wasn't in VAQ-33, but I worked with her when she was the squadron's Public Affairs Officer.

She was one of the most focused individuals I have ever known. We almost became roommates, and I remember her always joking and poking fun at me because I flew in C-130s. "Not me," she'd say, "my airplane has to have a pointy nose and afterburners, or I'll never be happy."

To me she was one of the chosen, because she was doing what so few people ever have the opportunity or talent to do, to live their dream.

Letter written November 1994 from Lt. Kitty Weidman, an NFO on a shore tour attached to the Coast Guard as a liaison officer

You don't know me, but I had the privilege to know your daughter.

I remember Kara best on the day of my sister's wedding. I was an usher and we somehow knew Kara was going to be late. So I saved her an aisle seat near the front. When she arrived, minutes before the ceremony began, the whole church literally gasped as I escorted her to her place. Her beauty and poise stunned everyone. And I felt like I had the actress Kathleen Turner on my arm. But she was real and not an image.

Letter dated 31 October 1994 from Bob Smith, brother of a college friend of Kara's

I was fortunate enough to be stationed with Kara in Key West. When thinking of Kara, her bright smile and wonderful laugh immediately come to mind. She's a terrific person! I truly admire her for following her dreams and taking all the risks that accompanied them. Her courage and ambition have opened the doors for many young women who wish to follow in her footsteps. She has touched the lives of everyone who knew her.

Letter dated 5 November 1994 from Lt. (jg) Amy Lyons, a general unrestricted line officer who had come to the squadron from the Naval Academy in 1992

I was the commanding officer of VAQ-34, the sister squadron of VAQ-33, and later the Operations Officer for the Fleet Electronic Warfare Support Group, the staff that served as the operational commander for both squadrons.

It was my pleasure to have known Kara and to have flown with her on at least one occasion. She was a superb aviator and naval officer, a total professional.

Kara, her shipmates in VAQ-33, and her friends in VAQ-34 demonstrated long before the Navy finally allowed them into fleet squadrons, that they had the "Right Stuff."

Her loss was a personal tragedy for me as I am sure it was for all those who knew her. But in your grief please find comfort in the fact that she touched the lives of many who will follow in her footsteps, encouraged by her example.

Letter dated 28 October 1994 from Capt. Rex Kibler, USN (Ret.)

Kara has, and always will have, a special place in my heart. In my 10 years as a naval flight officer there may be only 1 or 2 other pilots that have more flight time with me than Kara did. We logged well over 100 hours together. We worked well together as a team. Her enthusiasm and spontaneity rarely failed to lift the spirits of anyone around her. Kara's disregard for traditional barriers was not only evident in her quest for equality for female aviators, but she also chose to ignore the long standing rift caused by petty jealousy between female aviators and the wives of male aviators. Sherry often looked forward to detachments in which I was assigned and Kara was not, so they could spend time together without me to ruin their fun.

I know this is no consolation for you, because it doesn't even work for me, but it kind of sums up the vitality, the zest for life that had personified Kara: She did more and lived more in her 29 years than any of us could only dream of doing in a normal lifetime.

We have had something very valuable taken from us and my world will never be the same. I'll miss her.

Letter dated 3 November 1994 from Lt. Scott M. "Jelly" Hjelseth, Kara's good friend and fellow aviator

First, I would like to express how sorry and sad I feel about the loss of your daughter, Kara. She was much more than a great pilot. She was a great inspiration for all who she had been around. I knew Ms. Hultgreen for about 3 years while I was stationed with VAQ-33 in Key West, FL. She was the subject of conversation all the time. Of good conversation.

She was so much fun to be with. I remember this one time when I was getting ready to launch her out, and someone had dropped a tiny screw in the cockpit of the A-6. Needless to say, the maintenance officer had to postpone the flight until the screw was recovered. So LT Hultgreen and myself sat on the wing of the A-6 and began to talk. Without realizing, we had spent about an hour on the wing just talking. She made me laugh so much. I then realized what a good person she was inside. I will never forget that day as long as I live and I will never forget about Kara's memory. Well the very next memory I have of Kara was her going away party at a mutual friend of ours. Kara could not stop talking about how she was going to fly F-14s. I was so excited for her. She was so happy about being the first.

She was always smiling and laughing. I never ever saw her with a sad look or an upset attitude. She loved flying, even in the A-6. She had guts flying that plane considering all the things wrong with it and how old the planes were. I do remember telling Kara a joke at the party and how she could not stop laughing. I finally had my chance to make her laugh for the times she made me laugh.

Letter dated 28 October 1994 from AD2 Mel Gonzalez, a plane captain who was stationed at Key West with Kara

 *Notes*

Chapter 18 *The Combat Exclusion Laws*

1. Marina Pisano, "On the Wings of Women," *San Antonio Express-News,* 10 March 1991.

Chapter 19 *The NBC Interview*

1. Rhonda Cornum, as told to Peter Copeland, *She Went to War* (Novato, Calif.: Presidio Press, 1992), 50.

Chapter 46 *The Fortune Teller*

1. Patrick Pexton and John Burlage, "Combat Announcement Helps Women's Options," *Navy Times,* 10 May 1993, 14.

Chapter 49 *The Press*

1. Marina Pisano, "Night Landings Qualify S.A. Woman for Combat," *San Antonio Express-News,* 13 October 1994.

Epilogue *Sally's Story*

1. Pat Flynn, "F-14's Fate Sealed in Split Seconds," *San Diego Union-Tribune,* 1 March 1995.
2. Marina Pisano, "Navy Says Pilot's Plane Crashed Because of Engine Failure," *San Antonio Express-News,* 1 March 1995; Preston C. Pinson, "Investigation into the VF-213 F-14A Aircraft Accident on 25 October 1994 that Resulted in the Death of Lieutenant Kara S. Hultgreen, USN, and Injury of Lieutenant Matthew P. Klemish, USN," *Manual of the Judge Advocate General,* Department of the Navy, 22 February 1995, 22.
3. Robert J. Spane, "Anatomy of a Plane Crash," *San Diego Union-Tribune,* 13 April 1995.
4. Pinson, "Investigation," *Manual of the Judge Advocate General,* Department of the Navy, 22 February 1995, 18, 23.

5. Peter Garrison, "Aftermath, Compressor Stall," *Flying,* June 1995, 100.

6. Flynn, "F-14's Fate Sealed in Split Seconds."

7. Pinson, "Investigation," *Manual of the Judge Advocate General,* Department of the Navy, 22 February 1995, 13.

8. Jay B. Yakeley, "Investigation," *Manual of the Judge Advocate General,* Department of the Navy, 22 February 1995, 35.

9. Gregory L. Vistica, *Fall from Glory: The Men Who Sank the U.S. Navy* (New York: Simon and Schuster, 1995), 374.

10. Spane, "Anatomy of a Plane Crash."

11. Robert J. Caldwell, "Were the Simulator Tests Rigged?" *San Diego Union-Tribune,* 9 April 1995.

12. Scott Watkins, "Lost at Sea—A Fighter's Story," *Woman Pilot,* January–February 1995, 4.

13. Stanley R. Arthur, "Lt. Hultgreen Wasn't a 'Quota' Pilot," *Washington Times,* 28 May 1995.

14. Rolla Rich, "Setting the Record Straight," typescript dated 22 November 1994, intended for publication 25 November 1994 in the *Daily Record.*

15. Pat Flynn, "Pilot Qualified, Files Show," *San Diego Union-Tribune,* 20 November 1994.

16. Burns, Patrick J. "Letters to the Editor." *The San Diego Union-Tribune,* January 1998.

17. "Double Standards in Naval Aviation," *CMR Report,* no. 9, June 1995, 1.

18. Scarborough, Rowan. "Navy boss censures officer on records, Pilot gave files on female aviators," *Washington Times,* 19 March 1998, 10.

19. Peter J. Boyer, "Admiral Boorda's War," *New Yorker,* 16 September 1996, 73.

20. Michael J. Galpin, "Investigation," *Manual of the Judge Advocate General,* Department of the Navy, 22 February 1995, 31.

About the Author

Sally Spears holds undergraduate and law degrees from the University of Texas at Austin and practices law in San Antonio. She has lived and worked in Rumford, Maine; Greenwich, Connecticut; Chicago, Illinois; and Toronto, Canada. Sally is a member of the Defense Advisory Committee on Women in the Services. She has two other daughters and two granddaughters who live in Los Angeles. This is her first book.

The **Naval Institute Press** is the book-publishing arm of the U.S. Naval Institute, a private, nonprofit, membership society for sea service professionals and others who share an interest in naval and maritime affairs. Established in 1873 at the U.S. Naval Academy in Annapolis, Maryland, where its offices remain today, the Naval Institute has members worldwide.

Members of the Naval Institute support the education programs of the society and receive the influential monthly magazine *Proceedings* and discounts on fine nautical prints and on ship and aircraft photos. They also have access to the transcripts of the Institute's Oral History Program and get discounted admission to any of the Institute-sponsored seminars offered around the country.

The Naval Institute also publishes *Naval History* magazine. This colorful bimonthly is filled with entertaining and thought-provoking articles, first-person reminiscences, and dramatic art and photography. Members receive a discount on *Naval History* subscriptions.

The Naval Institute's book-publishing program, begun in 1898 with basic guides to naval practices, has broadened its scope in recent years to include books of more general interest. Now the Naval Institute Press publishes about 100 titles each year, ranging from how-to books on boating and navigation to battle histories, biographies, ship and aircraft guides, and novels. Institute members receive discounts of 20 to 50 percent on the Press's nearly 600 books in print.

Full-time students are eligible for special half-price membership rates. Life memberships are also available.

For a free catalog describing Naval Institute Press books currently available, and for further information about subscribing to *Naval History* magazine or about joining the U.S. Naval Institute, please write to:

Membership Department
U.S. Naval Institute
118 Maryland Avenue
Annapolis, MD 21402-5035
Telephone: (800) 233-8764
Fax: (410) 269-7940
Web address: www.usni.org